TEN INNINGS AT WRIGLEY

TEN INNINGS *at* WRIGLEY

THE WILDEST BALLGAME EVER, WITH BASEBALL ON THE BRINK

KEVIN COOK

A HOLT PAPERBACK

HENRY HOLT AND COMPANY   NEW YORK

Holt Paperbacks
Henry Holt and Company
Publishers since 1866
120 Broadway
New York, New York 10271
www.henryholt.com

A Holt Paperback® and ® are registered trademarks of
Macmillan Publishing Group, LLC.

The Library of Congress has cataloged the hardcover edition as follows:

Names: Cook, Kevin, 1956–, author.
Title: Ten Innings at Wrigley: the wildest ballgame ever, with baseball on the brink /
    Kevin Cook.
Other titles: 10 innings
Description: First edition. | New York : Henry Holt and Company, [2019] | Includes
    bibliographical references and index.
Identifiers: LCCN 2018047864 | ISBN 9781250182036 (hardcover)
Subjects: LCSH: Chicago Cubs (Baseball team)—History—20th century. | Philadelphia
    Phillies (Baseball team)—History—20th century. | Wrigley Field (Chicago, Ill.)—
    History—20th century. | Baseball—United States—History—20th century.
Classification: LCC GV875.C6 C66 2019 | DDC 796.357/640977311—dc23
LC record available at https://lccn.loc.gov/2018047864

ISBN 978-1-125-02-6837-2 (trade paperback)

Our books may be purchased in bulk for promotional, educational, or business use. Please
contact your local bookseller or the Macmillan Corporate and Premium Sales Department at
(800) 221-7945, extension 5442, or by e-mail at MacmillanSpecialMarkets@macmillan.com.

Originally published in hardcover in 2019 by Henry Holt and Company

First Holt Paperbacks Edition 2020

Designed by Kelly S. Too

Printed in the United States of America

D 3 5 7 9 10 8 6 4 2

For Pamela, Lily, and Cal

In Memory of Art Cook:
Birmingham Barons 1944
Kingston Ponies 1946–50
Ogdensburg Maples 1950–51
Union City Greyhounds 1951–52

CONTENTS

Philadelphia Phillies vs. Chicago Cubs
Wrigley Field
Chicago, Illinois
Thursday, May 17, 1979

Philadelphia Phillies	Chicago Cubs
Danny Ozark, manager	Herman Franks, manager

Starting Lineups

Bake McBride RF	Ivan DeJesus SS
Larry Bowa SS	Mike Vail RF
Pete Rose 1B	Bill Buckner 1B
Mike Schmidt 3B	Dave Kingman LF
Del Unser LF	Steve Ontiveros 3B
Garry Maddox CF	Jerry Martin CF
Bob Boone C	Barry Foote C
Rudy Meoli 2B	Ted Sizemore 2B
Randy Lerch P	Dennis Lamp P

Reserves

Mike Anderson	Larry Biittner
Ramon Aviles	Tim Blackwell
Jose Cardenal	Steve Dillard
Greg Gross	Mick Kelleher
Greg Luzinski	Sam Mejias
Tim McCarver	Bobby Murcer
Dave Rader	Scot Thompson

Pitchers

Doug Bird	Ray Burris
Steve Carlton	Bill Caudill
Larry Christenson	Willie Hernandez
Rawly Eastwick	Ken Holtzman
Nino Espinosa	Mike Krukow
Jim Lonborg	Lynn McGlothen
Tug McGraw	Donnie Moore
Ron Reed	Rick Reuschel
Dick Ruthven	Bruce Sutter

PROLOGUE: MAY 1979

I t was hotter than usual for spring in the Midwest. Temperatures pushed ninety degrees in May. Utility bills jumped, just as President Jimmy Carter had predicted when he warned Americans about a looming energy crisis. In Chicago, motorists lined up at filling stations as gas prices hit seventy-five cents a gallon.

Along Addison Street and Waveland Avenue, lake breezes carried disco tunes from cars and open windows. Donna Summer's "Hot Stuff." Gloria Gaynor's "I Will Survive." Rod Stewart's "Da Ya Think I'm Sexy?" Closer to Wrigley Field, organ music drowned out the disco. "The Star-Spangled Banner" a little after one p.m. on game days. "Take Me Out to the Ballgame" six and a half innings later.

Fans came to the ballpark from all directions. Some walked from the El stop at Addison; some paid a few dollars to leave their cars in somebody's driveway. One home owner held a hand-lettered sign: CUB FANS $5 OTHERS $25.

However they arrived, the fans had no trouble getting tickets. You could walk up while the anthem was playing and pay six dollars for a grandstand seat, a buck fifty for the bleachers. Every game was a day game and every day game was a party. Sure, there were suit-and-tie guys in the front rows, treating clients to an afternoon ballgame, but the usual crowd was neighborhood types, night-shift workers, nurses, waiters and waitresses, retirees, part-timers, and college students, dressed in shorts and jeans and T-shirts, baseball caps, painter's caps, sandals and sneakers.

The Chicago Cubs were one of the surprises of the first six weeks of the season. Thanks largely to cleanup hitter Dave "Kong" Kingman, whose towering homers sometimes crashed through windows across the street from the ballpark, the Cubs were over .500 at 16-15.

"Kingman was king of Chicago that year," recalled Ed Hartig, a Nielsen Company data scientist who moonlighted as the Cubs' official historian. Hartig considered the 1979 team one of the more interesting in a franchise history dating back to 1876. "Kong was king, but he didn't have much help. They weren't a rich, big-market club yet. The offense was basically Kingman and Bill Buckner. But they put on a pretty good show." Buckner, more of a pure hitter than Kong, a singles and doubles man whose batting average was often fifty points higher, batted third in the lineup, but that was about as close and he and Kingman got. The Cubs' two best hitters couldn't stand each other.

Rick Reuschel, the Cubs' roly-poly pitching ace, threw sinkers that hitters bounced into the high grass in front of the plate, grass the groundskeepers grew high to slow down those grounders. Despite a physique one teammate compared to a pile of laundry, Reuschel was cat-quick, often pouncing on ground balls before his infielders could get them. All-Star reliever Bruce Sutter closed games with a trick pitch, the split-finger fastball, which would in time be known as the Pitch of the Eighties. Behind Sutter the bullpen featured a pair of promising young pitchers, Willie Hernandez and Donnie Moore, but the rest of the pitching staff was average at best. And aside from Kingman and Buckner the lineup was a rotating cast of supporting players whose lack of power matched their lack of speed.

That's what Cub manager Herman Franks had to work with. A balding baseball lifer, Franks had spat, cussed, and chain-smoked his way through half a century in the game and knew a fourth-place club when he managed one. "The man invented grumpiness," recalled John Schulian, a *Sun-Times* sports columnist. "Herman Franks would sit in his office with his feet on his desk, eating chocolate donuts and smoking a cigar, ignoring questions."

"In Herman's defense, he had an impossible job," said Hartig. "If they had a popularity contest in that clubhouse, nobody would win. But he was keeping them close to first place."

"He kept them close for a month," Schulian said, "but they hadn't played most of the best teams. What was going to happen when the Phillies came in?"

The 1979 Phillies, winners of three straight National League Eastern Division titles, were making their first trip of the season to Wrigley Field that May, and they had a slugger of their own in the cleanup slot. Third baseman Mike Schmidt was the only National League hitter with more home runs than Kingman, and his supporting cast was better. Flashbulbs popped when Schmidt and the Phillies filed off the team bus in front of their Michigan Avenue hotel. There was Pete Rose, the hard-charging former batting champ who'd left Cincinnati for a free-agent contract that made him the best-paid player in the game at $800,000 a year. And Garry Maddox, who played center field so smoothly the fans called him the Secretary of Defense. And screwballing reliever Tug McGraw, who stuck out his tongue at fans who booed. And ace starter Steve Carlton, who stayed in shape with kung fu and refused to speak with reporters. With a league-leading $4.9 million payroll that nearly doubled the Cubs', Philadelphia was favored to win the division again. That added to the pressure on manager Danny Ozark, a tall, genial fellow with a gift for malaprop. Recalling an ovation on Opening Day, Ozark said, "It sent a twinkle up my spine." His mandate from the front office that year sent more of a chill: win or else.

The Cubs had won the opening game of the series, 7–1, on Tuesday, May 15, but on Wednesday afternoon Steve Carlton put the Cubs in their place with a three-hit shutout. The Phils' 13–0 victory put them three and a half games ahead of the second-place Montreal Expos, with

Chicago another two and a half back. That game was played in front of eighteen thousand fans and an equal number of empty seats—not bad for a Wednesday game, according to Hartig. "The neighborhood was a little seedy," he recalled. "The Cubs might draw ten thousand or less on a weekday, and in those days it was attendance and concessions paying the bills."

Like so much else about baseball in 1979, that was about to change.

During the '79 season, for the first time, Chicago's WGN-TV up-linked its programming to the Satcom 3 satellite and beamed Cubs telecasts to cable TV households around the country. WGN wasn't the first so-called superstation—that was Atlanta's WTBS, which got its start when deckhands ran a cable to Ted Turner's yacht so the Braves owner could watch his team's games. Thanks to cable, the Braves and Cubs were on their way to becoming national brands.

Cable TV rescued major-league baseball. At the end of a decade that saw football surpass baseball as the de facto national pastime, WTBS and WGN made baseball a habit for millions of viewers who never bought a ticket. (Another cable network, ESPN, built on the site of a former trash dump in Connecticut, also debuted in 1979.) ABC's *Monday Night Football* was already a pop-culture phenomenon, one of the top prime-time shows, while the major leagues had nothing but NBC's *Game of the Week* on Saturday afternoons. In the next decade cable would pour millions of dollars into baseball owners' pockets, remaking the sport. There were 850,000 cable households in 1979. Ten years later there would be 53 million.

TV money was one of three main factors driving the sport's transformation. The others were muscles and metrics.

Ballplayers of the '70s were skinny. Dave Kingman stood six foot six and weighed 210, roughly a pound of it mustache. Schmidt, the home-run king known around the Phillies clubhouse as "Muscles," was compared to a Greek god. "To have his body," Rose joked, "I'd give mine and my wife's, and throw in some cash." Yet the six-foot-two, 195-pound slugger was smaller than many of today's shortstops. Weight training was frowned on in major-league clubhouses. ("Makes you musclebound," old-timers said. "You can't get around on the fastball.") The '79 Phillies were ahead of the curve—they had the big leagues' first weight room—but they weren't so much bigger than ordinary Philadelphians. One reason was that steroids were barely a rumor in the '70s. Many if not most players took amphetamines—greenies or rat turds, depending on the pills' color. Others preferred cocaine. A few reportedly experimented with steroids or human growth hormone, but it wasn't until the '80s that baseball bodies ballooned like TV revenues. The '80s would end with the steroidal Oakland A's on top of the world.

Modern metrics would also reshape the game. Thirty-four-year-old Tony La Russa, who took over as manager of the crosstown White Sox in 1979, got razzed as "Egghead" and "Einstein" for poring over computer printouts. Fantasy sports, invented in the 1979–80 off-season by a dozen publishing-industry barflies at a Manhattan restaurant called La Rotisserie Française, would attract millions of fans by giving them skin in the game. At the same time a Kansas security guard who moonlighted as a statistician, Bill James, coined a term for the number crunching he introduced in his mimeographed *Baseball Abstract*: sabermetrics, named for the still-new Society for American Baseball Research. James's stats-driven approach would gain steam through the steroids era, the *Moneyball* era, and beyond. Today it dominates a sport whose every play is determined by stats, shifts, launch angles, exit velocities, and tendencies derived from deep data.

Baseball today perplexes a lot of '70s players. With all the mound conferences, pitching changes, shifts, and replay reviews, baseball seems to keep getting slower. A typical major-league game now lasts more than three hours, compared to two and half hours in their day. That's thirty minutes or more of dead time. Anyone who's been to a game lately knows there are no $6 seats anymore, or even six-dollar hot dogs. Many of the five-hundred-dollar seats behind the plate are empty—they're corporate seats. Ordinary fans pay hundreds of dollars for tickets and parking only to get soaked by vendors selling twelve-dollar hot dogs and fifteen-dollar beers. More and more young fans prefer football, basketball, even soccer.

Some old-timers say they barely recognize the game. But as Herman Franks said, "It's still goddamn baseball." In 1939, 1979, or 2019, "you throw the ball. You hit the ball." His club often dropped it, too.

Franks knew his job was on the line in '79. So did Ozark. In a sense the same was true of all their players. Even those with multiyear deals were playing for future contracts. Others were playing simply to stick around in the majors. Everybody had something to prove when the Phillies came to Chicago that May.

The rubber game of their three-game series would be a matchup of snakebit franchises famous for losing. As a cynical Cub fan said, it was almost a shame somebody had to win.

PART ONE

NATIONAL LEAGUE LEAST

THE CUBS: FOILED AGAIN

The Chicago Cubs were born to lose. They were cursed. Their die-hard fans said so. It wasn't just that Chicago's National League franchise hadn't won a World Series since 1908. Other teams had gone decades without winning, too. The Philadelphia Phillies had been in the league since 1883 and still hadn't won a World Series. What distinguished the Cubs was how consistently and entertainingly they stunk.

They were winners before they were lovable losers and traced their ancestry to a different animal—the whale. Their home diamond started out with a different name, too. Wrigley Field began its long life as Weeghman Park, named for the luncheonette tycoon who built it.

In the early 1900s Charlie Weeghman strolled the busy sidewalks of the Loop with a gardenia in his lapel, tipping his bowler hat to the ladies. Lucky Charlie, they called him. He had landed a restaurant job as a boy, filling coffee mugs for the builders, bankers, lawyers, aldermen, priests, and mobsters who made the town go. He soon moved up to maître d' and then manager, saving his wages and tips until he could open his own place. Weeghman's Lunch Room was a spotless, white-tiled cafeteria where working people could get a sandwich and a glass of milk for twenty-five cents. Chicagoans lined up to get in. Before long he had a chain of Lunch Rooms—America's first fast-food chain—that launched what the *Tribune* called a "cafeteria craze." By the time he turned thirty-five, his fortune amounted to $8 million (about $200 million today), more than enough to build a baseball park.

As a boy he'd pictured himself knocking doubles and triples like Cap Anson, the great first baseman of Chicago's National League baseball club, which played home games at the rat-infested West Side Grounds. After making his millions, Weeghman tried to buy the St. Louis Cardinals, but his wealth was a little too fresh for the silver-haired men who ran Major League Baseball. They turned him down. So he poured his money into a new league.

For the 1914 season the upstart Federal League of Base Ball Clubs placed teams in eight cities, including Chicago, to challenge the monopoly of the National and American Leagues. Their players were mostly big-league castoffs and never-wuzzes, but Weeghman had big plans for his Chicago Federals, cleverly nicknamed the Chi-Feds. As a first salvo against the game's establishment, he signed the Cubs' famous shortstop Joe Tinker.

Tinker had black hair spilling over a unibrow so pronounced you can see it on his Hall of Fame plaque. The Cubs' catalyst when they won four pennants and a pair of World Series, he had crossed into folklore in a 1910 poem by newspaperman Franklin Pierce Adams, a New York Giants fan:

> *These are the saddest of possible words:*
> *"Tinker to Evers to Chance."*
> *Trio of bear cubs, and fleeter than birds,*
> *Tinker and Evers and Chance.*
> *Ruthlessly pricking our gonfalon bubble,*
> *Making a Giant hit into a double—*
> *Words that are heavy with nothing but trouble:*
> *"Tinker to Evers to Chance."*

Weeghman signed the thirty-three-year-old Tinker as the Chi-Feds' player-manager for an unheard-of twelve thousand dollars a year. Four days later, he leased nine acres in Chicago's Lake View neighborhood. The land had been home to the city's Lutheran Theological Seminary until the seminarians decided their neighborhood was going to hell. They could barely hear themselves pray over the noise from trains clattering through the new El station on Addison Street. One seminarian recalled "smoke, dust, grime, soot, dirt, foul gases, railroading by night and day, whistles, ding-donging of bells." Weeghman leased the land for sixteen thousand dollars a year and hired architect Zachary Taylor Davis to build a ballpark there.

Davis had gotten his start at Louis Sullivan's firm, working alongside a twenty-one-year-old Frank Lloyd Wright. With $250,000 of Weeghman's lunch money to spend (about $6.3 million in today's dollars), he started from scratch less than two months before the Chi-Feds' 1914 season began. Davis and Weeghman hired hundreds of Chicago men to wield shovels, wheelbarrows, hammers, and saws and run mule teams and steam- and gasoline-powered engines on double shifts through February and March. From groundbreaking to Opening Day, they built the park in seven weeks.

They couldn't have done it without the sort of friends who can help a construction job. One of Weeghman's friends, New York mobster Arnold Rothstein, paraded around Chicago with flunkies like Legs Diamond, who enjoyed stabbing people who crossed his boss and cut out their tongues if they griped about it. This was five years before Rothstein fixed the 1919 World Series.

On April 23, 1914, a mile-long parade of motorcars and merrymakers led from the Loop to Weeghman Park to celebrate Opening Day. Ten brass bands played. A dozen fans in sombreros brought a live bull to the game. The park was built to hold fourteen thousand baseball bugs, as fans were called in those days, but more than twenty thousand packed the place that afternoon. Just before the game began, a car festooned with roses and carnations drove onto the field. Joe Tinker stepped out and waved to the crowd.

Tinker singled in three trips to the plate as the home team thumped the Kansas City Packers, 9–1. Chicago won again the next day. The Chi-Feds often outdrew the Cubs and White Sox—not only because they won but because Weeghman made baseball a bug-friendly experience. His concession stands sold the best ballpark food at fair prices. His team was the first to let fans keep foul balls, a policy that irked other owners, who had ushers chase down foul balls and return them to the field. Weeghman also pioneered Ladies' Day, letting women in free every Friday.

In the winter of 1915 he held a newspaper contest to give his Chi-Feds a better name. With Charlie's luncheonettes in mind, readers suggested that the team should be the Chicago Buns, Beefers, Doughnuts, or Pies. Windy Lads was another contender. In the end he decided to call his team the Whales. Weeghman's Chicago Whales chased the 1915 Federal League pennant with help from another former Cubs star, Mordecai Peter Centennial Brown.

Born in 1876, the hundredth anniversary of American independence, Mordecai Brown was a Hoosier who had lost much of his pitching hand in a boyhood accident. A mechanical corn shredder tore off most of the index finger and part of the pinkie on his throwing hand. To his delight he discovered that the accident didn't keep him from playing ball. In fact, the stubs of his fingers helped put spin on his curveball. After signing a minor-league contract with the Terre Haute Hottentots, "Three-Finger" Brown climbed quickly to the majors, landing with the Chicago Cubs. He won 26 games with a league-best 1.04 earned run average in 1906, when the Cubs won 116 games, running away with the National League pennant. Nine years later he helped lead Weeghman's Whales to a Federal League pennant on the last day of the season. Somehow the little ballpark held 34,212 fans that day, more than twice its official capacity. In one account, Chicago's baseball bugs "went Borneo" when the Whales clinched, rushing the field to mob Tinker, Brown, and the rest of the players.

After that season, Major League Baseball—the established National League and American League owners—bought out the Federal League.

Each Federal League owner received $600,000 to disband his team. (One club, the Baltimore Terrapins, refused and sued the major leagues for violation of federal antitrust laws. The case made its way to the Supreme Court, where the Terrapins lost. In an opinion by Justice Oliver Wendell Holmes Jr., the Court ruled that baseball was a game, not a business engaged in interstate commerce.) As part of the buyout settlement, Charlie Weeghman was allowed to buy the Chicago Cubs. Not only that, he got to add his Federal League players to the Cubs' roster. Tinker and Brown rejoined their former teammates, who were glad to move from the dilapidated West Side Grounds to the new baseball palace on the North Side.

Lucky Charlie was having the time of his life. He watched his Cubs from the owner's box and sometimes stayed after night fell on Weeghman Park. He kept a stable of horses in stalls under the grandstand. His favorite was Queen Bess, described by the *Chicago Tribune* as "an old, gentle bay mare." On summer nights the owner let Queen Bess run and graze on the field.

Weeghman's first major move as a National League owner was a blockbuster trade with the Philadelphia Phillies. In normal times the Phillies wouldn't dream of trading their ace pitcher, Grover Cleveland Alexander, who had led the league four seasons running with an average of thirty victories a year and taken the Phillies to their first World Series in 1915. But two years later, with a world war on and every American male between twenty-one and thirty subject to the draft, Phillies owner William Baker worried about Alexander's contract. Baker didn't want to pay his ace seven thousand dollars only to have him march off to France and get killed. When Weeghman offered to take Alexander off Baker's hands, the Phillies took the bait.

That winter, Baker traded Alexander to the Cubs for two part-time players and fifty-five thousand dollars—a massive amount of cash. It was the biggest trade in both teams' history to that point, and both teams came out on the short end. The Phillies would finish last fifteen times in the next twenty-five years.

Weeghman signed the great Alexander to a generous contract: eight thousand dollars a year whether he played or not, plus a five-thousand-dollar signing bonus and ten thousand dollars for Alex's fiancée. That made the owner a hero to Chicago fans just as war, recession, and a flu epidemic squeezed his finances. Restaurants closed. Baseball bugs stayed home.

Alexander won twice for the 1918 Cubs. Then the army called him up. The best pitcher alive spent seven weeks of trench combat, enduring bombardment from German howitzers that crippled him with shell shock.

His teammates went on to win the pennant with a record that gave them home-field advantage in the World Series against the American League champion Red Sox. To maximize revenue, Weeghman arranged a one-week lease with White Sox owner Charles Comiskey, whose South Side stadium held twice as many fans as Charlie's place. And so the Cubs hosted their games in the 1918 World Series at Comiskey Park.

They were favored in Game One against Boston lefty Babe Ruth. A pie-faced twenty-three-year-old who played the outfield on days he didn't pitch, Ruth blanked them in the opener, 1–0. During the seventh-inning stretch, a band played "The Star-Spangled Banner," which was then the U.S. Navy's anthem. Red Sox third baseman Fred Thomas, a sailor playing in the World Series on a furlough, spun and saluted the flag in center field. Others followed his lead. The fans stood and sang, some with hands over their hearts, and gave the tune's last notes a long ovation. After that, baseball owners made sure the song played at every Series game. Thirteen years later, Congress passed a law making "The Star-Spangled Banner" the national anthem.

The Cubs lost the 1918 World Series. There was talk that they'd thrown it. Their losers' share of $671 per man (to Boston's $1,100) was far less than mobsters like Arnold Rothstein would pay for a certain result. No one ever proved the Cubs were on the take, as Comiskey's White Sox would be the following year, but they had gone ten seasons without a Series title and would go oh-for-the-next-ninety-eight.

Charlie Weeghman might have gone bankrupt if not for William Wrigley Jr. The son of a Philadelphia soap maker who founded a chewing gum empire, portly, pomaded Wrigley kept his friend afloat with loans and purchases of stock in the team. Now, with two million soldiers shipping off to war, many of them chewing Wrigley's Spearmint and Juicy Fruit gum, Wrigley bought Cubs stock until he had it all. After that the old owner faded away.

Weeghman disappeared from public view until 1921, when he hosted twelve thousand Ku Klux Klansmen at a white-power rally on his farm in Lake Zurich, Illinois. Later he moved east and got back into the restaurant business just in time for the Depression to ruin him. Years later a newsman tracked him down. Weeghman was living out his days in a studio apartment in New York, wondering what had happened to his luck.

THE BALLPARK HE'D built was known as Cubs Park from 1919 until 1923, when Wrigley overcame his modesty and named it after himself. In 1927 he built a second deck that added eighteen thousand seats. Attendance crossed the million mark for the first time that season. The most famous patron was a chubby cigar smoker who sat in the first row: die-hard Cub fan Al Capone.

Capone used to roll up to the park in an armor-plated limousine with bulletproof glass and tommy-gun turrets. His outfit, the Outfit, ran bootlegging, gambling, narcotics, prostitution, extortion, and murder for hire in Chicago. When Scarface Al took in a Cubs game, players came over to pay their respects. One day it was catcher Gabby Hartnett smiling and posing for photos with Capone. When baseball commissioner Kenesaw Mountain Landis saw the photos, he sent Hartnett a telegram telling him to steer clear of unsavory characters.

Hartnett wired back: OK, BUT IF YOU DON'T WANT ME TO HAVE MY PICTURE TAKEN WITH AL CAPONE, YOU TELL HIM.

The Cubs won four National League pennants from 1929 to 1938, but always withered in October. In four World Series they won three games and lost sixteen. Still Chicagoans kept coming to Wrigley Field, even in the winter.

Starting in the '20s, Wrigley rented his field to the Chicago Bears of the new National Football League. George Halas, the football club's owner/coach/wide receiver/defensive end/ticket vendor, christened his team the Bears as a nod to their landlord, reasoning that bears are bigger than cubs. One Sunday, Bears fullback Bronko Nagurski barreled through the Washington Redskins, through the end zone, and banged his leather-helmeted head into the brick outfield wall. He jogged to the sideline, where Halas asked if he was okay. Nagurski said, "Yeah, but that last guy really gave me a lick."

Over the years the park hosted car shows, rodeos, even a ski-jumping contest. The ski jumpers stood atop a ramp that rose to the roof. They schussed to another ramp near home plate, took off, and came down like loud outs in center field. Still the park was best known for baseball teams that kept finding fresh ways to fall short. It was at Wrigley Field that Babe Ruth, now a New York Yankee, hit his Called Shot in the World Series of 1932. Or didn't. Historians say Ruth may have waved his bat to warn Chicago pitcher Charlie Root that the next line drive might take his head off. Scratchy game film, recently discovered, suggests they're right. Either way, Ruth hit a long home run on the next pitch and the Yankees swept the Series.

Wrigley died that year. His only son, Philip Knight Wrigley, a pipe-smoking yachtsman, never quite warmed up to baseball. The rowdy pastime, P. K. Wrigley said, was "too much of a sport to be a business and too much of a business to be a sport." To him, the Cubs were only one of the family's holdings, like the chewing-gum business and real estate including Chicago's landmark Wrigley Building and Catalina Island off the California coast. P. K. Wrigley abjured alcohol in his personal life but opened the taps at Wrigley Field as soon as Prohibition ended in 1933. Beer sales paid for renovations on the twenty-year-old stadium. The new owner rebuilt the outfield walls, bringing the diamond to its current shape: 400 feet to dead center, a cozy 368 to the power alleys, with recessed "wells" in the corners to create the longest foul lines in the majors, 355 feet to the left-field foul pole, and 353 down the right-field line. For a homey touch, he planted a dozen elm trees in tubs of dirt in the bleachers. That didn't work—the winds off Lake Michigan blew the leaves off the trees, and workmen carted them away.

Wrigley had better luck when he hired twenty-three-year-old Bill Veeck, the son of a Cubs executive, to plant ivy along the outfield walls in 1937. Veeck would grow up to be the maverick owner who sent a dwarf to bat for the 1951 St. Louis Browns. (Eddie Gaedel, wearing uniform number ⅛, stood three foot, seven inches and weighed sixty-five pounds. He walked.) Over the years Veeck's ivy grew lush enough to serve as Wrigley Field's version of Charlie Brown's kite-eating tree. Year after year a few gappers hop into the vines and disappear. Outfielders throw up their hands or point accusingly at the ivy, calling for a ground-rule double.

AFTER TRAILING PITTSBURGH by seven games in September, the 1938 Cubs roared back to cut the Pirates' lead to half a game. On September 28 Gabby Hartnett came to bat with the score tied in the bottom of the ninth. It was getting dark, the sun dipping behind apartment houses on Clark Street. With Wrigley Field lights fifty years in the future, Hartnett squinted at the pitcher. Finally he spied a pitch he liked. Hartnett's legendary Homer in the Gloamin' sent the Cubs ahead of the Pirates and got them back to the World Series, where the Yankees swept them.

P. K. Wrigley outfitted ushers in blue and gold suits with brass buttons. He hired young women in sundresses to pass through the crowd selling cigarettes, and made Chicago musician Roy Nelson baseball's first ballpark organist. At first, Nelson had no idea what sort of music to play. He chose what the *Sporting News* praised as "classic and soulful compositions. . . . What joy! A beautiful ballpark, delicious hamburgers with onions, a can of beer, victory and the restful, dulcet notes of a pipe organ." The Cubs would continue to provide burgers and beer if not many victories.

As other owners began installing lights in the 1930s for night games, Wrigley stuck to day baseball. He said he didn't want to keep the neighbors up at night. Critics wondered whether his policy was hurting the team. Only the Cubs had to reset their body clocks every road trip or homestand. Purists who praised the owner's defense of day baseball would have been disappointed to know that Wrigley had bought tons of steel to build light towers in 1941. When the Japanese bombed Pearl Harbor, he donated the steel to the war effort.

His team specialized in what were dubbed Cub Follies. During World War II, manager Charlie Grimm asked outfielder Lou Novikoff why he kept letting fly balls drop near the fence. Novikoff explained that he was afraid of vines. Asked why he'd tried to steal third with the bases loaded, he said, "I got such a good jump." His teammate Lennie Merullo set a record by making four errors in an inning. That same day, Merullo's wife gave birth to a son, and, in honor of Lennie's performance, they named the baby Boots.

In 1945 the Cubs made their lone trip to the postseason between the 1930s and the 1980s. They faced a Detroit club led by Hank Greenberg in the '45 World Series. Lieutenant Greenberg, just back from the Army Air Corps, won Game Two with a three-run homer. The Hebrew Hammer homered only once after that, but he wasn't the goat of the Series. A goat was.

Before Game Four, a tavern owner named Gus Sianis let his beer-drinking nanny goat, Sonovia, out of her pen at the Billy Goat Inn. Sonovia hopped into his car and rode with him to the ballpark, where Wrigley's ushers turned her away. Sianis couldn't believe it. Here he was in his pin-striped suit and silk tie, proffering two tickets—one for him, one for the goat. Sonovia wore a blanket emblazoned WE GOT DETROIT'S GOAT.

"If we can't go in," Sianis announced, "the Cubs will never win." Wrigley's private security guards blocked the way, and the Curse of the Billy Goat was born. The Cubs lost Game Four and went on to lose the

Series. They had been in seven World Series since 1908 and lost them all. They wouldn't reach another World Series for more than seventy years. But as George Will would note, "Cub fans like to say that any team can have a bad century."

THERE WAS NO baseball team at Dallas's Booker T. Washington High School, so Ernie Banks played softball. He was so good that baseball scouts began showing up at his church-league games. One paid the skinny shortstop an eye-popping fifteen dollars to barnstorm with a squad of black major leaguers. Before he knew it, Banks was turning double plays with Jackie Robinson, sitting in a dugout with Roy Campanella, Larry Doby, and Don Newcombe. Then he got drafted into the army.

Private First Class Banks served with an all-black unit at Fort Bliss, near El Paso, where he starred for the base's basketball team. After a game against the Harlem Globetrotters the team's owner, Abe Saperstein, called the young soldier aside. "Maybe you could play for us sometime," Saperstein said. Banks was too nervous to answer. It was the first time he'd sat beside a white man.

After his army hitch, Banks joined the Kansas City Monarchs of the Negro American League, who sold his contract to the Chicago Cubs in 1953. Nobody expected the twenty-two-year-old Banks to play much—what the Cubs needed was a roommate for Gene Baker, the shortstop they planned to make the first black Cub.

Baseball teams of the '50s still economized by having players room together on the road. Nobody would dream of asking a white player to room with a black one, so the Cubs brought Baker and Banks to the majors together. As it happened, Baker was nursing a sore muscle, so Banks played shortstop against the Phillies that day. He would start every game for the next two years.

Ernie Banks smacked forty-four homers in 1955, at the time the most ever by a shortstop. He was a fixture at short by the time Gene Baker got healthy, so Baker switched to second base. Cubs radio announcer Bert

Wilson, who nicknamed them Bingo and Bango, loved calling 6-4-3 double plays they turned with first baseman Steve Bilko: *"Bingo Bango Bilko and the Cubs are out of the inning!"*

In 1958 the shortstop with the Pepsodent smile batted .313 with forty-seven homers and 129 RBIs to win the National League's Most Valuable Player award. A year later Banks won again—the first National Leaguer to win back-to-back MVPs, even though the team finished fifth both years. Fans started calling him "Mr. Cub." Banks did his best hitting at the sunshiny park he dubbed the Friendly Confines.

"It's a great day for a ballgame," he said in all weather. "Let's play two!"

DURING THE 1960 home opener, one bleacher fan found the sun friendly and her clothes too confining. "The young lady did an impromptu and complete striptease," the *Tribune* reported.

A year later, while the Yankees' Mickey Mantle and Roger Maris chased Babe Ruth's record of sixty homers in a season, P. K. Wrigley decided that baseball managers were overrated. Wrigley opted for a rotating crew of skippers who worked like an umpiring crew, with one of them serving as manager in chief every four games. He called them the College of Coaches: Harry Craft, Lou Klein, Vedie Himsl, and El Tappe. (The last two aren't typos. Avitus "Vedie" Himsl and Elvin Tappe had played and coached in the big leagues for decades.) Wrigley's brainstorm turned out to be one of baseball's least successful experiments.

With the College of Coaches running things, the '61 Cubs came in seventh in an eight-team National League. In 1962 they finished ninth in a ten-team NL, six games behind the Houston Colt .45s, an expansion team, and ahead of another expansion club, the comically bad New York Mets. But even at their worst, the Cubs put on a show. During one game a vendor's hot dog cart caught fire and exploded in a spew of franks, smoke, and steam. Firefighters ran into the park from the firehouse across the street, hosed down the cart, and stayed to watch the game.

Wrigley ditched the College of Coaches. It didn't help, but there were signs of life as the '60s progressed. In 1966 they had Banks, now thirty-five years old, at first base. Third baseman Ron Santo won his third straight Gold Glove while batting .312 with thirty home runs. Out-fielder Billy Williams had twenty-nine homers. Shortstop Don Kessinger and second baseman Glenn Beckert turned more double plays than Tinker and Evers. Still the Cubs lost a league-worst 103 games. Their new manager was not amused.

Leo Durocher had had a respectable playing career as a shortstop in the 1930s, most notably with the St. Louis Cardinals team known as the Gas House Gang. Later, as the Brooklyn Dodgers' player-manager, he benched himself to get the talented rookie Pee Wee Reese into the lineup. In 1947 he welcomed Jackie Robinson to the team, only to get suspended for what the commissioner called "accumulated unpleasant incidents" including consorting with gamblers and stealing Hollywood actress Laraine Day away from her husband, who called Durocher "a love pirate." When he jumped from Brooklyn to the rival New York Giants in 1948, Leo the Lip invited Dodger fans to commit suicide. Now bald and fleshy at sixty-one, the Cubs' new manager mocked the aging Banks, ignored the front office, spat on umpires' shoes, insulted reporters, and steered the 1967 Cubs into the first division for the first time in twenty years. They finished third in '67 and '68. Then came a season to talk about.

The year 1969 transformed the major leagues. To the world outside it was the year of *Abbey Road*, Woodstock, the Manson murders, the Stonewall Riots, and five hundred thousand tons of American bombs falling on Cambodia, but to baseball it was the first year of divisional play and playoffs. A pretty good team now had a better shot at making the postseason.

On July 20, 1969, astronaut Neil Armstrong walked on the moon and the Cubs' Ferguson Jenkins beat the Phillies 1–0 to put Chicago five games ahead in the brand-new National League East. From then on the division was a race between the Cubs and the upstart New York

Mets. Cubs reliever Dick Selma led cheers from the bullpen, waving a towel. Ron Santo jumped into the air after each win, clicking his heels. By the middle of August, Chicago was nine games ahead.

The Mets, who had yet to finish better than ninth in their seven-year existence, were nothing much on offense but electric on the mound. Tom Seaver and Jerry Koosman headed the rotation. Nolan Ryan, a rawboned kid out of Alvin, Texas, threw one hundred miles an hour. Shaggy-haired reliever Tug McGraw baffled batters with his screwball. They won fourteen of sixteen to pull within four games of first-place Chicago. Durocher's Cubs won five in a row to stay ahead, but then collapsed. Maybe all the Cubs' day games wore them down, or maybe it was Durocher, who rode the starting pitchers he called "my horses" till they dropped. It was probably a combination of the two factors. Durocher wasn't the only manager guilty of riding his horses too hard, but he was the only one whose team played all its home games in midwestern afternoon heat. Randy Hundley caught 151 of the Cubs' 162 games that season, Banks played 155, Kessinger 158, Santo 160. Billy Williams played 163 games out of 162, including a tie that was called on account of darkness and replayed. Jenkins, Ken Holtzman, and Bill Hands, the team's top three pitchers, made 123 starts that season and completed 53. (In 2018, all major-league starters—more than 250 of them—combined to throw 42 complete games.) The three of them combined to pitch nearly nine hundred innings but faltered down the stretch while Durocher raged and called them names. When Holtzman got lit up in one start, the manager called him a "gutless Jew."

The Cubs lost eleven of twelve in September to finish eight games behind the Miracle Mets, who went on to upset the Baltimore Orioles in the World Series. The Mets capped their first decade with a championship while the Cubs closed their sixth decade in a row without one.

THE CUBS OF the early '70s relied on Jenkins, a six-foot-five righthander who won 21 games that year and 66 more in the next three seasons. In 1973, however, the thirty-year-old ace went 14-16 for a Cubs team that finished fifth in the six-team NL East. General manager John Holland thought Jenkins was showing his age. There was another factor: Holland didn't want too many black players suiting up for the Cubs. Not because he was prejudiced, Holland claimed, but because the team's overwhelmingly white crowds were. When the former Negro Leagues star Buck O'Neil, now serving as a Cubs scout, said, "Mr. Holland, we'd have a better ball club if we played the blacks," Holland didn't disagree. But the fans were already accusing him of making the Cubs look like a Negro League team, he said. So Holland traded Jenkins to the Texas Rangers. A year later, Jenkins led the American League with 25 victories. He would win 110 more on his way to the Hall of Fame.

The 1974 Cubs finished last despite twenty homers from outfielder Rick Monday and a .313 average from rookie third baseman Bill Madlock, who came from Texas in the Jenkins trade. That was almost enough losing for P. K. Wrigley, who could tolerate coming in fourth or fifth as long as the team turned a profit. The eighty-year-old owner had been a teenager when the Cubs last won the World Series, and that was before his father owned them. It was time for another experiment.

After a fifth-place finish in 1975, Wrigley replaced Holland with Eldred "Salty" Saltwell, the longtime chief of concessions at Wrigley Field, whom reporters dubbed "the general manager of hot dogs." Before the 1977 season, Saltwell traded Madlock, who wanted a raise after hitting .354 and .339 to win consecutive batting titles. He dumped Kessinger for a player to be named later, and never got around to offering pitcher Steve Stone a contract. Saltwell got fired after only one season but left Cub fans something to remember him by. It was his idea to put wire baskets atop the outfield walls to keep bleacher bums from sitting on the walls or jumping onto the field.

His successor was Bob Kennedy, who had managed the 1963–65 Cubs and the 1968 Oakland A's of Catfish Hunter and Reggie Jackson. Kennedy thought the Cubs could win if they made better use of a new way of acquiring players: free agency. As general manager, Kennedy assembled Chicago's roster the modern way, signing free agents and trading depreciating assets for futures. He stole Bill Buckner and Ivan DeJesus from the Dodgers—a good start, but the Cubs still needed a home-run hitter. Pitcher Mike Krukow joked about their "Rush Street offense." Like Chicago's North Side nightlife, it was "lots of singles and not enough scoring."

And so, in the winter of 1978, Kennedy spent $1.4 million to bring Dave Kingman to Chicago.

Kingman had grown up in Mount Prospect, Illinois, in the northwest suburbs many closer-in Chicagoans called the land beyond O'Hare. A four-sport star at Prospect High, he ran track, dunked for the basketball team, played wide receiver during football season, and set every record for the Prospect Knights' baseball team. In his last high school game he hit two home runs and pitched a two-hit shutout. High school hero Kingman had a long, clean-cut jaw and wore his hair in a crew cut. He grew his hair out at the University of Southern California, where he led the Trojans to the 1970 NCAA baseball championship.

A year later he was in the majors. In his first ten big-league at-bats, Kingman conked three home runs. Two were off Pirates ace Dock Ellis, the only man ever to pitch a no-hitter on LSD. (It was the '70s.) Kingman had the kind of power that put fannies in seats. He was with the Mets when he launched a blast at Wrigley Field that one writer swore "O'Hare could not have held." But he never lived up to his potential. Booed out of New York for falling down in the outfield and striking out two or three times a game, he acted like he didn't care. But now, following a disheartening 1977 season that saw him suit up for four different teams—the Mets, Padres, Angels, and Yankees—he was home, taking out his frustrations on the rest of the National League. He told reporters he wasn't fond of New Yorkers but liked Chicagoans. They liked him back after he hit seven homers in his first month as a Cub. He cooled off after that but still led the '78 Cubs with twenty-eight homers, two more than the other seven guys in the everyday lineup.

When the Phillies came to Wrigley in May 1979, Kingman had nine homers, second in the league to Mike Schmidt. He was also leading the league in strikeouts.

"Kingman kind of exemplified the Cubs," Ed Hartig said. "He was bad in interesting ways."

THE PHILLIES: UNLOVED LOSERS

The Philadelphia Phillies were mismanaged from the start. As of 1979 the Philadelphia National League ball club was the last of the major leagues' original sixteen franchises that had never won a World Series. They were oh-for-ninety-six years. Their 7,705 losses were the most in major-league history, 327 more than the Chicago Cubs. According to Frank Fitzpatrick, who covered baseball for the *Philadelphia Inquirer*, "It's easy to see why generations of Philadelphians never followed the examples of Chicago or Boston baseball fans in believing that their team was cursed. Cursed would have been an improvement."

The Phillies' first owner, sporting-goods tycoon Al Reach, bought the bankrupt Worcester (Massachusetts) Ruby Legs in 1883 and moved them to Philadelphia, where they debuted with an eight-game losing streak. Reach didn't believe in paying the two thousand or even three thousand dollars a year it took to sign star players. He remembered making twenty-five dollars a week when he was one of the first professional baseball stars in the 1860s. His Philadelphians came in last in the National League in 1883, their inaugural year, 46 games behind the Boston Beaneaters. Their best pitcher, John Coleman, had a record of

12-48. Some Phillies fans would say the team's history went downhill from there.

The club's first big star, pitcher-outfielder Charlie Ferguson, caught typhoid fever and died at age twenty-five. Philadelphia's next baseball hero, Napoleon Lajoie, jumped to the crosstown Athletics when the American League launched in 1901. Another early Phillies star, Ed Delahanty, paced the National League at one time or another in batting average (.410), homers (19), RBIs (137), and stolen bases (58). He led the senior circuit with 43 doubles in 1902, only to make a fatal error the following season. Kicked off a train for being drunk and obnoxious, Big Ed staggered into the Niagara River and was swept over the falls to his death. They found his body under the falls a week later, naked except for his shoes, socks, and necktie.

Reach built his team a home field, the Philadelphia Baseball Park. It burned down. He rebuilt it. A balcony in the new park collapsed, killing a dozen fans. He rebuilt again, hoping to recoup lost gate receipts, but even the weather was against him. The 1903 Phillies set a major-league record that still stands: nine rainouts in a row.

Reach gave up and sold out, leading to an era of mismanagement that cemented what Fitzpatrick would call the Phillies' "long, lamentable legacy of losing." At first, Charles Taft, half brother of President William Howard Taft, ran the club with sportswriter Horace Fogel, who treated fans to spectacles like a wedding on the pitcher's mound, with the bride and groom in a lion's cage and the lion serving as witness. Fogel proceeded to rename the team. "'Phillies' is too trite. It has come to mean a comfortable lackadaisicalness, the fourth-place groove," he announced. Henceforth, he said, the club would be the Philadelphia Live Wires. Everybody ignored him.

William Baker took over in 1913. A former New York City police commissioner, Baker was "entirely without knowledge of professional baseball," the *New York Times* reported. But when the Phillies finally won their first National League pennant in 1915, Baker was hailed as their savior. They won Game One of the 1915 World Series behind their thirty-one-game winner, Grover Cleveland Alexander, then lost the next four to the Boston Red Sox. They wouldn't win another pennant for thirty-five years. It would be sixty-five years before they won another World Series game.

It soon became clear that William Baker was cheap—even by the standards of the day, when all owners were tight with a nickel. To save on maintenance, Baker let sheep nibble the grass at the ballpark he had renamed the Baker Bowl. While other clubs sent teams of scouts to scour the country for talent, Baker's Phillies had just one scout. And while Weeghman's Chicago Cubs let fans keep foul balls, the Phillies called the police on Robert Cotter, an eleven-year-old fan who insisted on keeping a foul ball. A Philadelphia judge let the boy out of jail, lecturing Baker and his attorneys for "throwing small boys into prison because they took a ball. . . . I don't know whether you were ever boys, for if you were, you would know how they cherish the ball."

Baker's team carried on its losing legacy long after little Bobby Cotter grew up. Year after year they came in seventh or eighth in the eight-team National League. The Baker Bowl "bore a striking resemblance to a rundown men's room," wrote Red Smith in the *New York Times*. The crumbling park's most prominent feature was a Lifebuoy Soap ad on the right-field fence, with forty-foot letters spelling THE PHILLIES USE LIFEBUOY. One night a fan sneaked in with a paint can and added AND THEY STILL STINK.

Old-timers from those days told the story of a hotshot pitcher who came up from the minors around that time. He got tired of losing pitchers' duels. Finally the kid complained to Doc Prothro, the manager: "Pitching on this club, I'm not sure I'm in the big leagues."

Prothro said, "Son, don't you ever think you're not in the big leagues. We may not be a big-league club, but we play against them."

THE 1943 PHILLIES broke a streak of five consecutive last-place finishes by coming in seventh. That was the year they had a chance to change history.

The team was for sale again. One suitor was Bill Veeck, who had planted the ivy at Wrigley Field six years before. The fast-talking young executive claimed he could turn the Phillies from doormats to pennant winners in a matter of months, and he might have been right.

If he got the Phillies, Veeck said, he'd sign the top Negro League stars. Josh Gibson, Buck Leonard, Cool Papa Bell, Satchel Paige, Smokey Joe Williams—they'd come cheap and win a hundred games easy. If white Phillies players refused to play with them, Veeck would field an all-black team. That way, other owners wouldn't feel pressured to integrate their rosters—and millions of black baseball fans all over America would buy tickets to see the Phillies!

According to Veeck, his loose lips sank his plans. He told Commissioner Landis what he hoped to do, and the flinty onetime federal judge who ruled the game disapproved. The next thing Veeck knew, the National League took control of the Phillies and sold them to William Cox, a New York City timber merchant, "for about half what I was willing to pay."

Landis died the following year, and Veeck wound up buying the Cleveland Indians in 1946. After Brooklyn's Jackie Robinson broke the color line in April 1947, Veeck signed Larry Doby that July to be the second black major leaguer. The following summer he brought forty-two-year-old Satchel Paige to Cleveland. Paige, the oldest rookie in major-league history, called age a question of mind over matter: "If you don't mind, it don't matter." He went 6-1 that season as the Indians won the World Series.

Shortly after taking over the Phillies, William Cox fired Bucky Harris, the club's popular manager. But Harris had friends in the press box, and he let slip that he'd overheard the owner making phone calls to a bookie. Cox was promptly banned for betting on ballgames. He is the only owner ever kicked out of baseball; he and Pete Rose are the only ones to be banned for life since the 1919 Black Sox scandal.

Cox's successor was Robert Carpenter, whose family would run the franchise for the next four decades.

Carpenter's father, Robert Ruliph Morgan "Ruly" Carpenter, was a cynic's Horatio Alger story. Born in 1877, he grew up working in his father's hardware store, studied hard at MIT, landed a job at DuPont, and had the all-American gumption to marry the boss's daughter. He rose to be vice president of the conglomerate, which made plastics, insecticides, and agricultural aids. (See DuPont's 1910 pamphlet "Farming with Dynamite.") In later years the company introduced nylon, Freon, Teflon, Lycra, and Kevlar. At sixty-six, Ruly Carpenter was wealthy enough to buy the Phillies for four hundred thousand dollars and hand them over to his son.

The youngest club president in big-league history, twenty-eight-year-old Robert Ruliph Morgan Carpenter Jr., known as Bob, vowed to spend whatever it took to make the Phillies winners. "An heir has an obligation to put his money to work," he said. But if the new owner felt obliged to do the right thing, his manager didn't.

Phils manager Ben Chapman was a jug-eared Alabaman with a big mouth. As one of the game's leading bench jockeys, he couldn't wait to go after Jackie Robinson. When the 1947 Dodgers came to Philadelphia, Chapman heckled them unprintably. "Hey Pee Wee," he yelled at Brooklyn's Pee Wee Reese, "how you like playing with a nigger?" Chapman got fired in 1948 and never managed again, but the Phillies' charged racial history affected their fortunes for decades. They ignored a high school catcher from Philadelphia, Roy Campanella. They gave Alabama teenager Willie Mays a tryout but didn't sign him. (The Phils weren't the only club interested in Mays, just the only one that wanted to make him a pitcher.) They wouldn't have a black star until Rookie of the Year Dick Allen hit 29 homers in 1964, and Allen enjoyed his time in Philadelphia so much that he drew a message in the dirt with his spikes while playing first base: TRADE ME.

The Phillies' mismanaged history amounted to a long losing streak interrupted by one summer no Phillies fan ever forgot.

THE WHIZ KIDS of 1950 came together around the same time as Brooklyn's Boys of Summer, but are less remembered. They were the youngest team in the league. Center fielder Richie Ashburn, who would go on to the Hall of Fame and a long career in the Phillies' broadcast booth, arrived as a jut-jawed twenty-one-year-old from Tilden, Nebraska, his hair so blond that teammates called him Whitey. Pitching aces Robin Roberts and Curt Simmons were twenty-three and twenty-one, respectively. In the starting lineup only Eddie Waitkus, the nimble "Fred Astaire of first basemen," was out of his twenties. Waitkus was thirty and lucky to have lived that long.

The summer before, he'd received a message at the team hotel in Chicago: *Mr. Waitkus—It's extremely urgent that I see you as soon as possible . . . Room 1297A.* A bachelor on a road trip, he went upstairs and knocked. Ruth Ann Steinhagen, a pretty nineteen-year-old, invited him in. "I have a surprise for you," she said. A rifle. The next moments became the inspiration for Bernard Malamud's 1952 novel *The Natural* and the 1984 Robert Redford movie based on Malamud's book. She shot him. Waitkus almost died on the operating table, but fought his way back into playing shape in time to go three-for-five on Opening Day 1950.

The Phillies beat the National League champion Dodgers that day. The score was 7–0 when Jackie Robinson came to the plate in the top of the fourth with his usual swagger. "What do you think you're going to do, win the pennant?" Robinson asked Phillies catcher Andy Seminick.

Seminick said, "You bet."

Robin Roberts notched the first of twenty victories that day. With Simmons winning almost as often, the Phils took a seven-game lead in September. Jim Konstanty, a thirty-three-year-old junkballer, came out of nowhere to win sixteen games and save twenty-two. On September 20 Philadelphia topped the seventh-place Cubs to go seven and a half games up on second-place Brooklyn with ten to play. Then the Dodgers won seven in a row. Roberts and Konstanty each lost twice in the season's last week, and the Whiz Kids' lead was down to a single game with one to play.

On October 1 they met the Dodgers in a rematch of Opening Day, this time at Ebbets Field in Brooklyn. The Phillies sent Roberts—making his third start in five days—against Brooklyn speedballer Don Newcombe.

The teams went to extra innings with the score tied, 1–1. Both starting pitchers were still in the game. In the tenth, with Ashburn on second and Waitkus at first, Newcombe faced Phillies left fielder Dick Sisler, who was trying to make a name for himself.

Sisler was the son of George Sisler, one of the best hitters in major-league history. "Gorgeous George," a dimpled Ohioan, had retired with two .400 seasons, a career average of .340, and a plaque in the Hall of Fame. His son Dick, born in 1920, grew up hearing men say, "That's George Sisler's boy. He'll never be the hitter his dad was." They were right: Dick never batted .300.

His father was in the crowd at Ebbets Field that day; he worked as a scout for the Dodgers. George watched his son step up in the tenth with runners at first and second. Newcombe threw hard and Dick Sisler didn't want to get jammed; he was nursing a sprained wrist. Every fastball on the hands stung like hell. The Dodgers knew about Sisler's wrist and fed him fastballs that he fouled off. Finally they decided to cross him up with a fastball outside.

It wasn't as outside as they wanted. Sisler drove it over the left-field fence. The Whiz Kids were going to the 1950 World Series.

They lost.

The Yankees of Joe DiMaggio, Yogi Berra, Whitey Ford, and Phil Rizzuto swept them in four games. The Yanks had their second consecutive World Series title and thirteenth overall; the Phillies were still looking for their first.

They had scored all of four runs while getting swept in the last all-Caucasian World Series. (Mays, Monte Irvin, and Hank Thompson would play for the New York Giants in the 1951 Series.) Still, they rode the train home to a heroes' welcome at Philadelphia's Broad Street Station. The Whiz Kids were National League champions, the youngest club in the league, with better years in store, they thought.

But they came in fifth in 1951. The Phillies went on to finish third, fourth, or fifth every season until 1958, when they backslid to last and stayed there for another four years.

As the '60s began the only Whiz Kids left on the roster were Roberts and Simmons, both ten-year veterans. Roberts was thirty-three, still unfurling the silky powerful motion that had helped him lead the majors in victories four years running. A coal miner's son from Springfield, Illinois, Roberts came from a family of baseball fans who listened to the Cubs on WGN radio. Eleven-year-old Robin had been sitting down to dinner when Gabby Hartnett hit the Homer in the Gloamin' in 1938. (His happy mother spilled the potatoes.) Two years later he was an eighth-grade pitcher at a sports banquet when Grover Cleveland Alexander himself got up to give a speech.

The great Alexander was fifty-three and had been retired for a decade. He looked older than fifty-three. The boy knew Alexander had been the best Phillies pitcher ever and one of the Cubs' best, too. He was looking forward to a pep talk. Instead, the Hall of Famer's speech lasted less than a minute. Alexander stood, steadying himself. He said, "Boys, I hope you enjoy sports, but I warn you about one thing. Don't take a drink, because look what it has done to me." And then he sat down. He'd been deaf in one ear since the Great War, suffering seizures he blamed on shell shock and liquor. The great Alex would last another ten years, long enough to see Roberts and the Whiz Kids face the Yankees in the 1950 World Series, his last public appearance. He died a month later.

Roberts broke Alexander's team records. By 1960, having averaged thirty-nine starts and 301 innings per season during the '50s, he felt older than thirty-three. After a loss to the Reds on Opening Day, he wasn't the only one who felt that way. Phillies manager Eddie Sawyer, reflecting on the team's 0-1 record, told reporters, "I am forty-nine years old and want to live to be fifty." He retired on the spot. (Smart move: Sawyer would live to be eighty-seven.)

Nineteen sixty was the third of four straight last-place seasons for the Phillies. Roberts won twelve games and lost sixteen while getting to know a pair of new arrivals. One was a hulking reliever named Dallas Green, whose arm was no match for his confidence. The other was Gene "Skip" Mauch, a thirty-four-year-old former infielder, finally getting a chance to earn his nickname.

*   *   *

As a player, Gene Mauch eked out nine major-league seasons with the Cubs and five other clubs in the '40s and '50s. Like many future mangers, he was a scrapper with just enough talent to make the big leagues and enough brains to watch big-league managers at work and think he could do better. According to the *New York Post*'s Maury Allen, Mauch was "brash," a term Allen defined as "pushier than your humble ability would allow for."

Growing up in Kansas, Gene Mauch told anyone who'd listen that he was going to the majors—as a manager. They called him Skipper or Skip. In 1957, his ninth and last year as a player, Mauch hit a career-high two homers. He then talked his way into a job as player-manager of the Triple-A Minneapolis Millers, and led the Millers to the American Association pennant. The next year he did it again. So when Eddie Sawyer quit on Opening Day 1960, Phils owner Bob Carpenter gave Mauch the least-coveted job in the majors. Carpenter wanted a manager who was malleable and worked cheap. He got one who worked cheap.

Under Mauch, the 1960 Phillies finished last again. A year later they were twelve games worse. With the manager overturning the postgame buffet after yet another five-run defeat, the 1961 Phillies lost twenty-three in a row to set a major-league mark that still stands. They finished seventeen games behind the seventh-place Cubs. Then, a year later, they turned a corner. The '62 Phillies played small ball—first in the league in sacrifices, second in steals—winning 81 and losing 80 for their first winning record in a decade. Gene Mauch was the *Sporting News* Manager of the Year.

A year later his Phils jumped to 89-73. Suddenly relevant, they were picked to finish fifth in a fiercely contested 1964 National League pennant race, battling the Los Angeles Dodgers of Sandy Koufax and Don Drysdale; the San Francisco Giants, with Juan Marichal on the mound and a lineup featuring Willie Mays, Willie McCovey, and Orlando Cepeda; the Cincinnati Reds, with Rookie of the Year Pete Rose setting the table for Vada Pinson and Frank Robinson; the St. Louis Cardinals, with Ken Boyer at third and Bob Gibson just entering the prime of his career; and a Milwaukee Braves club featuring Hank Aaron, Eddie Mathews, and Warren Spahn. Even the Cubs had Lou Brock in his last Chicago season, scoring runs ahead of Banks, Williams, and Santo. Against all that the Phillies had Johnny Callison and hope.

Much of the hope centered on Jim Bunning, who had averaged sixteen victories over seven seasons with the Detroit Tigers. But there were two things the Tigers didn't like about Bunning. First, he was thirty-two years old. More important, he was the Tigers' representative in the new Major League Baseball Players Association—one of those clubhouse-lawyer types management could do without. When Bunning asked for a raise on his $39,000 salary, the Tigers shipped him to Philadelphia, where Carpenter welcomed the rotation anchor his manager kept pleading for.

Mauch was even more enthused about a broad-shouldered third baseman from Wampum, Pennsylvania. Wampum (population 1,085) was a coal-country town where Era Allen, a single mother who worked as a maid, raised nine children including Dick, who grew up tossing stones in the air and knocking them a mile. "I was always paying for window panes," Era said. A high school basketball All-American, her son chose baseball when the Phillies offered him seventy thousand dollars to sign a contract (about six hundred thousand in today's dollars). He bought his mother a house and went off to play ball.

Dick Allen hit professional pitches a mile, too. One of his minor-league shots broke a bulb in the top row of a hundred-foot light tower beyond the center-field fence. Newspapers called him the Wampum Walloper. Allen set hitting records at minor-league stops in upstate New York and Twin Falls, Idaho, but was appalled by what he saw when the Phillies promoted him to Triple-A Little Rock. Upon arrival he learned that he was the first black player the Arkansas Travelers ever had. Six years after Governor Orval Faubus sent the Arkansas National Guard to keep black students out of Little Rock Central High School, Governor Faubus attended the 1963 Travelers' home opener. A sign in the stands read LET'S NOT NEGRO-IZE OUR BASEBALL.

Allen dropped a fly ball that night. "It's tough to play when you're frightened," he said after the game. He won the fans over with a thirty-three-homer year that earned him another promotion. The following March he reported to spring training as a big leaguer and discovered that the team had told the press his name was Richie Allen, a name the Phillies must have considered more fan-friendly than Dick.

"Please call me Dick," he said. "I don't know how 'Richie' started. It makes me sound like I'm ten years old. Anyone who knows me well calls me Dick. I don't know why, as soon as I put on a uniform, it's Richie."

By any name he raked. "His hands are so fast it's unbelievable," Mauch said after the rookie walloped a pair of homers at Wrigley Field. With Callison and Allen batting third and fourth, the new-look '64 Phillies took over first place in June. The Reds and Giants stayed close, but it was the Cardinals who worried Mauch, with Curt Flood in center, Brock (filched from the Cubs in a midseason deal) in left, Ken Boyer at third, and Bob Gibson pitching every fourth day. His worries seemed misplaced in the middle of September, when St. Louis sat six and a half games behind Philadelphia with two weeks to play. There were twelve games left on the schedule. When the first-place Phillies flew home from a West Coast trip, Mayor James Tate waited at the airport to welcome them home along with a hundred or so fans, all singing the local radio hit "Go-Go Phillies '64." Bob Carpenter began printing World Series tickets.

A night later, Cincinnati had Frank Robinson at bat in a scoreless game with a runner at third and two out. That's when the runner, Giraldo "Chico" Ruiz, tried to steal home. Ruiz's mad dash startled his manager, Dick Sisler, the Phillies hero of 1950. It also startled the Phillies. Ruiz slid under the tag at the plate to score the game's only run.

Mauch threw a postgame tantrum: "Chico fucking Ruiz beats us on the bonehead play of the year!" That loss trimmed the Phils' lead in the pennant race to five and a half games with eleven to play, and Mauch seemed to panic. He pitched Bunning and left-hander Chris Short on short rest, hoping to clinch the pennant. Both lost twice while St. Louis won seven of eight to slip past Cincinnati into second place. And who should be the Cardinals' secret weapon but Curt Simmons, Robin

Roberts's old roomie. At thirty-five the aging Whiz Kid was throwing harder than ever, winning four times in two weeks as St. Louis cut the Phillies' lead to half a game.

Mauch sent Bunning back to the mound on the last day of September. Making his third start of the week, his ninth of September, Bunning hung a second-inning slider to Tim McCarver, the Cardinals' light-hitting catcher. McCarver stroked a two-run homer. St. Louis never looked back, and Curt Simmons was on his way to his eighteenth victory, a World Series ring, and an eight-thousand-dollar raise.

Mauch found an upside to his team's collapse. He said a 92-win season was nothing to sneeze at. The *Inquirer*, *Bulletin*, and *Daily News* didn't see it that way. They harped on the "Pholdo" of ex-genius Gene's "Phutile Phils."

"The first thing I'm going to do," Callison said, "is find a place to hide."

At spring training a few months later, the manager refused to talk about any Pholdo or Phlop. "We're looking forward to 1965," Mauch said. When ABC Sports asked for an interview, he said, "I won't talk about last year." ABC's Howard Cosell told him that this would be fine—no questions about last year.

Cosell brought a TV crew to Clearwater, Florida, where the Phillies held spring training. He and Mauch shook hands and sat down. When the red light blinked and they were on-camera, Cosell began: "Gene, how did it feel to blow a six-and-a-half-game lead with twelve games to play?"

Mauch said, "Fuck you, Cosell." He got up and went back to work.

His clubhouse wasn't much more peaceful than before. In July 1964, backup outfielder Frank "Big Donkey" Thomas, a former seminarian who had given up priestly studies to play baseball, started a fight with Dick Allen. "Hey Richie! Richie X!" Thomas yelled, referring to Malcolm X. Allen knocked him down with one punch. Big Donkey came up swinging—swinging a bat into Allen's shoulder.

"There's a firm rule—you never swing a bat at another player," Callison said. The Phils put Thomas on waivers. A year later, the last-place

Cubs signed and then released him. That was the end of Thomas's fifteen-year major-league career.

Allen made the 1965 National League All-Star team. The following year he slugged forty home runs, slashing .317/.396/.632. In 1967 he led the league with a .404 on-base percentage, but by then he wanted out of Philadelphia. He showed up late for team flights. He missed meetings. In 1968 Mauch gave Phils owner Carpenter an ultimatum: "Either Allen goes or I go."

The owner fired Mauch. A year after that, following a thirty-two-homer campaign, Allen demanded a boost on his seventy-thousand-dollar salary. Carpenter traded him to the Cardinals, the Phillies' rivals in the new National League East, for a package including Curt Flood.

Flood was a three-time All-Star who'd heard Philadelphia fans boo Allen for five years. Of course they had a right—they'd paid for tickets—but it seemed to Flood that they booed black players louder. Flood was black like Allen, a proud professional like Allen, but nowhere near the hitter Allen was. Flood was settled in St. Louis, raising a family there. And the Cards were contenders, as attested by his 1964 and 1967 World Series rings, while the Phillies were losers. Most of all, as Flood wrote in a letter to Commissioner Bowie Kuhn, "After twelve years in the Major Leagues, I do not feel that I am a piece of property to be bought and sold irrespective of my wishes."

With backing from players' union leaders like Jim Bunning as well as the Major League Baseball Players Association's new executive director, Marvin Miller, Flood sued Major League Baseball for the right to play for a team of his choosing. It took two and a half years for *Flood v. Kuhn* to reach the U.S. Supreme Court.

The Court ruled against him. Justice Harry Blackmun, writing for a five-to-three majority, upheld the baseball owners' right to buy and sell players as they pleased. Citing the Court's 1922 ruling against the Federal League's Baltimore Terrapins, and quoting from "Casey at the Bat," Blackmun granted that the reserve clause binding players to their teams was "an anomaly" in labor relations and admitted that Major League Baseball was a form of interstate commerce. Still the Court ruled that the game was immune to federal antitrust laws due to its unique place in American life. Society's interest was not in freeing baseball players, Blackmun wrote, but in keeping this "aberration confined to baseball."

Flood, Miller, and the players lost that case but went on to win the war. The union kept suing, chipping away at the owners' antitrust exemption. Miller, a labor organizer with a dark mustache and a shock of swept-back silver hair who had come to the Players Association from the United Steelworkers union, worked with player representatives including Joe Torre and Brooks Robinson to lead a strike in 1972, the first players' strike in modern sports history. A year later, the owners agreed to federal arbitration of some players' salaries. An arbitrator finally voided the reserve clause in 1975. Now assured a bigger piece of the pie just as television began to enrich baseball owners beyond their fathers' dreams, the players would see their share of revenue reach 38 percent by the end of the 1970s, turning ballplayers into millionaires. In the fifteen years before Marvin Miller came to the players union in 1966, the average big-league salary had crept from $12,000 to $19,000. Fifteen years later it was $325,000. The game's economic transformation changed everything, just as the Phillies were finally figuring out how to win.

PHILADELPHIA FANS WERE still booing in 1979, but things were looking up. Much of their success was the handiwork of Paul Owens, who had been the Phillies' minor-league director since 1965. Known as "the Pope" for his resemblance to Paul VI, Owens signed and developed three promising college shortstops: Ohio University's Mike Schmidt, Stanford's Bob Boone, and Sacramento City College's Larry Bowa. (Schmidt and Boone shifted to third base in the minors; after that, Boone got a look at Schmidt and switched to catcher.) The Pope then drafted high school slugger Greg Luzinski out of Notre Dame Prep in suburban Chicago. After becoming general manager in 1972 he made shrewd trades, acquiring reliever Tug McGraw from the Mets before the 1975 season, and then center fielder Garry Maddox from the Giants and right fielder Bake McBride from the Cardinals. Owens and the Phils' new manager, Danny Ozark, took the novel approach of treating players as grown men.

Under Ozark, the Phillies won three straight division titles only to flop in the playoffs. Pete Rose and the Reds swept them in the 1976 National League Championship Series, and the Dodgers knocked them out in 1977 and 1978. After that, Owens and club president Bill Giles convinced owner Robert Ruliph Morgan "Ruly" Carpenter III, grandson of the original Ruly, to open his wallet for the last puzzle piece. On December 5, 1978, they signed Pete Rose for four years and $3.2 million.

The biggest gamble of the new free-agent era owed a debt to TV's growing influence. When Carpenter balked at Rose's price, WPHL, which telecast Phillies games, kicked in six hundred thousand dollars.

At thirty-eight, Rose was slowing down, but he was still a .300 hitter with doubles power and versatility. He'd been an All-Star third baseman for four straight seasons, but Philadelphia had Schmidt at third, so Charlie Hustle switched to first base. Leadership meant more than position, he said. He hadn't switched teams for the first time in his sixteen-year career to teach guys how to field, he said. "I'm here to teach 'em how to win." His contract gave Philadelphia the highest payroll in baseball. It was the exclamation point on a message from the front office: Division titles aren't enough. Win or else!

According to Phillies reliever Rawly Eastwick, "Pete was all energy, and that's what we needed."

"We had the best talent already, but something was missing," shortstop Larry Bowa said. Asked what Rose was supposed to bring, Bowa had to think about it. "Charisma, or whatever," he said.

For the first six weeks of the 1979 season, it was working. As the Phillies came to Chicago to close a two-week road trip, they had the best record in baseball.

"They needed a leader," Rose said, "but it's not like I walked in and said, 'Follow me.' Schmidt was already the best player in the league three or four days a week. I just did my thing. Play hard with no phonyism.

He saw that and pretty soon he's the best player seven days a week. And they knew I wasn't only there for the money, because Philadelphia didn't offer the most money." In fact, Cardinals owner August Busch Jr. had offered Rose a Budweiser dealership if he signed with St. Louis. Pirates owner John Galbreath had offered racehorses. Said Rose, "I went to Philly to win."

PART TWO

TEN INNINGS

TOP OF THE 1ST

PHILADELPHIA	—0	0	0
CUBS	—0	0	0

Due up for the Phillies: McBride, Bowa, Rose

It was a Thursday in Chicago, mostly sunny with the wind blowing out. The players started their workdays as usual, the Cubs driving from suburban homes and Streeterville condos to the players' parking lot on Clark Street, looking up to check the flags around the ballpark. The visiting Phillies looked out their hotel windows to see candy wrappers and businessmen's hats blowing north up Michigan Avenue.

"In Chicago, the first thing you do is check the wind," Phils catcher Bob Boone said. "If it's blowing out, you can't wait to get to the park. Unless you're a pitcher."

Fans began arriving around noon. Soon there were dozens and then hundreds walking a block from the Addison El stop to Wrigley Field. Pamela Marin and Helen Rosenberg, a waitress and a college student, both twenty years old, paid a buck fifty each to sit in the bleachers. "When we got inside I had a Frosty Malt and Pammie had an Old Style. We sat back to work on our tans," Rosenberg recalled. "Then we heard Ronnie Woo Woo."

Ronnie "Woo Woo" Wickers, a leather-lunged fan who attended every home game, strode through the crowd yelling "Cubs *woo!* Cubs *woo!*" at the top of his high, reedy voice, never seeming to pause for breath. He name-checked the Cubs as they took the field for the top of the first. "Buckner *woo!* Kong *woo!*" The Cubs' old-fashioned home whites were baggier than the visitors' nylon uniforms. All nine Cubs sported mustaches, from outfielder Mike Vail's gingery bristles to first baseman Bill Buckner's black street-sweeper. The park was only half full. The game-time temperature was sixty-eight degrees, warming up along with Cub pitcher Dennis Lamp.

The curly-haired, bespectacled Lamp had a plug of chewing to-bacco bulging his cheek. He wasn't the Cubs' scheduled starter. Mike Krukow had been expected to pitch, but he came down with a slight case of elbow soreness, as some pitchers tended to do when the wind was blowing out at Wrigley. Lamp had injury issues of his own; he'd spent two weeks fighting blisters on his pitching hand. He treated the blisters the way ballplayers often did, covering them with superglue when they popped. His middle finger was still bluish from the glue, but he'd been glad to see a new baseball in his shoe when he got to his locker that day, the traditional signal that he was the starting pitcher.

"Lamp *woo!*"

The umpire, wearing black pants, a white shirt, and a short-billed black cap, signaled to the mound. Lamp squinted in for a sign from catcher Barry Foote.

Arnold Ray McBride, the Phillies' leadoff man, was the son of a Negro Leagues star who'd gone on to be a bricklayer. McBride had mutton-chop sideburns and an Afro his batting helmet could barely contain. Teammates called him Shake 'n Bake or just Bake.

Lamp's sinker started at the level of McBride's knees, then dived. "*Swing and a miss and we're underway,*" Cubs announcer Jack Brickhouse said.

Lamp's next pitch was his slurve, quicker than a curve with a sharper break. McBride looped it to left for a single. That brought Larry Bowa to the plate. Bowa was a 150-pound shortstop with a .287 average and a short fuse. He had no power but he'd kill you with slap hits and hard slides. If not the doggedest competitor in the league, he might be runner-up to the guy who was coming up next. As Bowa kicked dirt in the batter's box, Pete Rose leaned on his bat in the on-deck circle. With his Rolls-Royces and eight-hundred-thousand-dollar-a-year contract, six times the average big-league salary, Rose was the poster boy for free agency. He was eager for his ups. "A day like that, you can't wait to take a swing," he said. He watched Bowa slap Lamp's next pitch to the left-field gap.

Dave Kingman had a chance to catch the ball. Diving for it with the grace of a falling tree, he missed it. Kong wasn't paid for defense. "*Kingman tried*," Brickhouse told WGN viewers as Bowa pulled into second base with a double, McBride holding at third with nobody out.

Rose came to the plate batting .346. He told himself not to be overanxious. *Overanxious* was one of those revealing baseball terms, a reminder that anxious is the usual state. Rose took a slurve from Lamp for ball one. Lamp signaled to the umpire—he wanted a new baseball. The new one didn't feel right in his bluish fingers, either, so he called for another. Rose smacked this one on one hop right back at the pitcher. McBride, leading off third, took a step toward the plate. Lamp threw behind him and McBride was out.

"Lamp *woo!*"

Mike Schmidt came up with men at first and second, one out. Schmidt was leading the National League with a dozen home runs. Kingman stood second with nine. At his early-season pace, Schmidt looked like he might challenge Roger Maris's record of sixty-one in a season. And he loved to hit at Wrigley. On the team bus from O'Hare he'd smiled, looking forward to three games at Wrigley, and said, "I might hit four." After a solo homer on Tuesday and a two-run shot yesterday, he was halfway there with a game to play.

Lamp rubbed up the ball, gingerly. He and his infielders could get a force at any base. A double play gets him out of the inning.

Schmidt swung at the first pitch he saw, a sinker that didn't. It came in belt-high, but Schmidt got under it, sending a routine fly to Kingman in left. At least it looked routine until it caught the wind, which averaged seventeen miles an hour that afternoon, gusting to thirty. At first, Kingman seemed to have plenty of room. Drifting back onto the warning track, he had an extra ten feet thanks to the well in the wall created when P. K. Wrigley rebuilt the fences in 1937. Shielding his eyes, Kingman reached up for the ball and watched it carry out of his reach.

"*Back she goes, back, back, back,*" Brickhouse said, his voice rising. "*It's a home run and three runs are in!*"

Lamp's shoulders sagged. He'd thrown eight pitches and the score was 3–0. Not much of a present for his wife, Janet, who had a seat in the wives-and-girlfriends section behind the backstop. It was her birthday.

With one out, left fielder Del Unser singled. Then Garry Maddox singled. Maybe this wasn't Lamp's day. Relief pitcher Donnie Moore started getting loose in the Cubs' bullpen.

Bob Boone, batting seventh for the Phillies, wasn't accustomed to coming up in the top of the first. He'd ditched his shin guards on his way to the bat rack. Boone was a second-generation ballplayer who saw every play, every pitch, in context, and in baseball there's nothing but context. His father, Ray, had been an All-Star third baseman for the Detroit Tigers who once led the American League in RBIs. Bob grew up around big leaguers and signed his first autograph when he was eleven. He'd been practicing his fielding with his dad and some teammates on the Chicago White Sox when a fan mistook him for second baseman Nellie Fox. Eleven-year-old Bob was big for his age. He signed Fox's name and went back to shagging flies.

Through his father, Boone was connected to the generation of Joe DiMaggio and Ted Williams. His father's fondest memory had nothing to do with his All-Star appearances (including a homer off Robin Roberts in the 1954 All-Star Game) or his league-leading 116 RBIs in 1955. What Ray Boone prized most was the year he batted .205 with one measly home run and 11 RBIs for the 1960 Boston Red Sox, the last season of his thirteen-year career, because Ted Williams was his teammate that year. Williams had been Ray's idol since his high school days, when the Splendid Splinter set hitting records nobody could break, not even Ray Boone, the second-best ballplayer ever to come out of Herbert Hoover High School in San Diego. Ray went on to be a Red Sox scout, and he made sure his son met the great Williams, Nellie Fox, and other Hall of Famers. Bob grew up thinking of his father's friends as guys with the best job in the world. "So you pay attention," he recalled.

In college Bob Boone played for Stanford against Dave Kingman's USC Trojans, and he played alongside Kingman in a summer league in Alaska, where they were teammates on a club called the Goldpanners. Now he took a pitch inside. He fouled off the next one. Lamp's third pitch to Boone, a sinker, hung over the inside corner. Boone got all of it, sending a high liner over the forty-foot screen beyond the well in the left-field fence.

"*Kingman looks up. . . . Another home run and it's six to nothing!*" Brickhouse said.

In the bleachers, Helen Rosenberg turned to her friend Pamela and said, "Typical Cubs."

Ten minutes into the game, Herman Franks climbed from the dugout to take Lamp out of his misery. The Cubs' manager was more annoyed than usual. A hard-nosed baseball man in the Leo Durocher mold, Franks had coached for Durocher, stolen signs for him, commiserated with him about how soft modern players were. The way his Cubs fell apart against Philadelphia turned his stomach. The Phillies had won fifteen of their last twenty games at Wrigley Field, and here they go again.

The Phillies were high-fiving in the dugout. The high five was new, invented two years earlier by the Dodgers' Dusty Baker and Glenn Burke. Franks thought it was bush.

Franks took the ball from Lamp and gave him a pat on the butt. "Fuck of a day, kid," he said, and Lamp trudged to the dugout. He'd entered the game with a 2.36 earned run average. After allowing six runs in ten minutes, he left with an ERA of 4.42.

Janet Lamp was running late that day—family duties on her birthday. She hurried to her seat behind the backstop and asked, "Where is he? How's he doing?" Nobody wanted to tell her.

The manager handed the ball to Donnie Moore.

Donnie Ray Moore had a round face and a thin mustache. He threw hard but his second pitch, a slider, was mediocre. Moore had grown up in Lubbock, Texas, where his father drove a truck and his mother worked as a maid. When Donnie was ten his half brother, Ronnie, was run over by a car and killed.

The boys' father, Conaway Moore, was strict. If Donnie misbehaved, he got a whipping. But Conaway also showed the boy how to play baseball, even taught him to switch-hit because switch-hitters had a better chance to make the big leagues. But nobody had to teach the kid how to throw a fastball past older boys; as a pitcher, Donnie Moore began making headlines as a fourteen-year-old high school freshman. After Conaway mentioned that pro scouts didn't like scouting black neighborhoods, Donnie transferred to all-white Monterey High. The only black kid in a school with more than a thousand students, he led Monterey to the state baseball championship, starting and winning all nine of the team's playoff games. When the coach said he didn't have to pitch every game, Donnie said yes, he did. He wanted to make sure no pro scouts could miss him.

Scouts liked his fastball but some said he was moody, one of those baseball terms with a subtext. Words like *scrappy*, *plucky*, and *gritty*, for instance, generally applied to players who were white and not obviously gifted, like Pete Rose and Bill Buckner, while *moody* often meant black and less than deferential. Dick Allen, Bobby Bonds, and Reggie Jackson were moody. The Phillies' Garry Maddox and Bake McBride had been called moody, as much for their Afros and beards as for anything they said or did. But Moore really was moody. As a kid he'd moped after losses. One day he lipped off to a white shopkeeper in Lubbock. A sheriff's deputy tracked him down and gave him a beating, and when Conaway Moore heard about that, he gave him a worse one. After that Donnie kept to himself even more, except when he was with his high school sweetheart, Tonya. Sometimes he cried in Tonya's arms. She married the schoolboy star when they were both nineteen, with nobody in attendance but their year-old daughter, Demetria.

He'd surprised the scouts and delighted his father by reaching the majors at age twenty-one. But that was four seasons ago. Now twenty-five, Moore had spent four years going up and down between Chicago and the minors and he thought the Cubs were screwing with him. This was the second day in a row that Franks had used him as a mop-up man, pitching in a lost cause. That showed what the organization thought of Donnie Moore.

He took the ball from Franks. When his name was announced, hardly a clap arose from the crowd of fifteen thousand.

Moore started strong, striking out Phillies second baseman Rudy Meoli. He looked impatient on the mound, holding his glove up, demanding the ball, ready to strike out the next guy. There was no need to get fancy with Phillies pitcher Randy Lerch, who came to bat with two singles in twenty at-bats on the year, for a slash line of .100/.100/.100. Lerch got fastballs.

With the count full, he lofted one of them into the wind over shortstop. Moore turned to watch the ball carry over shortstop, over the gap in left field, over the wall and into the bleachers for an opposite-field home run.

The bleachers rejected the ball. Schmidt's homer had caromed off a catwalk back onto the field; Boone's had left the park entirely. This one rattled around until a fan nabbed the baseball and then, per Wrigley Field tradition, chucked it back into left field. Souvenir or no souvenir, that's an enemy homer.

A yellow 7 went up on the scoreboard beside PHILADELPHIA, yellow because the half inning wasn't over yet. Yellow numbers were subject to change.

Bake McBride came up for the second time in the inning. He hit a pop toward the Cubs dugout. Third baseman Steve Ontiveros gathered it in, and the top of the first was over. Moments later a white 7 replaced the yellow one.

BOTTOM OF THE 1ST

PHILADELPHIA	7		—7	7	0
CUBS			—0	0	0

Due up for the Cubs: DeJesus, Vail, Buckner

In the bleachers, Helen Rosenberg polished off her Frosty Malt. She and Pamela Marin made friends with a couple sitting nearby who were passing a pipe around. When the Phillies took the field, the fans turned their attention to the right fielder jogging their way.

"Hey Bake!"

"Bake potato!"

"Look up here!"

McBride tipped his cap to the bleachers and settled into his spot in right field.

Mike Schmidt toed the dirt near third base, grooming his territory. Seeing utility infielder Mick Kelleher in the Cubs dugout, he pointed to the 20 on Kelleher's jersey and the same number on his own jersey. "I was saying that might be the score today," Schmidt told a reporter later. "Twenty to twenty."

Larry Bowa shouted at the pitcher. "Seven runs," he called to Lerch. "That enough for you?" Lerch and Bob Boone had just become the first pitcher-catcher duo in major-league history to homer before they took the field. (Forty years later, they are still the only ones.) A six-foot-five left-hander with a delivery that was mostly knees and elbows, Lerch uncorked a first-pitch fastball.

Cubs leadoff man Ivan DeJesus had a slashy swing and a fan club that called itself Jews for DeJesus. He took a half swing and dumped a single over second base.

"*You've gotta hold your breath today*," Richie Ashburn, the old Whiz Kid, said on the Phillies' radio broadcast. "*The Cubs can launch the ball out of this ballpark also. I've got a feeling this might wind up about 19 to 12.*"

Right fielder Mike Vail lined an 0-2 pitch for another single. That brought up Bill Buckner, one of two ornery cusses at the heart of the Cubs lineup.

Buckner hailed from American Canyon, California, a Napa Valley community of strivers. When he was thirteen, his father committed suicide. Marie Buckner, a police stenographer, went on to marry a highway patrolman who didn't much like his stepson until he discovered that Billy was the best high school ballplayer for a hundred miles around. Hall of Famer Joe Gordon, then scouting for the California Angels, said Buckner had "the finest swing I ever saw in a prospect." The Los Angeles Dodgers selected him in their legendary draft of 1968, along with Steve Garvey, Ron Cey, Dave Lopes, and Bobby Valentine. As a twenty-year-old minor leaguer with the Triple-A Spokane Indians, Buckner broke his jaw in an outfield collision with Valentine. There were reports that he'd be out five weeks. Instead, Buckner missed one game. According to Spokane manager Tom Lasorda, "He learned to spit and swear with his jaw wired shut."

Soon Billy Buck was a star, batting .314 and swiping thirty-one bases for the pennant-winning Dodgers in 1974. He called Pete Rose his role model. "I play like Pete, full-out all the time," he said. A year later he tore up his left ankle sliding into second base. Two surgeries went so badly there was talk of amputation. Buckner recovered, but his speed was gone. From then on he played hurt every day. He taped the ankle. He often took half a dozen pregame aspirins. The *Sun-Times'* John Schulian called him "an ambulatory cripple." But he could still hit.

With two on and nobody out, Buckner took Lerch's first pitch outside. He took ball two to gain control of the count, the way he liked it. He took a strike.

He'd been heartbroken in 1977 when the Dodgers traded him to Chicago for another ex-phenom, Rick Monday, who was best known for keeping two protesters from burning an American flag on the field in the bicentennial season of '76. Buckner saw the trade as an insult. "It's very questionable whether Monday is a better hitter than I am," he told reporters. In the next two seasons he batted .304 while Monday hit .241. Buckner became a fan favorite to the lunch box crowd at Wrigley. He figured he was the new Mr. Cub until somebody better came along.

Choking up on the bat, he swung at Lerch's fastball, broke the bat, and fisted a looper to short right field. The ball fell in. DeJesus scored and there was a yellow 1 on the center-field scoreboard under Philadelphia's white 7.

Dave Kingman took his time stepping into the batter's box. Cheers mixed with several shouts of "Kong *woo!*" At six foot six, Kingman loomed over Phillies catcher Boone and the umpire.

Kingman and Buckner steered clear of each other. As hitters, they were opposites. Buckner with his level swing and .293 career average saw his rival as a one-trick horse who either homered or struck out, while Kingman (career average .232) viewed Buckner as a plinker who settled for singles. Buckner was the Cubs' union rep, with two more years in the league and more friends in the clubhouse, but there was no doubt which player Chicago liked better. Nineteen seventy-nine was the season conductors on the El announced the Addison stop as "Kong Stadium—Wrigley Field!"

Kingman let Lerch's first pitch go by. The next delivery was more his style, a fastball on the outer half of the plate. He stepped into it, his thirty-five-inch, thirty-six-ounce Louisville Slugger connecting with an audible *clack* as the ball took off over the bleachers.

"*A Waveland Avenue homer for Dave Kingman,*" Brickhouse called it. "*Hoo boy, did he tag it!*"

"*Way, way out of here,*" said Phillies announcer Andy Musser. "*A real mooner that sailed off his bat on a mighty arc to left field!*"

The fans were on their feet, enjoying the show at Kong Stadium. One was DePaul University basketball coach Ray Meyer. Two months earlier, his Blue Demons had reached the NCAA Final Four, losing by two points to Larry Bird and Indiana State, who went on to lose the final to Magic Johnson and Michigan State. Meyer had shaken Kingman's hand before the game and asked him, Chicagoan to Chicagoan, to hit one for DePaul. Now the sixty-five-year-old Meyer was as happy as the bleacher bums.

With the score 7–4 and still nobody out, Bob Boone joined Phillies pitching coach Herm Starrette at the mound to talk to Lerch. They agreed they were still ahead by three and let's get 'em.

Cubs third baseman Steve Ontiveros grounded out, allowing the Phillies to exhale. But then center fielder Jerry Martin doubled, and that was enough for Philadelphia manager Danny Ozark to send Lerch to the showers. Like Dennis Lamp, Randy Lerch had warmed up for the game as long as he had pitched. Like Lamp, he'd recorded only one out. Lerch didn't wait for Ozark to reach the mound; he flipped the ball to the manager on his way off the field.

The Phils turned to Doug Bird, a six-foot-four, 180-pound right-hander who'd achieved trivia status by being nicknamed after another tall, skinny pitcher of the era, Detroit's Mark "the Bird" Fidrych, the 1976 American League Rookie of the Year who was known for talking to the baseball between pitches. If Mark Fidrych's nickname was "the Bird," Phillies fans reasoned, they would call Doug Bird "the Fidrych."

Barry Foote, the Cubs' stout catcher, was the kind of guy bench jockeys greeted with dietary advice: "Throw in a salad!" But he was strong. As the seventh batter of the inning, Foote greeted Bird with a liner to right. Bake McBride tracked it down for the second out. Next up: second baseman Ted Sizemore, who singled to bring Martin home with the Cubs' fifth run. That meant that both teams would bat around in the first inning, Donnie Moore coming to the plate.

Moore was a good-hitting pitcher with a .250 average in three big-league seasons, but relievers don't bat much. This would be his first at-bat of 1979. Batting left-handed like his father taught him, he took a palmball from Bird. That was a show of respect from the other pitcher, a first-pitch breaking ball. It came in six inches outside, but the umpire called it a strike. Umps sometimes enlarged their strike zones with pitchers at the plate; some also enlarged their strike zones during the last game of a series. The last game was "getaway day" for the visiting team and the umps, everyone thinking about how soon they might get to the airport after the game. Moore just shrugged. He had enough to think about, knowing he'd have Rose and Schmidt batting for the Phillies in the top of the second inning. But Bird's 0-1 fastball surprised him by coming right down the middle, and Moore reacted like a hitter. He leaned into the ball, driving it to the gap in right-center. Bake McBride and Garry Maddox chased it to the ivy while Moore legged out a triple, driving in Sizemore with the Cubs' sixth run. Moore stood on third with his hands on his knees, catching his breath. With a triple and a homer today, he and Phillies pitcher Randy Lerch were slashing 1.000/1.000/3.500.

In the press box, Dave Nightingale of the *Tribune* remembered a joke. A dad shows up late for his son's Little League game and asks what's the score. "Pop, we're down fifteen to nothin'," the boy says, "but don't worry. We ain't been to bat yet."

Tonya Moore yelled for her man from the seats behind the plate. Donnie had a triple and the Cubs were coming back! The two of them had driven to Wrigley that morning with Donnie's friend Ray Burris, another Cub pitcher, and Ray's wife, Regina. They'd made plans to go to dinner after the game.

Shortstop Ivan DeJesus, batting for the second time, hit a lazy fly ball to right field. The wind caught it. Bake McBride lost the ball for a second. Moore was about to score the tying run when McBride stutter-stepped and trapped the veering ball against his shoulder.

"The craziest game ever," Bowa called it. "And then the second inning started."

TOP OF THE 2ND

| PHILADELPHIA | 7 | | —7 | 7 | 0 |
| CUBS | 6 | | —6 | 7 | 0 |

Due up for the Phillies: Bowa, Rose, Schmidt

After allowing a homer to the opposing pitcher to fall behind by seven runs in the first inning, Moore still had a chance to win the game.

The Cubs had used him in the first three games of the season, all losses. Each time, Moore entered with the team trailing by at least three runs. In a dozen appearances since, he had won once and lost twice in ugly outings that left his earned run average at 5.14. Through the season's first six weeks, opponents were batting .337 against him. His fastball touched ninety-five miles an hour but his breaking pitches needed work, particularly the split-finger fastball he practiced in the bullpen. Of course there was time to turn his season around—it was only May— but the way manager Herman Franks used him was enough to drive a man to drink. After four years of shuttling back and forth between the majors and minors, it seemed Moore's only distinction was having one of the best-looking wives in any league. He was trying to keep them both from getting sent back to Wichita.

Larry Bowa led off the top of the second. One of five All-Stars in the Phillies' lineup, he jumped at Moore's first pitch and slapped a grounder that rabbited down the first-base line. Bowa sprinted for first, picturing his second double of the game, while Bill Buckner lurched toward the ball and Moore ran to cover first base. He knew he'd better get there in time.

Buckner, according to Bill James, "had more assists per game than any first baseman in baseball history," a stat suggesting great range. But the opposite was true. Due to the constant pain in his legs, Buckner insisted that pitchers cover first on every ball hit his way. He'd field a grounder two steps from first base and wait, pointing at the bag. Cub pitchers knew they'd get an earful from Buckner if they didn't cover.

Moore was on his way, but this time Buckner waved him off and tagged the bag himself.

That out was a break for the Cubs. Instead of a runner on base with the big boys coming up, the bases were empty. Maybe Tonya Moore was right when she told Donnie his luck was going to change. "Do your best and let God do the rest," she said.

Pete Rose took a breaking ball, watching it right into the catcher's mitt, a little outside. With his beady eyes and caffeinated hustle, the twelve-time All-Star had a lion's heart and a mind like a pocket calculator. No player knew more about his own numbers. Rose knew that the run he had scored in the first inning, the 1,677th of his seventeen-year career, one more than Mickey Mantle, had made him baseball's all-time leader in runs scored by a switch-hitter. He kept the Phillies' PR people posted on things like that.

When clubhouse jokers like Tug McGraw called him Old Man, Charlie Gristle, or Pete Moss, Rose mentioned his World Series rings and Rolls-Royces. At thirty-eight he was on his way to yet another season with two hundred hits and a .330 average. Like Buckner, who looked up to him, Rose was a thinker with a quick, level swing, working counts until the odds shifted his way.

The Cubs' game plan was to be aggressive with Rose. In pregame meetings, catcher Barry Foote and pitching coach Mike Roarke agreed: go after him, get ahead in the count. They remembered what Ferguson Jenkins used to say: "Walking Pete Rose is asking for trouble."

Rose took another ball outside to run the count to two balls and no strikes. Moore didn't want to fall further behind. The situation called for a fastball. So did Foote. Of course Rose was thinking the same thing.

Moore's fastball crossed the inside corner at the knees. Barry Foote waited for a strike call that never came. Without fully turning to face plate umpire Dick Cavenaugh, Foote expressed his belief that Cavenaugh was a bleary-eyed, drunken scab. And this was more than just a catcher working an ump. It was a fact. The major-league umpires had gone on strike that spring, demanding better pay and a pension plan. "We have no health care, no job security, no tenure. Our pension plan is a joke," veteran ump Ron Luciano told the *Washington Post*. With the real umps on strike, the owners hired "replacement umpires" who performed so badly that many writers and fans thought they were cheapening the game. Finally, just as the Phillies arrived in Chicago, the owners gave in. The real umps got a 401(k) plan, higher per diems, and a new minimum salary of twenty-six thousand dollars, which was five thousand more than the players' minimum. But they wouldn't return to work until the coming weekend. That left Cavenaugh, a college ump who later admitted he was nursing an epic hangover that day, calling balls and strikes at Wrigley Field.

Moore hid the ball in his glove and spread his index and middle fingers along the seams. His windup and delivery were the same as for his fastball, but at release he yanked downward as hard as he could.

The pitch looked like a fastball, Rose recalled years later, but "ducked down" at the last instant. He had seen a pitch behave like that before—Gaylord Perry's spitball. But this one wasn't a spitter. It was the pitch that would make Donnie Moore a millionaire.

Moore hadn't harnessed it yet, but he had seen what the split-finger fastball could do. That was back in the Texas League in 1975, when he and Bruce Sutter were teammates on the Midland Cubs, two rungs down from the majors. Moore was twenty-two, Sutter a year older, both of them middling prospects. Moore was more highly regarded, but that wasn't saying much. As their minor-league manager put it, "When

Bruce Sutter is ready for the big leagues, that's the day the Communists take over."

Fred Martin, the Cubs' roving minor-league pitching coach, turned up at Midland's Christensen Stadium one blazing West Texas day. His specialty was the kind of trick pitch failing prospects tinker with. As Sutter would recall on the day of his Hall of Fame induction, "He told me to spread my fingers apart and throw it just like a fastball." A weathered Oklahoman who'd thrown a forkball—a diving changeup gripped with two wide-spread fingers—during his own brief career, Martin taught a new wrinkle on the forkball. His own fingers weren't long enough to throw it perfectly, but if a longer-fingered pitcher spread his grip even more and threw it like a fastball, yanking downward at release, the pitch dived at the last split second, making it cruelly difficult to hit. Sutter mastered it quickly and called the pitch a miracle, "a new way to get hitters out." Throwing Martin's so-called splitter, he rose from Double-A Midland to the National League All-Star team in fifteen months, arriving in the big leagues in the year Communist forces took over Vietnam.

Every batter knows what a fastball looks like. Spinning at about twenty-two hundred revolutions per minute, or almost forty per second, it creates a partial vacuum just above and ahead of the ball as it zips through the air. A good fastball sizzles audibly in flight. More important is how it looks: the spin creates an optical illusion so that the ball appears to resist gravity. Though all pitches descend on the way to the plate, hitters swear the best fastballs actually rise.

A split-finger fastball is thrown the same way, but the odd grip reduces its spin. At only fifteen hundred rpm, the ball resists gravity less. The difference is enough to trick hitters who have spent most of their lives training their eyes and fast-twitch muscles to hit regular fastballs. The split-finger pitch seems to "fall off the table," they say, or "disappear" as it reaches the plate.

Seeing his Midland teammate go from Texas League suspect to major-league All-Star, Donnie Moore asked Martin to teach him the pitch. Moore's fingers weren't quite as long as Sutter's, but when he got the timing just right the ball dipped. Unfortunately, Moore's splitter seemed to have a mind of its own. Sometimes, instead of dipping, it hung and practically asked to be hit out of sight. More often it dove into the dirt or caromed off the catcher's knee.

He worked hard on his splitter, but it was still a work in progress. It was the reason Tonya wouldn't catch him anymore. His wife was athletic and tough in a way he admired. She used to catch for him on off days as he worked his way up through the minors, wearing a mitt and mask but no other equipment. Then her husband tried Fred Martin's pitch. Donnie's splits buzzed under Tonya's mitt, banging off her shins and ankles. One day she threw down the mitt and told him he could get another catcher or a divorce.

Four years later at Wrigley, Rose took Moore's ducking pitch at knee level. "I wasn't looking for that," he remembered. "Moore had a fastball, a decent curve, and not much else." Making a show of himself as usual, he ran to first on the walk.

Mike Schmidt stepped into the batter's box. His practice swing was like Kingman's, leisurely but threatening. Donnie Moore wasn't intimidated. He said hello with a fastball. Schmidt took it.

Moore's next delivery was more to his liking. Schmidt uncoiled, but fouled it straight back. "*He's going for it,*" Richie Ashburn said on the radio. "*The hitters can't wait to get up there and swing the bat. We might see grown men cry on that mound today.*"

Two pitches later, with a count of a ball and two strikes, Schmidt swung again. This time his thirty-five-inch, thirty-two-ounce Adirondack connected about half an inch below the ball's sweet spot, shooting a pop fly almost straight up. Second baseman Sizemore thought he had a play on the ball. Then the wind wafted it past shortstop DeJesus, who called for the ball, then backpedaled madly as the breeze carried it behind him. He grabbed it for the second out.

That brought up Del Unser, a second-generation big leaguer playing for his fifth team in eight years. He was in the lineup because Greg

Luzinski, the Phillies' regular left fielder, was hurt. Unser had been an everyday player until 1976, when he homered in consecutive at-bats for the Mets in St. Louis. The Cardinals didn't appreciate that. The next time up he got a fastball on the elbow. From then on, Unser could never fully straighten his arm. A part-timer after the injury, he'd batted .235 over the past three seasons. Still he hit left-handed with decent power, a combination that can keep a thirty-four-year-old in the majors past what might ordinarily be his sell-by date.

Moore missed with a changeup. Cub manager Franks leaned on the railing in the home dugout, eyeing his pitcher. The oldest manager in the big leagues at sixty-five, he had parlayed the small salaries of his playing and coaching years into a real-estate fortune he called his fuck-you money. With a belly that cast a shadow over his belt, Franks baited umpires, cussed out reporters, and bossed batboys around. But like his mentor and hero Durocher, another old-school hard-ass, he knew the game inside out. In the second inning on a day like this, with his Cubs in the middle of a stretch of thirteen games in thirteen days, his job was to get through the day without burning too many of his relief pitchers' arms. He stood on the top step of the dugout, clapping his hands, urging Moore to get the third out.

Unser fouled a pitch straight back. That made three hit-me pitches Moore had gotten away with in the last couple of minutes. Maybe it was his day after all.

His wife and his manager were always telling Moore to trust his stuff. Herman Franks would tell him this was no day to dick around like Picasso: rear back and throw the heater that got you to the big leagues! But a man's best pitch isn't always the right choice. It's not the right choice if you throw it at the wrong time. Like every hitter on both teams, Unser had been dying to get up there and swing. A fastball was just what he wanted.

Moore's next pitch was another changeup. It was a beauty, too, the ball drifting over the outside corner while the hungover umpire twitched but did not pull the trigger. Ball two.

With the count two and one, Foote signaled fastball. Moore nodded.

He stretched, casting a sidelong look at Rose, the runner at first, then kicked and threw the fastball Unser was hoping for.

Unser whacked it toward the ivy. Rose, taking off with the crack of the bat, rounded second base as right fielder Mike Vail reached up and caught the ball.

BOTTOM OF THE 2ND

PHILADELPHIA	7	0			—7	7	0
CUBS	6				—6	7	0

Due up for the Cubs: Vail, Buckner, Kingman

Donnie Moore found a seat in the dugout. If the Cubs could score a couple of runs, he had a chance to be the winning pitcher. After all, Buckner and Kingman were coming up again.

The Cubs' stars managed to keep their distance even while batting back to back. They approached the bat rack from different directions. "Buckner and Kingman were the reason we had a dysfunctional clubhouse," one of their teammates recalled. "Our two big stars were both me-first guys."

With Buckner in the on-deck circle and Kingman watching from the dugout, Doug Bird faced Cubs right fielder Mike Vail, whose catch had just ended the Phillies' half of the inning. Vail proceeded to rip his second single of the game to left field. The Cubs now had eight hits and had made only three outs.

Buckner, batting .257 with three home runs and fourteen RBIs, knew his stats to the last decimal place, like Pete Rose. He struck out even less often than Rose. The two of them were throwbacks to the game of a generation earlier, when strikeouts were embarrassing. Buckner had batted .323 for the '78 Cubs with only seventeen strikeouts in 470 trips to the plate.

He took a strike, then slapped a slider over the mound. The ball dribbled into center as Vail went to third. Cheering Buckner's second single of the game, the crowd got louder as the next hitter took a practice swing.

"*And here's Mr. Kingman,*" Brickhouse told Channel 9 viewers.

Shirtless guys in the bleachers beat their chests for Kong. They watched Kingman reach his bat out and tap the dirt on the far side of the plate, showing the pitcher he could cover the outside corner and then some.

"*King Kong Kingman hit a moonshot in his first at-bat,*" Andy Musser reminded Phillies fans. "*Runners at first and third with nobody out.*"

Kingman didn't work counts. He, too, was a throwback, but not to pure hitters like Joe DiMaggio and Stan Musial who hated striking out. He was more in the Mighty Casey mold.

He drilled Bird's first pitch toward third base. Schmidt snagged it with a flick of his glove, pure reflex. Most third basemen would throw to second right away in hopes of starting a double play. Not Schmidt, who was now in the fourth of nine consecutive Gold Glove seasons. Holding the ball, he looked at the runner at third. Mike Vail had no choice—he'd be out easy if he tried to score. So he stayed where he was. Only then did Schmidt fire the ball to second base, having burned a split second he knew he could spare. With Kingman loping toward first, the Phillies still had time to double him up.

Bleacher fans who'd been hoping for a three-run homer sat down again. "That was a bummer," Helen Rosenberg recalled. "After all that action in the first, we might not even score? I was almost bored till we saw the garbage truck."

A streets and sanitation truck had been chugging west on Waveland Avenue, trailing a plume of smoke. A minute later the back of the truck burst into flames. Fans climbed to the top of the left-field and center-field bleachers to watch smoke from the trash truck's tailgate carry past the apartment building at the corner of Waveland and Kenmore and the firehouse next door. One fan bumped another, spilling his beer, setting off a scuffle. Others cheered the firefighters who came pouring out of Engine Company 78 to hose down the truck.

While that was going on, Steve Ontiveros grounded out. The second inning ended with zeroes on both sides.

Donnie Moore headed back to the mound.

PHILADELPHIA	7	0		—7	7	0
CUBS	6	0		—6	9	0

Due up for the Phillies: Maddox, Boone, Meoli

Moore had made it through an inning and two-thirds with one run allowed—the homer by Phillies pitcher Randy Lerch. With the pitcher's spot in the Cubs' batting order coming up soon, Moore knew he would be done for the day if he could get through the top of the third. Franks would call it a gutty performance. He might even give the kid a chance to prove himself in the late innings of a future game. To make that more likely, Moore needed three outs.

But that was the wrong way to think of it. Like most pitchers, he had been told again and again never to think he needed three outs because triple plays are few and far between. He needed one out. The pitcher's job is to get the guy at the plate.

Garry Maddox, the Phillies' Gold Glove center fielder, swung at a fastball and popped it into the wind. Mike Vail and Jerry Martin converged in right-center field. Vail made a sliding try at a basket catch. The ball bounced off his arm for a pop-fly double. That was bad luck for Moore, who had made a good pitch. He knew what his wife would say: keep believing.

He threw Bob Boone a fastball near the knees. Maybe a couple of inches low. Cavenaugh, the scab umpire, called it strike one. Boone turned toward him—only partway so as not to show up the ump in front of the fans and TV cameras—and asked if he had ever given any thought to calling balls and strikes with some minimum level of bleeping professionalism, a sentiment he got across in fewer words.

With the count 1-0, Moore threw another changeup. Foote didn't usually call for changeups when Moore was on the mound. The change was his third-best pitch. But hitters were overeager on a day like this. You want to use that against them. It was the right call—Boone swung early and cued the baseball off the end of his bat—but the wrong result for the Cubs, a dying quail that plopped in front of Kingman in left field as Maddox rounded third. Moore ran behind the umpire to back up the throw to the plate.

Kingman corralled the ball and came up throwing. He heaved it past the plate, the catcher, the umpire, and Moore, all the way to the brick wall under the backstop, for his fourth error of the season. It was 8–6 Philadelphia.

"*Everything was hit hard in the first,*" Richie Ashburn said on Phillies radio. "*But the Phillies now have put together a couple of looping base hits. Of course the outfielders are playing so deep today you're going to see those short fly balls drop in.*"

Moore trudged up the front of the mound. He took off his cap and mopped his forehead with his sleeve. He'd faced two batters in the inning and made them both look bad. Still they had a run in, a man on second, and nobody out.

Rudy Meoli took a fastball at the knees. Maybe an inch low. Cavenaugh called it strike one. "*Barry Foote was doing a lot of complaining in the first couple of innings,*" Ashburn said, "*and maybe it's starting to pay off. The plate umpire seems to be giving him some borderline pitches.*"

Phillies infielder Rudy Meoli was the kind of player described in pitchers-and-catchers meetings as "not a hitter." He was in the lineup because the regular second baseman, Manny Trillo, was hurt. Meoli, batting .180, sent a fly ball to center for the inning's first out. That out, according to twenty-first-century metrics, raised the Cubs' chance of winning the game from 24 percent to 27 percent. Their chances improved with the Phillies' pitcher batting next. And Doug "the Fidrych" Bird was no hitter at all. With a career batting average of .000, he perched in a far corner of the batter's box as if the plate were radioactive.

"*It doesn't look to me like he could reach an outside pitch. Or half the plate*," Phillies announcer Harry Kalas said.

"*He'd be murder on a pitch about a foot inside, though*," Ashburn said.

And Moore walked him. Walked the worst hitter he would face all year—and he didn't believe it himself, never mind what Herman Franks was muttering in the dugout. Walked the pitcher to bring up the leadoff man with two runners on base.

Moore stood on the mound rubbing up the ball. Franks sat in the home dugout between coaches Peanuts Lowrey and Mike Roarke, looking pained.

It was only the third inning and Bake McBride was up for the third time. Moore and Foote fooled him with yet another changeup. McBride got a little more bat on this one than Boone got on his cue shot a minute before, but the result was the same, a fly ball that parachuted safely to earth in short left field. It was deep enough to allow Boone to score the Phillies' ninth run. Moore had fooled three good hitters in this inning and got three pop-ups. On any normal day that would get him out of the inning. Instead it was this: two in, two on, only one out.

Some managers would go to the mound to reassure a frustrated pitcher. They'd say something to the effect of "Chin up, it's bloops and bingles. Get the guy at the plate." But Franks stayed in the dugout. Moore had to wonder if the manager intended to leave him out here to give up eight or nine runs if that's what it took to save another bullpen arm. A pasting like that would get him a pat on the butt for taking one for the team, but the stain on his numbers would last. Management would point to his inflated ERA when they sent him to Wichita. He'd met guys in the minors, good pitchers who got lit up one day in the big leagues, got sent down, and were never heard from again.

There was "*stirring in the bullpen*." Announcers often call it stirring, not shaking, muddling, or musical chairs, when pitchers shift around on the bullpen bench while one picks up his glove and starts lobbing pitches to the bullpen catcher. This time it was left-hander Guillermo "Willie" Hernandez. That suggested Franks wasn't planning to use Moore as a designated shock absorber. At the same time it meant Moore might be showering before the third inning was over.

Larry Bowa, one-for-two with a double, banged a liner past Moore's cap for a single to center. Bird stopped at third. The bases were loaded with Pete Rose coming up, Schmidt on deck.

"*Twenty hits in this game*," Ashburn noted, "*in the top of the third.*"

Foote went to the mound to give his pitcher a breather. Their mound conference also gave Willie Hernandez more time to warm up. Moore stood on the mound looking at Rose, who was yanking his helmet down over his Buster Brown haircut. With a grounder and a walk, Rose hadn't joined what Kalas called the Philadelphia hit parade. He knew his first-inning grounder had dropped his average to .344.

Rose liked seeing relief pitchers a second time. Most of them had limited repertoires. Rose had seen how quick Moore's fastball was today: low to mid-nineties. He'd seen a split-finger pitch but discounted it; Moore hardly ever threw one. More interesting was the changeup, his third-best pitch. He'd been throwing a lot of them, knowing hitters would be swinging out of their shoes.

Foote crouched behind the plate and put down a sign. Catchers usually get credit for calling a game, but their signals—typically one finger for a fastball, two for a curve, three or four for other pitches, with variations if there's a runner at second—are suggestions. Catchers like to think of themselves as the smartest guys on the field, which they often are. They tend to be take-charge types, but they can boss pitchers around only so far. They can put down one finger all they want. They can switch from index to middle finger if they want, but the pitcher decides what he's going to throw.

Moore went into his fastball motion, but his forearm and hand slowed down at release. The pitch left his hand at the usual release point but came to the plate in slow motion. Another changeup. Rose was waiting for it. He drilled it to left-center. Kingman jogged after the ball as two runs scored and Rose pulled into second. The Phillies led 11–6.

Franks went to the mound.

It was Moore's turn to leave the field, shaking his head as if to clear it. Five hits and a walk in the third inning added up to five runs against him (including the Lerch home run in the first), and he was responsible for the runners at second and third.

Moore watched Willie Hernandez lob four outside pitches, walking Mike Schmidt intentionally the old-fashioned way. The bases were loaded again. The Phillies had batted around again.

Del Unser topped a bouncer toward first that Buckner reached too late for a throw to the plate. He tagged Unser for the second out as Bowa came home. The score was 12–6.

Garry Maddox was up next, batting for the second time in the inning. At twenty-nine, Maddox was coming off a typical season: he'd hit .288 in 1978 with eleven home runs, sixty-eight RBIs, and thirty-three steals. He figured he was lucky to be alive.

Ten years earlier, as a nineteen-year-old army infantryman, he had slogged through the Vietnamese jungle and huddled in foxholes. He also suffered chemical burns to his face. The army never informed Private Maddox—who had enlisted at the height of the antiwar, draft-dodger late '60s—whether it was Agent Orange that burned him. All he heard was that he'd suffered "friendly fire." Whatever the toxin was, it blistered his skin and made it painful to shave, so he grew a beard. His first big-league team, the Giants, had a no-facial-hair policy, but waived it for the Vietnam vet whose hair and whiskers helped set a new style for black players in the '70s.

"I loved Garry Maddox for his glove, but even more for his hair," recalled another Phillies center fielder, Doug Glanville, who would patrol Maddox's beat twenty years later. "His beard and his Afro were cool. They sent a message: grow it, be free." Glanville went from the playgrounds of Teaneck, New Jersey, to a nine-year career in the majors before joining ESPN as a baseball analyst. Looking back, he said,

"From the age of eight I had two goals in life. One, make it to the big leagues. And two, grow my hair like Garry Maddox's and feel the power of the 'fro."

Mets broadcaster Ralph Kiner was the first to say that two-thirds of Earth's surface was covered by water and the rest was covered by Garry Maddox, but the Secretary of Defense was more than a glove. "He was quiet confidence," a teammate said. During his rookie year with the Giants, there was talk that Maddox might be the next Willie Mays. The hype wasn't fair to either man. Mays, the best player in National League history, had seen other young players get hung with the same label—and never to their advantage. The most highly touted "next Willie Mays" was Bobby Bonds, who enjoyed the attention until it dawned on him that he'd be seen as a flop if he didn't hit and field like Mays. Which he didn't.

In April 1972, playing for the Giants' Triple-A team in Phoenix, Maddox hit .438 with nine homers in eleven games. The big club brought him up. "After I went hitless in my first two games, Willie came to me," he told a writer. Mays gave the rookie a glove, a pair of spikes, and a bit of advice. "Don't crouch so much at the plate. Wait on the pitch a little longer." Maddox started hitting, and a month later the Giants traded the forty-one-year-old Mays to the Mets. The next day, Maddox replaced him in center. When reporters asked his opinion of the trade, he responded like a good soldier: "I'm here to follow orders. I figure the men running this ball club are a whole lot smarter than I am."

They weren't. In 1975 they traded him to the Phillies for first baseman Willie Montanez. Maddox became a fan favorite and celebrity chef in Philadelphia, hosting a charity barbecue outside the ballpark every summer. Pete Rose saw him as "the quiet type, a hell of an outfielder and a pretty damn good hitter."

In the third inning at Wrigley, Willie Hernandez threw a curve that Maddox poked toward Kingman in left. "*A high fly*," Jack Brickhouse called it. "*Pretty deep back there, the wind's got it, back she goes . . . home run! Oh boy, the seventeen-mile-an-hour wind did it for Maddox.*"

While Maddox rounded the bases, Bowa popped out of the visitors' dugout to yell at the Cubs: "We're kicking your ass today!" No Chicago player disagreed. It was hard to argue against a 15–6 lead.

The game's fifth home run closed the book on Donnie Moore: two innings pitched, six hits, two walks, seven runs. His ERA had ballooned from 5.14 to 7.43, one of the worst in the league.

With the bases cleared, Willie Hernandez faced Bob Boone. One of five future All-Star closers who would pitch in this game, including Moore, Hernandez had been trying to tame a trick pitch of his own, the screwball that would win him the American League's Cy Young and Most Valuable Player awards in 1984. But he had no intention of starting the next hitter with a screwball. He greeted Boone with a pitch to the thigh.

"*That's something Hernandez had to do*," Ashburn told listeners, "*to keep his self-respect.*"

Boone shrugged it off. A fastball to the elbow can feel like a hammer smacking your funny bone, but the thigh's not so bad.

Getting plunked on a meaty part like the thigh or butt could leave a bruise—the ball's stitches were often visible in the bruise—but a pro pretends it doesn't hurt. Boone picked up the baseball, gave it a bored look, and flipped it aside on his way to first base.

Rudy Meoli, the only Phillie without a hit, promptly singled to left, sending Boone to second. Then Doug Bird struck out to end the Phillies' eight-run inning. The Cubs came off the field to sarcastic cheers.

No major-league game had ever featured more scoring in the first two and a half innings.

"The thing of it is," Rose said, "we were just getting going."

PHILADELPHIA	7	0	8				—15	14	0
CUBS	6	0					— 6	9	1

Due up for the Cubs: Martin, Foote, Sizemore

Clunking to his locker in his spikes, Donnie Moore entered a clubhouse the size of a small apartment. He could shower if he wanted. With nobody flushing toilets in the Cubs' gloomy clubhouse, the showers might stay hot. He could shower, shave, and put his street clothes back on, or just sit in his uniform and pop a beer. There was no protocol for knocked-out pitchers except that they were not allowed to leave the clubhouse. They had to stay at the scene of the crime so the press could ask postgame questions.

At 1,275 square feet, the home clubhouse at Wrigley Field was slightly roomier than the one at Fenway Park in Boston, its rival for worst in the majors. "You could hardly call it a clubhouse," said Cubs historian Ed Hartig. "It was more of a rat-infested hole in the wall with a few hooks and showers. There were high schools that had better locker rooms." Before and after games, the Cubs had just enough room to keep from bumping butts with the next guy over. There was a bank of sinks, shaving mirrors, and toilet stalls that had hosted sixty-five years of practical jokes. What's funnier than pouring a bucket of ice on a guy who's trying to take a dump?

Moore liked a postgame beer. Many teams today ban alcohol in clubhouses (except for champagne celebrations) due to front-office worries about image problems. What if a visitor posts an iPhone picture of players guzzling beer? What if one of them drinks too much in the clubhouse and crashes his car on the way home? But in 1979 there was a cooler full of Old Style in the Wrigley clubhouse.

A beer took the edge off. Moore could shift to whiskey later, when he and Tonya were alone. They might fight, but they always made up. She couldn't join him on the road in the big leagues as much as she used to when they were coming up—too much long-distance travel when she had their six-year-old daughter and a baby, Donnie Jr., to look after. But she made up for it on homestands. When *Cosmopolitan* asked Tonya how to make a baseball marriage work, she said, "When Donnie goes on the road, the first night is hard, but you can't be a crybaby. To keep things working, I make it real interesting when he comes home. Some baseball wives will leave the car at the ballpark for their husbands. I always pick him up, even if it's four in the morning. I'll throw on a little coat with nothing on underneath. It's never boring!"

For all their fights, the Moores' life wasn't boring.

JERRY MARTIN LED off the last of the third for the Cubs. Like Bob Boone and Del Unser, Martin was a second-generation major leaguer. His father, Barney Martin, had been a thirty-year-old minor-league veteran when he made his big-league debut for the 1953 Cincinnati Reds, managed by Hall of Famer Rogers Hornsby. He pitched a scoreless inning against the St. Louis Cardinals, then gave up a couple of runs. To his everlasting credit, Barney Martin retired Stan Musial on a grounder to short to escape more trouble. And that was it. The Reds returned him to the minors and he never made it back. He was one of 1,523 baseball mayflies whose careers lasted a single day.

Jerry Martin followed his father's path from South Carolina to the big leagues, but stuck around longer. He rode the Phillies' bench for four seasons before being traded to Chicago a month before spring training in 1979. In an eight-player deal, infielder Manny Trillo went from Chicago to Philadelphia, where he promptly broke his arm (moving Rudy Meoli into the lineup), while the Cubs got three everyday players: Martin, Barry Foote, and Ted Sizemore. Herman Franks had the three ex-Phillies batting sixth, seventh, and eighth in today's batting order.

Martin could play all three outfield positions. He batted right-handed and preferred the ball above the belt. His weaknesses included sliders low and away, and cocaine. With a salary of $125,000, worth about $450,000 in today's dollars, a player like Martin could afford to party. There was no shortage of pot smokers in and around the game in the late '70s, but baseball was more suited to booze at night and speed during the day. Every clubhouse featured players who popped the Dexedrine pills called greenies. "I took them," one retired All-Star admitted. "A lot of guys did, and there was nothing wrong with it. Greenies didn't make anybody stronger or faster, they'd just wake you up a little. It's a long season." Red juice, a liquid amphetamine some trainers dispensed, was popular, too. Willie Mays reportedly introduced younger players to red juice. By the time cocaine became fashionable in the '70s, baseball players were ready. "You have to picture a bunch of horny, jet-lagged young guys who think they're rich, rolling into a bar," this retired player said. "That's pretty heady stuff. It's like, 'We're here and we're buyin'!'"

Four years later, after a trade to Kansas City, Martin would be arrested for cocaine possession along with his Royals teammates Willie Mays Aikens and Willie Wilson and a former teammate, Vida Blue. The so-called Kansas City Four were by no means the only ballplayers snorting coke in those days, but each served three months in a federal penitentiary. They were reportedly the first active major-league players to do prison time. As Aikens admitted to the press, "I was a tremendous junkie. Every game, I used drugs." Martin was never like that, more of an occasional user. "Pure hell," he called the scandal. "I'll tell you what I thought about in prison—opposing pitchers." The other offenders resumed productive careers—Aikens hit eleven homers in half a season the following year—but not Martin. He would hook on briefly with the Mets in 1984, hit .154, and get released, a casualty of the biggest drug scandal to hit baseball before the steroid era.

Five years before all that, in May 1979 at Wrigley Field, Martin slapped a grounder to the hole on the left side of the infield between Bowa and Schmidt. Bowa ranged to his right, gloved the ball, and threw to first. His throw beat Martin to the bag for the first out.

Foote came up, the catcher with puffy black hair and a mustache almost as bushy as Buckner's. With the count 1-1, he took a palmball for a strike. Doug Bird's palmball, the same quirky change-of-pace pitch Jim Konstanty employed so well for the 1950 Whiz Kid Phillies, was choked back in the hand so that the middle and forefingers barely touched the ball, reducing its spin so that it floated past the batter at seventy to seventy-five miles an hour. Foote swung before it got there.

At this point, Bird had thrown him a palmball with the count 0-1 and another at 1-1. Foote didn't expect him to set some sort of palmball record by throwing three floaters in a row. He got the fastball he was looking for and drove it at the third baseman. Schmidt got his glove up in time to deflect the ball. He scrambled after it, gathered it up, and threw across the diamond to Rose for the second out. "*Foote does not motor all that well,*" Harry Kalas told Phillies fans in the understatement of the inning.

For the first time all afternoon there were two outs and nobody on base. Ted Sizemore changed that, wafting a windblown single to right.

Down by nine runs with two out, Herman Franks let Willie Hernandez go to the plate for his first at-bat of 1979. Like many major-league pitchers, Hernandez had been a legendary hitter in his youth, smacking baseballs all over the lot for every team he played on from boyhood games in Puerto Rico up through high school, but he was no match for professional pitching. In four minor-league seasons his best batting average had been .167. As a big leaguer he had a single in seventeen at-bats for a slugging percentage of .059. He took a strike, then reacted to Bird's 0-1 curveball as if he'd never seen one. "*He checked his swing,*" Kalas said, "*and fell down in a clump at the plate!*" Hernandez lay flat on the ground, facedown. He got up and struck out.

With the game out of reach, there was so little crowd noise you could hear individual voices: "C'mon!" and "Beer here." One fan sneezed.

The teams traded places with the score 15–6. According to a latter-day metric called wWE (winners' win expectancy), the Phillies had a 99 percent chance of winning the game.

PHILADELPHIA	7	0	8		—15	14	0
CUBS	6	0	0		— 6	10	1

Due up for the Phillies: McBride, Bowa, Rose

Bake McBride led off the fourth, batting for the fourth time. With the Cubs down by nine, Hernandez went after him. A fastball set up a curve McBride swatted at and missed. He bounced the next one foul toward the Phillies' dugout. Danny Ozark reached for it but couldn't make the play—no applause for him. After that, pitcher and hitter staged a two-minute skirmish. Hernandez went for the kill with a pair of fastballs, a sidearm curve, and then a surprise sidearm fastball. McBride fouled them all off. Finally, on the eighth pitch of the at-bat, McBride lifted a fly ball to Jerry Martin in center field. The ball carried, but Martin followed it back toward the warning track and hauled it in to scattered applause.

Larry Bowa was next. With the count 0-2 he took a fastball for strike three. Unfortunately for the Cubs, Dick Cavenaugh called it a ball. Barry Foote stamped his foot. Any catcher would have been upset. Any catcher would have asked himself, Couldn't this scab ump go a single at-bat without missing a call? Didn't he know a missed call means more than any one particular pitch, that it affects the rest of the at-bat if not the rest of the inning or the game? Each pitch of every at-bat was a cloud of contingency made up of variables like release point, deception, velocity, spin, desire, the sun, the wind, the footing in the batter's box, sometimes the dreaded "flu-like symptoms" that were newspaper code for a hangover—a balance of factors that had evolved over more than a century of professional baseball. Blown calls upset the balance.

Still up there after three strikes, Bowa grounded a single to left for his third hit.

Now Pete Rose was up with one on and one out instead of two outs and the bases empty. Foote didn't need to glance to his right to know who was on deck.

Batting right-handed against the lefty Hernandez, Rose was already one for two with two runs scored and two RBIs. He took a strike, then swung through a changeup. Rose nodded as if to say *Good pitch*. Hernandez was ahead in the count again. His 0-2 delivery came in at the knees. Foote held the ball where he caught it, framing it for the ump to see. Again Cavenaugh ruled it a ball.

Hernandez stood on the pitcher's rubber. He stepped off. Foote called time and went to the mound to commiserate. "*Foote's been very upset by calls from the home plate umpire*," Richie Ashburn said.

They thought they'd get Rose with a backdoor curve. It started a foot outside and came sneaking back to the plate. Rose lashed it to the opposite field for an RBI double. Bowa's run made it 16–6.

As Rose could have told you, it was his fifth double of the three-game series. Hernandez looked skyward for help. He'd done his job against Bowa and Rose, a pair of pests, and in the eyes of God he'd struck them both out. With a real umpire he'd be out of the inning. Instead he had Rose leading off second, one run in, one out, Mike Schmidt at bat, and no options for his next move. "*Schmitty predicted he'd hit four home runs in this three-game set*," Andy Musser reminded Phillies fans. The Cubs didn't want to let that happen. They walked Schmidt intentionally for the second inning in a row.

Ordinarily that would bring up Greg Luzinski, a burly power hitter so strong he'd once pulled a line drive that the third baseman jumped for; the ball kept rising and cleared the fence. With Luzinski hurting, the job of protecting Schmidt in the lineup fell to Del Unser, a less intimidating hitter. The idea that one batter can protect the one before—getting

Schmidt better pitches to hit, in this instance, from pitchers worried that the next guy might hurt them—makes sense but has never been proven. Like clutch hitting, it might be a myth based on anecdotal evidence. Either way, the onus was on Unser to make the Cubs pay for walking Schmidt.

He bounced a double-play ball to second base that should have ended the inning. Ted Sizemore flipped the ball to Ivan DeJesus, who bobbled it. DeJesus got the out at second, but Unser, hustling down the line, beat the throw to first. First baseman Buckner shook his head like he couldn't believe it. Rose went to third. The inning went on.

Garry Maddox, overeager, swung at a curve in the dirt for strike one. Hernandez's next pitch was off the plate as well—six inches outside—but Maddox took a rip at this one, too, looping a fly ball that fell between outfielders. Rose scored Philadelphia's seventeenth run. Maddox, sliding into second, pulled a muscle in his thigh. Backup outfielder Greg Gross went in to run for him as Maddox limped off the field. The Secretary of Defense was finished for the day after four innings with a single, two doubles, a homer, and five RBIs. A few fans headed for the exits, looking for something better to do with the rest of the afternoon.

Bob Boone, two-for-two with a homer and four RBIs of his own, stood in. Rather than plunk him again, Hernandez paid Boone a different compliment. He walked him intentionally to load the bases.

Rudy Meoli was the eighth man to bat in the inning. If the Cubs got him out they would keep Philadelphia from batting around for the third time in four innings.

He grounded out to short. "*Whaddya know,*" Brickhouse said on WGN. "*We finally retired the side!*"

"I thought about leaving," one fan remembered, "but Kingman was coming up again pretty soon. I was up for that."

BOTTOM OF THE 4TH

PHILADELPHIA	7	0	8	2	—17	17	0
CUBS	6	0	0		— 6	10	1

Due up for the Cubs: DeJesus, Vail, Buckner

The Cubs had the top of the order coming up against Doug Bird. Now in his fourth inning of relief, Bird floated a 2-2 palmball past Ivan DeJesus for strike three. With one out, Mike Vail took a palmball, then lined a fastball to left for his third single of the day. Bill Buckner worked the count to 3-1 before skying one to left. This one didn't carry, as Del Unser put it away for the second out. The home fourth was starting to look like a quick inning, but nobody was heading for the exits.

"Dave!" a fan shouted. "Let's go, Daaave!"

Stone-faced as usual, Kingman checked his swing on a palmball that wasn't his style. Strike one, the umpire said.

Kingman was batting a sensational-for-him .285, twenty points better than Buckner, with power numbers that projected to fifty-two homers and 141 RBIs over a full season. The Giants, Mets, Padres, Angels, and Yankees, who had all dumped him, would have liked to have those numbers. Of course it was impossible to say if he'd have numbers like that in San Francisco, New York, San Diego, or Anaheim. His previous teams all played in pitchers' parks. (Yankee Stadium favored left-handed power but not right-handed sluggers like him.) Wrigley Field was the best hitters' park of all. What was more, Kingman claimed he was happy, even relaxed, to be back in his hometown, catching trophy-size

salmon and trout on the lake and visiting his widowed mother, Cap-
tola, known as Cappy, who still kept all his clippings. He was even
thinking of opening a restaurant in Chicago.

"I'm finally putting it all together. I guess the key was learning about
myself," he said.

Bird's 1-1 pitch was over his head. The crowd, such as it was, less
than fifteen thousand before some gave up and left, clapped along with
the fanfare played on the ballpark organ and yelled "Charge!"

Kingman fouled the 2-1 pitch straight back to the screen, a near
miss. Then Bird missed with a slider and the count was full. He rubbed
the ball up, looking in to see what his catcher wanted. Boone held
down one finger. With an eleven-run lead you go right at him.

Kong fouled this one straight back, too. Again he didn't miss by
much. It was the kind of foul ball that has a scent, a slight whiff of
burnt leather as the fast-moving bat scorches a bit of the ball's cover.
Again the crowd yelled "Charge!"

Vail, the runner at first, took off with the next full-count pitch, giving
him a fine view of the shot Kingman launched over the left-field ivy,
the bleachers, and Waveland Avenue.

"And there she goes!"

Modern metrics and technology suggest that the best launch angle
for home runs is around thirty-five degrees. Higher than that and the
ball starts falling before it reaches extreme exit velocity. The only visual
record of the ball Kingman hit is grainy WGN video. It shows his blast
taking off at forty degrees or more, which turned out to be just what a
fly ball needed with the wind gusting to thirty miles an hour.

This ball seemed to gain speed on the way up. It cleared the forty-foot
screen behind the bleachers and kept going. Several guys watching
from the roof of the four-story apartment building across the street saw
it coming. They leaned over the roof's railing to see if they could catch
it. The ball almost got there, bouncing off the building on a lower floor.

Kingman jogged around the bases looking at the ground. Cheers
and whistles followed every step. He touched the plate and walked to
the dugout, shaking hands with the batboy, who smacked him on the

butt. Excited fans banged the top of the Cub dugout and reached out as Kong went down the steps, but he never looked up.

Philadelphia still led by nine, 17–8. Bird's spot in the batting order would be coming up in the fifth for the Phillies; he knew he'd be out of the game after this inning. One more out and he's in the clubhouse with three earned runs against him in three and two-thirds innings. Not good but not the sort of career suicide that could happen at Wrigley on days like this.

Bird had to be happy to see Steve Ontiveros with two out and nobody on. The Cub third baseman, his right cheek full of chewing tobacco, spitting a brown glob into the dirt at his feet, was 0-for-2 with two weak grounders. But Bird's happiness was short-lived: Ontiveros, choking up two inches on the bat, socked a fly ball into the breeze for the Cubs' third homer—his first of the year. The score was 17–9.

Bird was reeling. The next batter was Jerry Martin, batting .272 with two home runs on the season. He whacked another fly ball, this one to center field, the wind carrying it. Substitute outfielder Greg Gross, the interim Secretary of Defense, chased it back to the warning track. He chased it until his shoulders were up against the ivy four hundred feet from home plate. Martin's fly ball died in his glove, just short of the wire basket on the wall, for the third out.

PHILADELPHIA	7	0	8	2		—17	17	0
CUBS	6	0	0	3		— 9	13	1

Due up for the Phillies: Bird, McBride, Bowa

As the Phillies prepared to bat in the fifth, Tug McGraw got his left arm loose. The thirty-four-year-old reliever had spent four innings amusing himself in the visitors' bullpen down the right-field line. "Wrigley Field was my favorite bullpen," McGraw recalled. "It's right there by the fans—you could trade baseballs for hot dogs and peanuts." In the days before selfies, fans settled for bullpen balls, autographs, and handshakes. McGraw added waves to the better-looking female Cub fans while watching Randy Lerch allow five runs and Doug Bird four more. "Can't nobody get nobody out?" he remembered thinking. "I could stop all this foolishness."

Phils manager Danny Ozark sent Greg Luzinski to lead off the inning, pinch-hitting for Doug Bird. Luzinski was Philadelphia's answer to Kingman, a homer-hitting outfielder who had led the National League in both RBIs and strikeouts. Known as the Bull for his beefy build, the blond left fielder was among a dozen former All-Stars on the Philadelphia roster, but he'd slumped all April and so far in May. "The team's not hitting and I'm not hitting," he told reporters. "I'm so messed up I don't even know what I'm doing wrong." Then he pulled a leg muscle, which was why Del Unser was playing left field this week.

Luzinski stepped gingerly to the plate. "Bull might be hurt," another player said, "but he could fall out of a hospital bed hitting."

Willie Hernandez pitched Luzinski carefully and ended up walking him. Ozark then dispatched Nino Espinosa, a scrawny pitcher, to pinch-run for Luzinski.

In the radio booth, Richie Ashburn noted the change. "*This scorecard is uncipherable*," he added.

Bake McBride grounded a single past first baseman Buckner, putting runners at first and second for Larry Bowa. "*Bowa's had a good day, two singles and a double*," Ashburn reminded listeners. "*Larry's probably over the .300 mark now.*" At a time when stats were updated at the end of the game rather than instantly, announcers guessed. Ashburn had it right: Bowa was at .301.

Choking up enough to show two inches of bat between his hands and the knob, Bowa hit a pop fly down the right-field line. Mike Vail, auditioning for a Cub Follies blooper reel, pulled up at the last instant, and the plummeting ball almost hit him on the foot. Nino Espinosa wheeled around third, losing his helmet to reveal the Phillies' biggest Afro. He touched home to boost the visitors' lead to 18–9. McBride stopped at third base as Bowa pulled into second.

A few more fans got up to go. The rest watched Cubs third baseman Steve Ontiveros and shortstop Ivan DeJesus come in a step on the infield dirt. Herman Franks didn't want Pete Rose bunting, though a bunt was the last thing on Rose's mind. Rose swung away, rolling a grounder to DeJesus, who dropped it. He retrieved the ball and dropped it again. McBride scored, Bowa took third, and Rose was safe at first. There was still nobody out.

Now behind by ten, the Cubs had to face Mike Schmidt. Hernandez set him up with breaking stuff and fooled him with a two-strike fastball, a pitch the twenty-nine-year-old Schmidt might have swung at and missed a couple of years earlier, when he led the league in strikeouts, but after six years in the majors he was maturing as a hitter. He fouled it off to stay alive. The *Inquirer*'s Frank Fitzpatrick called Schmidt "an enigma, always tinkering with his swing." That made him less predictable and more dangerous. Schmidt and Hernandez scrapped their way through a nine-pitch at-bat. Hernandez finally walked him for the third time, with ball four as the better part of valor. The Phils had loaded the bases for the fourth time in five innings. Hernandez paced around the mound.

Del Unser's sacrifice fly brought Bowa home with Philadelphia's twentieth run. Rose, the runner at second, tagged up and showboated to third, sliding around the tag, reaching through a cloud of dust to get a hand on the bag.

Greg Gross came up, batting in Garry Maddox's spot. Gross sent a fly to medium-deep left field. Kingman tracked it back to the warning track. Kong reached up and snagged the ball just short of the wall while Rose took off from third, hotfooting it home, his helmet flying off, Charlie Highlight.

Hernandez let his breath out. Another mile an hour of wind blowing out to left would have meant four runs instead of the one on Gross's sacrifice fly. Even so, Philadelphia had its biggest lead yet, 21–9.

The Phillies had batted around again. In the Cubs' dugout, Franks flashed four fingers. "*Herman Franks is still employing baseball strategy here, walking Bob Boone intentionally to get to Rudy Meoli,*" Ashburn said. "*The scorecards we have, well, you just can't make any sense out of 'em. . . . We're only in the fifth inning and my scorecard is spilling over into the sixth.*"

After another long at-bat, Hernandez walked Meoli to reload the bases. Now the Phillies' manager had a choice to make. Lucky for Hernandez, perhaps, Ozark let Espinosa, who pinch-ran for Luzinski and came around to score earlier in the inning, bat for himself. The spindly pitcher had a career batting average of .164. He swung at the first pitch, tapping a grounder to second baseman Ted Sizemore, who fumbled it. To the fans' relief, the ball dropped between Sizemore's spikes. He picked it up and fired to first to end the top of the fifth.

PHILADELPHIA	7	0	8	2	4		—21	19	0
CUBS	6	0	0	3			— 9	13	2

Due up for the Cubs: Foote, Sizemore, Hernandez

Bruce Newman of *Sports Illustrated* wondered if he'd stumbled onto a scoop. "I was working on a Pete Rose story, not a game story," Newman remembered. "Everyone expected Rose to make the Phillies tougher, to make them winners. Nobody expected me to call the office on a Thursday afternoon, raving about this crazy thing going on."

As if to add to the game's zany vibe, Frank Edwin McGraw Jr. took the mound for the last of the fifth. Philadelphia's third pitcher of the day hailed from Martinez, California, a working-class East Bay town where his father, known as Big Frank, ran a water treatment plant. As a baby he'd nursed so hungrily that his mother, Mabel, called him Tugger. More than three decades later Tug McGraw was still tugging on life. During his first decade in the big leagues he'd seen his pay grow from six thousand dollars to more than a hundred thousand, enough to keep his Porsche full of high-test gas, his wine cellar stocked with hundred-dollar bottles, and his heart full of song. "Ninety percent of my salary I spent on booze and women," he said. "The other ten percent I wasted." In his Mets days he'd helped his friend Joe Namath perfect the booze-and-broads lifestyle at Namath's Upper East Side nightclub, Bachelors III. On road trips to Chicago, McGraw could be found at the Playboy Club. Bowa was on his way to breakfast one game day when

McGraw staggered into the team hotel and asked the desk clerk for a wakeup call at eight o'clock. The clerk said, "Sir, it's eight-fifteen now."

McGraw once refused a trade to the American League, saying, "I don't believe in the DH." Asked if he preferred Astroturf or grass, he said, "I never smoked Astroturf." His repertoire included the screwball, his out pitch, as well as what he called his Peggy Lee "Is That All There Is?" fastball, a "Cutty Sark" fastball that sailed, and a "Bo Derek" cutter named for the movie sexpot because it had "a nice little tail on it." McGraw even named his home-run balls. They were "Sinatras," crooning "Fly Me to the Moon" all the way to the plate.

Now thirty-four, with a tender elbow, a 1969 World Series ring, and 132 major-league saves to his credit, he entered the game with a 1.59 ERA and a plan to stop all this nonsense: throw strikes.

"McGraw was a presence, especially on that team," Philadelphia sportswriter Frank Fitzpatrick recalled. "Schmidt was always churning inside, brooding over his at-bats. Steve Carlton, their ace, was quiet. He'd freeze out the press. One night his personal catcher, Tim McCarver, did postgame interviews for the whole club. McCarver gave a few quotes as Carlton, then went around the empty locker room pretending to be everybody else—a great audition for his TV career. . . . McGraw was the biggest personality in the clubhouse—at least until Rose came from Cincinnati. McGraw was a veteran, pretty famous, with a lot to say. That team needed a leader, but can you have a flaky left-handed relief pitcher for a leader?"

After his warm-ups, McGraw and his catcher huddled in front of the mound. Boone would recall saying that they should keep it simple. "Tuggles," he said, "we got you a twelve-run lead. Try not to screw it up." Boone bossed pitchers around if they needed it, but McGraw didn't need motivating, he needed settling down. Some of the tall tales other players told about him were true, like the one about the time Tug struck out Orlando Cepeda and got so worked up about it that he hyperventilated. The trainer had to give him a tranquilizer shot. McGraw floated back to the mound and won the game.

Boone jogged back to his spot between the plate and the hungover umpire. At bat was his opposite number, Barry Foote, who had been Boone's backup for the past two seasons in Philadelphia, before the trade to the Cubs over the winter. Foote had a stronger arm but less flexibility than Boone, who had mentored him when they were with the Phillies. Foote nodded hello to Boone and stepped into the batter's box. In the Philadelphia outfield, Del Unser, Greg Gross, and Bake McBride each moved a few steps toward left field, knowing Foote was a dead-pull hitter. Mike Schmidt leaned forward at third, twitching his glove open and shut. Bowa shifted a couple of steps to his right. Rose played well off the bag at first. Boone squatted behind the plate and showed McGraw one finger.

Foote pulled a Cutty Sark over the semi-shift for a single to left. McGraw wasn't worried, not with a twelve-run lead. He induced a double-play ball from Ted Sizemore. (Double-play balls, like other delightful arrivals, are often "induced.") It was an easy play for Schmidt, a three-time Gold Glover, and he booted it. McGraw could only roll his eyes at his buddy Schmitty. Mr. Franchise Player, who carpooled to home games with Tug, was creating a hostile work environment. Instead of two out and none on, McGraw had the opposite.

Pinch-hitter Steve Dillard, batting for Willie Hernandez, walked to load the bases for the Cubs. What was left of the crowd—paid attendance 14,952 minus a couple hundred who had left—got louder.

With DeJesus at bat, McGraw missed with a curve. Boone went partway to the mound to confer with his pitcher.

"What do *you* want?" McGraw asked.

"Outs would be good," Boone said.

Both of them were attuned to the screwy side of their jobs, but this was starting to get serious.

McGraw said, "My arm hurts." After fourteen years of throwing screwballs—the arm-killing reverse curve that bent away from right-handed hitters, the pitch Willie Hernandez was hoping to master—he had only so many left.

"Okay, we'll throw fastballs."

Missing with a Peggy Lee, a Cutty, and a curve, McGraw walked

DeJesus to force in the Cubs' tenth run. Still leading by eleven, he got Mike Vail on a pop-up. With one out and the bases full, he had a chance to escape further nonsense. A double play would end the inning.

Bill Buckner took a fastball. Ball one. In the stands Ronnie Wickers yelled, "Cubs *woo!* Buckner *woo!*"

Buckner's batting stance favored his ankle. His legs didn't quite fill his uniform pants, but his chest and arms were bulky by 1979 standards, chiseled by the hours he spent in the batting cage. Many Chicago players admired him. Fans might see Kingman as this year's Mr. Cub, but when the union asked the Cubs to choose a player representative, they elected Buckner. Choking up an inch on his black bat, he took another pitch to get ahead in the count, 2-0.

McGraw came back with a cutter for a strike. He and Boone didn't think Buckner would be looking for another one, but this pitch stayed straight, belt high on the outer half. Buckner triggered his short quick swing, sending a line drive toward the bleachers in right.

"*Deep to right field,*" Jack Brickhouse called it. "*Hey, hey, kiss it goodbye, a grand slammer by Buckner!*"

The ball took almost four seconds to reach the dancing bleacher bums, who kept this one. Buckner took half a minute rounding the bases, slowing down to offer Bowa a few choice words. He touched the plate with Chicago's fourteenth run on the game's eighth homer. Maybe this wasn't such a bad day for the Cubs after all, at least for the hitters. On his way to the dugout Buckner shook hands with the next batter, Dave Kingman, giving him a go-get-'em slap on the back.

"*Twenty-one to fourteen. Sounds like an Eagles game,*" said Ashburn.

Boone went back to the mound. As he recalled later, "I was trying to keep a straight face."

"What's so funny?" McGraw said.

"Well, I got a three-run jack and you're in the shit. Bowa thinks it's funny, too."

Bowa joined them. "Hey, we can win if we hold them to two touchdowns," he said.

The Phillies returned to their positions. McGraw stood on the mound, ten inches higher than the rest of the field, as commanding and lonesome a place as there is. He liked to console himself with thoughts of how insignificant a place it was on a cosmic scale: "Ten million years from now, when the sun burns out and Earth's just a frozen ice ball hurtling through space, nobody's going to care if I got this guy out or not."

Kingman was scroogie bait, a big right-handed pull hitter. But McGraw was conserving screwballs. He invited Kingman to take a rip at a fastball that was outside enough to keep him from pulling it. Kong fouled it off.

"*Kingman can taste it,*" said Brickhouse. "*He went after that one and he jumped at it.*"

Soon the count was 1-2. McGraw and Boone felt pretty good about that. Year after year, batters hit below .180 on 1-2 counts. At the same time, the Phillies' battery didn't want to feed Kong a cookie. If McGraw was at his best he might wipe Kingman out with a screwball that looked like a Sinatra until it swooned off the outside corner. As it was, he tried one and missed, then nibbled with Cuttys and Bo's. With the count 3-2, McGraw missed low and inside. No big whoop—Tug proceeded to strike out Steve Ontiveros, who provided no protection for Kong if you believe in that sort of thing, and faced Jerry Martin with two out and Kingman at first. The Cubs had scored five runs this inning, but one more out would end the fifth with the Phillies still seven runs ahead.

Jerry Martin was one for three with a double. He fouled off a cutter. McGraw then missed before sneaking a Peggy Lee under Martin's bat for strike two. Boone called for a fastball outside, but it leaked back to the strike zone. Martin swung hard. WGN's microphones caught the *clack* of bat on ball and transmitted it to Satcom-3, which beamed it to TV sets from coast to coast. Greg Gross chased the ball to the center-field ivy but watched it carry about ten feet farther than Martin's long, loud fourth-inning flyout and come down in the second row of bleacher seats.

"*Ooh, I can't believe it!*" Ashburn said. The score was 21–16.

Tuggles had allowed seven runs in fifteen minutes. Only four were earned, but still. He could do without a catcher who thought it was funny. Boone, gunning a new ball back to the mound, said they might need another touchdown.

Barry Foote, batting for the second time in the inning, pulled a double to left. That was enough for Danny Ozark, who signaled for Ron Reed to come in from the bullpen.

McGraw's ERA had jumped from 1.64 to 4.50, but his sense of humor led the league. Leaving the field to an ovation from Cub fans, he tipped his cap.

Ron Reed was the Phillies' fourth pitcher in five innings. At six foot six—Kingman's size—he was one of the tallest men in the majors. He'd been a college basketball star at Notre Dame, setting a record by averaging eighteen rebounds a game, and spent two seasons with the NBA's Detroit Pistons before switching to baseball.

"Reed was a misanthrope," Frank Fitzpatrick said. "He hated everybody." Reed had forty-nine big-league saves to his credit. His loopy windup helped him distract hitters from the lack of hop on his fastball, which topped out around ninety miles per hour, and he kept hitters guessing by mixing in a slider, curve, and a modified palmball he called a slip pitch. When Reed first came up from the minors in 1966, his Atlanta Braves teammate Hank Aaron said, "The last kid I saw with so many pitches was Juan Marichal." Eight years later Reed was the starting and winning pitcher the night Aaron broke Babe Ruth's home-run record. Five years after that he was a thirteen-year veteran on a hot streak. He entered the game with a record of four wins, one loss, and an earned run average of 0.42. He'd gone twenty-one innings without allowing a run.

"*Reed is in the ballgame to try to restore some order,*" Richie Ashburn said.

Ted Sizemore, batting for the second time in the inning, was two for three with an RBI. Reed started him off with a forehead-high fastball, which Sizemore swung under. Reed's second pitch, just like the first, got the same result. With the count 0-2, Sizemore slapped a slip pitch up the middle. The ball was on its way to center field when Bowa, racing over from shortstop, intercepted it and threw to first to beat Sizemore by a step.

After seven runs on four hits, the Cubs were finally done in the fifth.

TOP OF THE 6TH

PHILADELPHIA	7	0	8	2	4		—21	19	1
CUBS	6	0	0	3	7		—16	17	2

Due up for the Phillies: McBride, Bowa, Rose

Rookie Bill Caudill came out to pitch for the Cubs. He was a lean, clean-shaven Californian, medium-sized at six foot one and 190 pounds, with a compact delivery of a low-nineties fastball and several unreliable off-speed pitches. That mix put him in the vast middle class of major-league pitchers who get outs if they can get ahead in the count and nibble at corners, but not if they fall behind and need to aim for more of the plate.

After signing a pro contract right out of high school, Caudill left his native Los Angeles for Little Rock; Trois-Rivières, Quebec; Little Rock again; and Indianapolis, throwing major-league fastballs while working on those secondary pitches. He'd made his big-league debut only five days before, when the twenty-two-year-old right-hander fanned four Astros in a three-inning stint. Herman Franks then used him to mop up the final three innings of yesterday's 13–0 loss to the Phillies, but that outing didn't go so well. Caudill coughed up five runs, two on a long homer by Mike Schmidt.

There was no sign as yet that the rookie would one day become an All-Star reliever, one of five famous closers to suffer on this Thursday afternoon. He would eventually be known for something else as well: his loyalty to a minor-league teammate. After Scott Boras, an infielder who washed out at the Double-A level, got his law degree from the University of the Pacific and became an agent, Caudill became his first client. In time Boras would make him a millionaire with help from stunts like hiring a plane to fly a banner over Toronto the year Caudill lost favor with Blue Jays manager Jimy Williams: JIMY—GIVE CAUDILL THE BALL. Boras would become the king of baseball agents, perhaps the most powerful man in the sport, a new sort of agent combining Marvin Miller's aggressive tactics and Bill James's statistics, spinning dossiers full of modern metrics into nine-figure contracts. After he retired, Caudill would go to work for Boras as a talent scout. For now, though, at the outset of his major-league career, he was hunting strikes against the Phillies' leadoff man.

Bake McBride, three-for-five, swung and missed a fastball, then took another for strike two. Caudill kicked with a quirky twitch of his left ankle as he delivered the 0-2 pitch, another fastball that McBride waved at.

The home crowd's cheers were twice as loud as an inning before, now that the Cubs had cut the Phillies' lead from twelve runs to five. McBride spun on his heels and retreated to the dugout as the Cubs threw the ball around the horn—Foote to Ontiveros to Sizemore to DeJesus, who returned it to Caudill—the age-old celebration of a strikeout. The baseball goes around the horn again and again during pitchers' duels, but this was the first time the Cubs had done it today.

Larry Bowa, four for five with four runs scored, took a fastball. He swung late at another fastball, got a piece of yet another. Here was an approach Herman Franks liked—a rookie comes in and pours six fastballs in a row down the strike zone. Rather than trying to paint corners, the rookie was pumping gas. He made pitching look easy—until Bowa popped a two-strike fastball over the shortstop's head.

Philadelphia's twentieth hit brought up Pete Rose again, to the usual Chicago boos. Caudill stuck with his aggressive approach. The three-time batting champ took a pair a fastballs to fall behind in the count, 0-2. He then drilled a liner to left that carried straight to Kingman, who hauled it in for the second out.

Caudill was now in the same fix he'd been in the day before: a runner at first with two out and the league's most fearsome slugger coming up next.

The flags on Wrigley's ramparts had been pointing straight out to left all day, but the wind was fickle. Mike Schmidt's first-inning homer would have been a routine fly ball without it. Greg Gross's fifth-inning fly two hours later had died at the fence. When the wind blew off the lake Chicagoans called it the Hawk, a chilly draft that froze noses in winter. Gusts from other directions changed spring afternoons in other ways. In 1969, Hank Aaron hit a towering fly that cleared Wrigley's left-field fence only to encounter a wall of wind that carried it higher and backward until the ball dropped into Billy Williams's glove. That day's wind was so pitcher-friendly that Ken Holtzman went on to throw a no-hitter without striking anybody out—one of only three no-strikeout no-hitters in major-league history.

This day's pitchers had no such luck. Facing Schmidt with the elements against him, Caudill knew that the breeze in his face was strong enough to take a tick off his fastball. No matter; his fastball was hopping. He barely glanced at Foote's fastball sign before nodding.

"Schmidt had an aura," *Sports Illustrated*'s Bruce Newman said. "Rose and Tug McGraw had personality and he didn't, particularly, but there was kind of an intake of breath when he came up. He looked dangerous, not for his physique as much as his swing. Even his practice swings looked dangerous. He was like Kingman that way. They were the most feared hitters in the league and utterly different. Kingman took all-or-nothing swings and practically sneered at singles. Schmidt was quieter, more of a purist, a real baseball player. He said his dream was to bat .340. But whatever Schmidt said about his batting average, he still wanted to hit more homers than Kingman."

Batting .274, with a home run and three walks on the day, Schmidt took a level practice swing. He watched a fastball go by for strike one. Caudill was throwing darts.

Caudill missed twice, then released another dart that Schmidt swung through while Bowa, the runner at first, stole second.

Bowa bounced up cursing. He'd jammed his ankle on the bag, which was not a bag like the sawdust-filled canvas bases of the game's early days but a square mounted on metal studs and anchored in concrete. The bases at Wrigley Field and other parks in 1979 were harder than those of earlier decades but softer than today's bases, which are about as yielding as a fire hydrant. Made of hard rubber, painted bright white for visibility on TV, modern bases cause numerous injuries to sliding players' feet, ankles, knees, thumbs, and fingers. A breakaway base patented in 1979 would prevent injuries and save hundreds of disabled-list stints, but would cost more. Not a lot more—probably no more than what the 2014 Nationals paid Bryce Harper during his rehab after he sprained his thumb diving into an anchored rubber base or the 2017 Angels paid Mike Trout after he tore a thumb ligament the same way— but the owners have never been willing to switch to breakaway bases. The players' union hasn't pushed for them.

Bowa shook the bees out of his ankle. As a veteran on a loosey-goosey club, he had the green light to steal, but his sixth stolen base of the year gave Chicago the option of walking Schmidt again.

With first base open, Schmidt called time. He stepped out of the box. The Cubs weren't going to put him on this time. The kid was throwing too well. Caudill's job was to go after Schmidt but don't give him anything to hit.

Caudill shaved the outside corner with what looked like strike three, but the umpire said no. With the count full, Caudill missed inside. Schmidt trotted to first with his fourth base on balls. His windblown first-inning homer was still his only hit but he was building his stats, slashing .500/.800/4.000 for the day.

"*The Phillies have a plane out of here tonight,*" Andy Musser told his listeners in Philadelphia at 3:40 p.m. "*Not till a little after seven, and it's a good thing.*"

With runners at first and second, Caudill buzzed three fastballs past Del Unser. The Cubs came off the field with the sun starting to sink behind the grandstand. They had twelve outs left.

| PHILADELPHIA | 7 | 0 | 8 | 2 | 4 | 0 | | —21 | 20 | 1 |
| CUBS | 6 | 0 | 0 | 3 | 7 | | | —16 | 17 | 2 |

Due up for the Cubs: Dillard, DeJesus, Vail

Steve Dillard led off the Cub sixth. He had pinch-hit and walked for Willie Hernandez and stayed in the game to play second base. A journeyman infielder who'd started his career with the Red Sox, Dillard had a special fondness for the game's vintage ballparks. "The Red Sox, to me, had the greatest place to play in the American League, and I thought Chicago was the greatest place to play in the National League," he said. In both cities "the fans are crazy about their teams."

He never played much in either town. In four seasons Dillard had never hit more than one homer or driven in more than fifteen runs. Halfway through May he was 0 for 5 for the season, still looking for his first hit of 1979. Looking uphill at six-foot-six reliever Ron Reed, he chopped a grounder past the mound. The crowd, getting louder by the inning, went crazy for Dillard as he legged out an infield single.

DeJesus batted next, an aggressive slasher from Santurce, Puerto Rico. Scouts liked to say that Puerto Rican (and Cuban and Dominican) players were free swingers because "nobody ever walked their way off the island." Spanish-speaking players were thought to be hotheaded, spicy in temperament, swinging at everything. You wouldn't know from the stereotype that DeJesus walked more often than his famously disciplined teammate Bill Buckner.

This time he swung freely at Reed's first pitch, stroking a long drive to center. Gross chased it and nearly got to it, but the baseball carried over his head and caromed off the ivy. Dillard stopped at third, DeJesus at second.

"*Oh boy*," Ashburn said on Phillies radio, "*here we go again.*"

Cub fans yelled and stamped their feet, waved their fists, whistled between their teeth—a ruckus Reed intended to stifle.

Mike Vail, a part-time player like Dillard, was three-for-four so far, enough to lift his batting average from .333 to .409. Vail swung halfway out of his socks at Reed's first delivery to him. The fans, now reacting to every swing, got quieter when Vail came up empty. Then they began clapping in foot-stomping rhythm. A minute later Vail chopped a 2-2 pitch to Bowa, who threw him out as Dillard scored and DeJesus went to third. Philadelphia's lead was down to four.

Bill Buckner moved from the on-deck circle to one of his biggest ovations since Opening Day. Buckner, three-for-four with a grand slam, worked the count to 3-1. If the *Inquirer*'s Frank Fitzpatrick was right about Ron Reed's misanthropic leanings, this ump was doing nothing for his opinion of humanity. "That guy cut the strike zone in half," Danny Ozark said of Dick Cavenaugh. "He took a lot of strikes away."

Buckner fouled off a fastball to run the count full.

Reed's 3-2 slider came in where he and Bob Boone wanted it, knee-high above the plate's black border on the outside edge. Buckner, protecting the strike zone, flicked his bat at it. He topped the ball but got enough of it to send it bounding over the mound. Bowa charged, took it on a short hop, and threw in one motion while Buckner, digging for first on his rickety ankles, found a new gear. He sprinted up the line while Rose stretched for the throw and stamped on the base within a split second of the ball's hitting Rose's mitt. Out. Still, a run scored to make it a three-run game, 21–18. In the middle of the biggest slugfest in a century, the Cubs just got two runs on a pair of RBI groundouts.

WGN's cameras showed the crowd on its feet. "*A standing ovation for*

Kingman, and also for Buckner," Lou Boudreau told Channel 9 viewers. *"That's five RBIs for Buckner today. He ties Kingman at the present time."*

There was ease in Kingman's manner as he reached out to touch his bat to the outside corner.

The catcher said, "Hi, Dave."

"Hello, Boonie."

The two of them had been friendly rivals playing college baseball, and teammates on the Alaska Goldpanners. They'd kept in touch the way baseball friends who aren't close friends do, by chatting on the field before and during games. Boone, remembering Kingman's days at USC, liked to needle him by saying, "You're still just a pitcher to me." Kingman would give him a little screw-you smile and strike out. Or hit a home run. Today Boone settled into his crouch and asked him a question.

"So where you want it? Middle in?"

Kong thought that was funny. "Are you psyching me out?"

"You're damn right. Nothing else is working."

Kingman stared coolly at Reed. Their face-off was the season's first in which pitcher and hitter totaled thirteen feet tall.

Reed started him out with a fastball belly button–high. Kingman strode on his front foot and started his bat. The baseball never knew what hit it.

"High, kiss it goodbye!" Boudreau shouted.

Ashburn was even louder. *"Long drive—oh! Way out of the ballpark, way across the street. Oh brother! Oh boy! That one's in Milwaukee!"*

Kingman went into his home-run trot while bleacher bums went Borneo. Boone stood up, pulled off his mask, and watched the ball rocket over the bleachers. "There was a second when everybody in the park was watching that ball, thinking, 'Holy crap,'" Boone recalled. Suddenly it was 21–19, a close ballgame again.

Boudreau said, *"It hit the porch of the third house across Waveland Avenue! And I thought he hit the last one hard!"*

Today, Major League Baseball's Statcast technology employs

Doppler radar guns and HD cameras to measure the speed, spin rate, and launch angle of every pitched and batted ball at twenty thousand frames per second. Nobody dreamed of such precision in 1979. Even so, the WGN video suggests that Kingman's third homer of the day had an exit velocity of 115 to 120 miles per hour and a launch angle between forty and forty-five degrees.

Kingman rounded the bases with his head down. He touched hands with the on-deck batter, Steve Ontiveros, and walked to the dugout, ignoring the fans reaching out to him.

In the press box, sportswriters quizzed one another about tape-measure homers they'd witnessed. Was this one longer than Kong's house-hitting blast of '76, when he was with the Mets? Longer than Mickey Mantle's 565-footer in 1953? According to Newman's *Sports Illustrated* story, it carried "an estimated six hundred feet on the fly."

Newman went out to interview the family that lived at 3711 North Kenmore Avenue, where the ball came down. Neighborhood homes "have become pillboxes in which families sit trembling in their cellars as Kingman bombards their facades," he wrote in a jolly report on what he called The Game. Newman quoted Diane Reyes, who'd been minding her own business one afternoon when a baseball came crashing through a window. "The Cubs pay for the broken windows, but they take the balls back," she said. "It would be nice to have something to remember Kingman by besides a pile of busted glass."

Kingman's shot was the tenth home run of the game. According to wWE it boosted the Cubs' chance of winning from 12 percent to 20. The Phillies had never given up more than six homers in a game in their long history; the Cubs had already hit six, and it was only the sixth inning.

Ron Reed wanted a new ball. He rubbed it up as if to crush it and went after the next batter, Ontiveros, who took Reed's first pitch a foot outside. Cavenaugh called it a strike. A pitch later, Ontiveros banged a one-hopper up the middle. Reed speared the ball with his bare hand, flung it to first, and was on his way off the field before the baseball was safe in Rose's mitt. After allowing one earned run in the season's first six weeks, he'd just given up three in an inning.

After recording the out, first baseman Rose spiked the ball the way he did with third outs on the artificial turf at Veterans Stadium. On Wrigley's dirt it kicked sideways.

TOP OF THE 7TH

PHILADELPHIA	7	0	8	2	4	0	—21	20	1
CUBS	6	0	0	3	7	3	—19	20	2

Due up for the Phillies: Gross, Boone, Meoli

In the Philadelphia dugout, Danny Ozark told Ron Reed not to worry. "A game like this, the first thing you do is see if you've got any broken bones," he said. Reed told him he was good for another inning at least.

Bleacher fans salaamed as Kingman jogged out to his position in left. In the Cubs' broadcast booth, Lou Boudreau narrated a slow-motion replay of Kong's third home run. *"Whacko! Now watch the youngster on the porch."* The video showed a fuzzy figure hurrying down the stairs at 3711 North Kenmore, chasing the baseball. *"That is the fourth house from Waveland Avenue. It bounced on the porch of the third house, and where that youngster is, is the fourth house!"*

Ballhawks and reporters paced off the distance at well over 530 feet. Or was it 550? Either distance made this wallop longer than Kong's homer in '76.

Caudill fell behind in the count to Greg Gross, the substitute outfielder, leading off the seventh. He was trying to stay away from Gross's power, which was occasional. Barry Foote let Dick Cavenaugh know that a real ump, as opposed to some gym teacher trying out for the job, would have called Caudill's first pitch a strike. He gave Cavenaugh a second chance, calling for another fastball. Ball two. Instead of 1-1 or even 0-2, Foote and his pitcher were down in the count. They didn't want to walk Gross on a day when forty baserunners had already touched the plate, and Gross knew that as well as they did. Even Ronnie Woo Woo knew Caudill had to throw a strike now.

Caudill threw a fastball for strike one. He then reared back and flung the next one past the hitter as well. Gross was getting Linda'd, a '70s baseball term referring to Linda Ronstadt, whose song "Blue Bayou" captured the way that fastball just blew by you. Now Caudill was effectively ahead in the count. At 2-2 he couldn't walk the hitter with his next pitch, but he could strike him out.

Gross fouled off a fastball. He checked his swing on the next, this one flirting with strike three. That could have been the first out, but the umpire's right hand never moved. The count was three and two.

Some players claim that full counts favor the pitcher. Others say it depends. Baseball's sheer measurability would soon make it possible to quantify the odds of a hit, walk, home run, or strikeout on every count, but third-decimal analysis of each butterfly effect in each ballgame was decades away. In 1979 Franks, Foote, and Caudill relied on intuition. In their day as today, a 2-1 count was thought to be neutral, the only neutral pitch after the first one. Most seat-of-the-pants metrics of the '70s saw full counts as neutral, too, but that view was wrong. In fact, they favor the pitcher by several percent.

Caudill surprised nobody by throwing a full-count fastball. Gross was quicker than before, not quick enough to pull the ball but to sock it off the wall in left-center, just under the basket that caught home runs. Kingman misplayed the carom as Gross sped around second toward third.

"*The ball bounds away*," Andy Musser said. "*Kingman giving chase . . .*"

Gross's triple was the game's first since Donnie Moore's three-bagger six innings before. For the moment the Phillies had twenty-one runs on twenty-one hits: four home runs, a triple, six doubles, and ten singles. This latest extra-base hit brought up Bob Boone, who had helped turn Andy Musser's scorecard into *"something for a mathematician"* with a home run, four RBIs, a pair of walks, and a hit-by-pitch. "They hadn't got me out yet," Boone recalled years later. "I couldn't wait to get up there."

Franks made a daring call: he brought his infield in. Such a move would make sense in the seventh inning of a pitchers' duel, but few managers would try it in a 21–19 melee with three innings to play and the wind howling out. Players and coaches often claim that playing the infield in boosts the batter's average by a hundred points. A recent study pinned the number at eighty-three points, which would turn Boone from a guy with a .265 average, his career norm at the time, into a .348 batting champ. He made Franks's move irrelevant by ripping another extra-base hit to the opposite field, a double to right-center, scoring Gross and giving Philadelphia a little breathing room at 22–19.

"*Now, come on*," Jack Brickhouse told Cub fans. "*Let's not come this close and then give 'em that big lead again.*"

To complicate matters for the home team, having Boone at second base forced them to change signals, which they'd already done half a dozen times. Foote could no longer call for a fastball with one finger and a curve with two, not with a baserunner who could relay his signs to the batter. When the runner at second was a catcher like Boone, who could easily decipher most sets of signals, the new signs might involve reversed or "upside-down" signals (four fingers for a fastball, one for a change, and so on), indicator signs to say, in effect, "the next one's the one that counts," fist pumps, thigh taps, the occasional intimate scratch.

Rudy Meoli griped about a called strike that had been below his knees and an inch or two outside. Caudill's next fastball came in knee-high over the outside black. Meoli took this one, too, and his gripe may have registered because Cavenaugh called it a ball. Now, for the umpteenth time, both teams were peeved at the inexperienced ump.

Caudill held the ball behind his back, twirling it between his fingers. He waited for Foote to run through a handful of signs before nodding yes. He came to his set position, cradling the baseball in his glove just under the Cubs logo on his chest, then rocked into his motion and strode for the plate, releasing the 2-2 pitch at batting-practice speed. It moved at such an unhurried pace that Meoli had time to think, twitch, think again, and leave the bat on his shoulder while the best changeup of Caudill's first week in the majors floated past for strike three.

Caudill let out his breath. One man down, two outs to go. And the Phillies were about to do him a favor by letting the pitcher bat. Ozark was counting on Ron Reed to give him that one more inning.

Reed, the former Notre Dame basketball star, demonstrated how difficult it is to hit big-league pitching whenever he tried. A multisport legend in high school and college, he had flailed at hundreds of major-league pitches since 1966, his rookie year, and made contact with a few. Homerless in 579 at-bats for his fourteen-year career, the equivalent of one full season for an everyday player, he'd batted .147 with 182 strikeouts.

Hitters as weak as Reed get the fondue treatment: gas, heat, and cheese. Caudill's first fastball was a strike, but he missed with the next two, then buzzed one so high that Foote had to stand up to corral it. Again Caudill aimed at the opposing pitcher's NBA-size strike zone; again he missed and Reed had the thirteenth walk of his fourteen-year career. It was a rookie mistake on Caudill's part, but a double play would get him out of trouble.

"And here's Herman Franks," Musser said, *"emerging slowly from the Chicago dugout. As Herman walks out he is calling the home plate umpire, Dick Cavenaugh, over, and he's going to make a double change."*

"Franks was managing for his job," said Ed Hartig, the Cubs' historian. "Not that he needed the job, with all the money he had, but who wants to get fired?"

Franks brought relief pitcher Ray Burris into the game and sent Bobby Murcer to replace Mike Vail in right field. Carrying a scrawly lineup card to the ump, he announced that Murcer would occupy the pitcher's spot in the Cubs' batting order, with Burris going into Vail's number-two slot, a double-switch that would bring Murcer to bat in the bottom of the inning.

Caudill, to his surprise, was finished after an inning and a third. But he was still in the game in a numerical sense: he was responsible for the men he left on base. If they scored, the runs would count against his record. On the other hand, if the next pitcher kept them from scoring, his responsibility would go away like a sin forgiven. That's why his favorite player in the world, at least for the next few minutes, was Burris, the game's ninth pitcher.

Franks plodded back to the dugout to see how his strategies would work out.

Burris was the son of African American sharecroppers who grew cotton, hay, and barley in southeast Oklahoma, near Idabel, where the summer heat liked to hit triple digits. From the age of five he picked cotton and stacked hay. He also churned butter, which old-timers liked to say was the best exercise God ever made for building hand and wrist strength. Burris went on to star at Southwestern Oklahoma State, then signed with the Cubs and rose through their farm chain in a year. In 1975 the twenty-four-year-old Burris won fifteen games and lost ten for the fifth-place Cubs. He won another fifteen in the bicentennial season, signed a seventy-five-thousand-dollar-a-year contract, and then, suddenly, couldn't get anyone out.

"There was nothing wrong with my arm. It was a performance issue, bad performance," he recalled. In the first year of his lucrative new contract he won fourteen, lost sixteen, and led the league in home runs allowed. His next season was worse. "Finally Herman Franks came to me to say they want me in the bullpen, in middle relief. I said fine. 'Give me the ball whenever you want.' Wind blowing out? Top of the order coming up? If you just give me a chance to promote myself, to show I can still pitch, I'm fine."

If the manager had wanted a fresh arm this afternoon, Burris wasn't it. He'd pitched four innings the day before. He didn't know exactly why Franks was using him to relieve a younger, possibly stronger right-hander, and didn't need to know. "From the time I got up in the bullpen all I was thinking was, *Keep the ball down.* I expected I could locate my fastball, but didn't know about the slider. People think the wind helps hitters. It can hurt pitchers, too. If you're throwing into a twenty-mile-an-hour wind, your fastball doesn't get there as fast, but it affects a slider more. The ball won't spin as much in a headwind, so you want to stay away from the slider." He planned to throw sinking fastballs and use his slider mainly for display purposes, "more as a taste pitch" out of the strike zone, giving the batter a look at a fat one he wasn't going to get in a spot where he could hit it.

Pitcher and catcher met on the mound. "Give me a low target," Burris told Barry Foote. "We're going to think ground balls." Foote returned to the plate and flashed a signal that didn't matter. They were going to throw fastballs until further notice. Burris peered in at Foote's mitt, even with the level of Bake McBride's knees, but aimed lower. "I'm starting that pitch at the bottom of the catcher's butt, so it's never a strike even if it might look like one."

McBride was twitchy in the batter's box, kicking dirt, pulling his batting gloves tighter. After the umpire called "Play," he took a hack at a low fastball and missed.

"*Burris has his sign from Foote,*" Musser said of the pro forma sign, "*and the one-strike pitch . . . swing and a miss, strike two.*"

At 0-2 the Cubs' battery resumed signaling for real. Burris shook off signs until he saw the one he wanted. "I pretty much called my own game. No offense to Barry, a good catcher, but I'm the one who has to live with what happens." He went into his stretch, shooting the runners a look, digging his fingertips as deep as he could into the ball's leather skin, indenting the ball a little to make it spin more.

McBride let the slider go. It skipped in the dirt. The count was a ball and two strikes.

Burris gave him another taste with the same result. "Now it's two and two," Burris recalled thinking, "and I'm not going to fool around anymore. I'm going after him." He reached back for a fastball McBride waved at, striking out.

Larry Bowa, batting for the seventh time, crouched in the batter's box, bouncing on the balls of his feet, optimistic. Five-for-six with two doubles, four runs scored, and a stolen base, he jabbed at the first pitch and hustled down the first-base line, cussing all the way at his crappy little inning-ending two-hopper to second.

BOTTOM OF THE 7TH

PHILADELPHIA	7	0	8	2	4	0	1		—22	22	1
CUBS	6	0	0	3	7	3			—19	20	2

Due up for the Cubs: Martin, Foote, Murcer

The seventh-inning stretch was a special occasion in Chicago, but not yet at Wrigley Field. At Comiskey Park, where the exuberant Harry Caray called White Sox games, owner Bill Veeck liked the way Caray sang along when ballpark organist Nancy Faust played "Take Me Out to the Ballgame." One night in 1976—the year Veeck briefly outfitted his Sox in short pants—the owner sneaked a live microphone into the broadcast booth. Fans adored Caray's cheery, bullfrog-voiced rendition. Soon singing along with Harry became a tradition, one that would follow Caray when he jumped to the Cubs in 1982. But in '79, few Cub fans sang along with Wrigley Field organist John Henzel. The stretch was a last chance to grab a beer or take a bathroom break.

Ron Reed completed his warm-ups for the last of the seventh from a mound that was lower than when he first reached the majors. From 1904, early in the dead-ball era, until 1968, Reed's third season in the big leagues, the pitcher's rubber had been fifteen inches off the ground. But 1968 was the year the Tigers' Denny McLain went 31-6 to become the first thirty-game winner since Dizzy Dean in 1934, while the Cardinals' Bob Gibson posted an earned run average of 1.12 and the Dodgers' Don Drysdale pitched six shutouts in a row. Pitchers threw 279 complete-game shutouts that season (compared to 19 in 2018), and the owners decided that hurlers had broken the game. In 1969 the height of the mound was reduced to ten inches.

Reed had been an All-Star with the Braves in 1968, a tall man striding down-mountain. But he didn't much care how high the mound was; even at its new, lower height he was effectively seven and a half feet tall. He never made another All-Star team, but he did win eighteen games in '69. After joining the Phillies seven years later, he moved to the bullpen and led the team with seventeen saves in 1978, eight more than Tug McGraw.

Reed did all that with a pedestrian fastball that never got within hailing distance of ninety-five miles an hour. Some fans and rookie hitters expected more from such a big man, but he made up for his lack of velocity with expert control of a slider, a curve, and a slip pitch he choked between his thumb and forefinger. Similar to Doug Bird's palmball, the slip pitch behaved like a blend of a changeup and a curve. Some pitchers today throw a version they call a churve. Whatever you call it, Jerry Martin was looking for it.

Martin, two-for-four with a homer and a double, got a fastball instead. Coming out of Reed's lengthy windup, it looked a little quicker than it was, and even his low-octane gas gave the batter only a tenth of a second to judge the ball's direction and spin and decide whether to swing. Martin fouled it off the bat handle, the kind of off-kilter contact that stings. He swung at the next pitch, too, rolling it to Bowa, who gobbled it up and threw him out.

Barry Foote's two hits in the Cubs' seven-run fifth had raised his average to .198. He swung through Reed's next pitch. At this point some of the fans had to be thinking this was typical Cubs: they needed baserunners, but had now seen three pitches in the inning and swung at them all.

Foote hit a bouncer to third. Schmidt played the ball on a hop. The three-time All-Star had three Gold Glove awards in the trophy room at his home in Delaware County, but this grounder clanged off his leather glove for his second error of the game.

"*Ordinarily you see Mike suck those up like a vacuum cleaner,*" Richie Ashburn said.

Bobby Murcer came up next. It hadn't been long since Murcer was the New York Yankees' star center fielder, batting cleanup behind Thurman Munson and Roy White. The Yanks' pitching staff at the time featured wife-swapping starting pitchers Fritz Peterson and Mike Kekich. It was the '70s.

Bobby Ray Murcer had torn up high school pitching in Oklahoma City and signed his first pro contract with the same Yankees scout who had signed his idol Mickey Mantle. Comparisons to Mantle chased him up through the minors. Murcer split his $10,000 signing bonus between investments in his father's jewelry store and his father-in-law's grocery, and went off to New York City, arriving just as the Yankee dynasty was falling apart. He soon became a bright spot for the mediocre Yankee teams of the early '70s. In 1971 he batted .331 with twenty-five home runs and ninety-four RBIs. He stole fourteen bases. His .427 on-base percentage was the best in the majors, .002 better than Willie Mays's. Murcer started in four consecutive All-Star games. His 1974 salary of $120,000 made him the highest-paid player in Yankees history. The team's new owner, George M. Steinbrenner III, told him, "You'll be a Yankee as long as I own this team." A year later the Boss traded him to San Francisco for Bobby Bonds. Murcer was crushed.

He batted .279 and drove in 181 runs in two seasons for the Giants, who shipped him to the Cubs in exchange for batting champ Bill Madlock. By then Murcer had a reputation for being brittle. First he tripped over his luggage and broke his arm. He broke a finger throwing a punch in a bench-clearing brawl. He hit twenty-seven homers in 1977, his first year as a Cub, but fell off the map with a miserable nine homers in '78. At thirty-two he was one of the bigger busts in recent Cub history. A year later he was a platoon outfielder.

Murcer stepped in from the left side and watched Reed's pitch miss the outside corner. Cavenaugh called it strike one. Reed stretched again, checking the baserunner, Foote, who was taking about a one-foot lead off first. Reed kicked his long left leg and delivered a pitch that Murcer fisted to right field for the Cubs' eleventh single and twenty-first hit of the day.

Herman Franks had four hitters left on his bench. With one out and runners at first and second, he sent Larry Biittner to hit for Steve Dillard. Biittner, the potential tying run, was a thirty-two-year-old out-fielder–first baseman whose role on the club was to pinch-hit and play first base when Buckner's injuries acted up. "*A tough hitter here,*" Jack Brickhouse called him. "*He almost always gets a piece of the ball.*" Year after year, Biittner put the ball in play more than 90 percent of the time.

Murcer led off first base. Foote, the runner at second, took a step toward third.

Biittner usually took the first pitch, but this wasn't a usual day. As Bob Boone put it, "Swinging at the first pitch was getting contagious." Biittner lashed at Reed's first delivery to him and got just enough of it to squib it to Bowa, who ran to second and threw to first for an inning-ending double play.

Reed had kept his promise: he gave the manager an inning at least.

TOP OF THE 8TH

PHILADELPHIA	7	0	8	2	4	0	1		—22	22	2
CUBS	6	0	0	3	7	3	0		—19	21	2

Due up for the Phillies: Rose, Schmidt, Unser

Pete Rose stepped in against Burris to open the eighth. He was having what Harry Kalas called *"for this game, a mediocre day, two for five with two doubles."*

"Rose was a great hitter, a born hitter," Burris recalled, "but not the kind you worry so much about. He might hit the ball hard but he's not trying to go long Johnson on me."

Rose let Burris's first pitch go by, turning to watch it into Barry Foote's mitt. Dick Cavenaugh called it a strike. Then Burris missed twice, and his 2-1 fastball got more of the plate than he wanted. Rose punched it past the pitcher's feet into center field for a single. Rounding first, bluffing as if he might take off for second, he had his forty-seventh hit of 1979, a pace that would give him 224 over a full season. As Rose well knew, that would be the second-highest total of his seventeen-year career. The new Phillie was now batting .353.

Schmidt came up for his third official at-bat. He had a closed stance, maroon and white batting gloves on both hands, and an uncommon line for the day: three-run homer, popout, walk, walk, walk, walk.

"A hitter that good, with power, you'd never pitch the same way twice," Burris remembered. "Schmidt and Rose, I'd show them a slider for a taste to keep them honest—not for a strike but to plant the seed that I might throw it for a strike. Sometimes I'd go against the grain with Schmidt, a pattern I wouldn't normally use. This time I wanted to go in first, then down and away."

The Cubs' other pitchers had nibbled with Schmidt. Burris started him with a fastball. Schmidt took it for a strike. The next one buzzed under his elbows—another called strike that did not sit well with Schmidt. For Burris, though, the at-bat was ideal so far. He didn't want to risk another home run, not after the Cubs had sliced Philadelphia's lead from a dozen runs to three. Burris remembered another game against the Phillies at Wrigley, three years earlier, when the Cubs built a 13–2 lead only to see Schmidt take Rick Reuschel deep twice, Mike Garman once, and Paul Reuschel (Rick's brother) for a fourth home run in the tenth to lead the Phillies to an 18–16 victory. Schmidt is still the only player ever to hit four home runs in a game at Wrigley Field.

But Burris was feeling pretty powerful himself. He was throwing as if he had the wind at his back instead of in his face. His choice for the 0-2 pitch: "Down and away, but in the zone. I wanted to go aggressively after him."

Schmidt swung and launched Burris's low-outside fastball on a high arc to right field. Bobby Murcer looked up for it, shielding his eyes with his glove. Right field was Wrigley's sun field in the late innings, afternoon sun pouring over and through the gap between the upper deck and the grandstand. Murcer, a two-time Gold Glover, backtracked. From his perspective the baseball was a dot surrounded by sun. He reached for the falling dot—and caught it. Schmidt took a right turn to the visitors' dugout, shaking his head. How much had he missed that one by?

With one out, Burris could see his way to the end of the inning. Pitchers may be trained to think one batter at a time, but one batter hitting into a double play gets you out of trouble in a stroke, so keep the ball down.

A cluster of fans started a round of rhythmic clapping as Del Unser stepped into the batter's box. The Cubs' plan for Unser was simple, Burris said: "He's going to get a fastball." No nibbling, no taste-pitch sliders, and no disrespect meant. Unser could hit a mistake a long way, especially on a day like this, but he was no Mike Schmidt.

Rose marched a couple of steps off first as Unser took strike one. Unser chopped the next fastball toward Buckner at first. Burris hurried over to take the throw, knowing Buckner demanded that pitchers cover. "But he waved me off." The limping first baseman jogged over to record the out as Rose took second. "That was a vote of confidence," Burris recalled, "like Buckner was saying, 'You're doing good for us, save your energy.'"

Greg Gross, the next batter, was one-for-one with a triple since replacing Maddox in center. As Kalas noted, that meant the Phils' center fielders were "*five for five with two doubles, a single, a homer, a sacrifice fly and a triple.*" It went unnoticed that they had hit for the cycle.

Gross got fastballs and sliders at knee level. Cavenaugh called the first one a ball, the next a strike, the next a ball. Gross bounced the 2-1 pitch to Buckner, who fielded it and looked up to see Burris running hard to cover first and return the compliment.

BOTTOM OF THE 8TH

PHILADELPHIA	7	0	8	2	4	0	1	0		—22	23	2
CUBS	6	0	0	3	7	3	0			—19	21	2

Due up for the Cubs: DeJesus, Burris, Buckner

Philadelphia's three-run lead belonged to Ron Reed, taking the mound for his fourth inning of work. In the left-field bleachers, Helen Rosenberg's mind wandered. "We hadn't had a homer for how long, two innings?" she remembered thinking. She found herself appreciating how the Phillies' form-fitting nylon uniforms "highlighted their butts" better than Chicago's home whites. "Modern marketing—but it worked," she said.

Ivan DeJesus came up for the sixth time. The Cubs needed baserunners more than ever now; again their leadoff man took a rip. He grounded Reed's fastball to Schmidt's left, into the hole between third and short, but Larry Bowa scooped the ball up and fired to first. Too late—DeJesus had an infield hit. For the fifth time the Cubs had led off an inning with a single.

Herman Franks sent Scot Thompson to hit for Burris, the first Cub pitcher to escape the afternoon undamaged. His line: one and two-thirds innings, one hit, no runs. "I put a zero on the board and had a shot at a W," Burris recalled, "considering we had Bruce Sutter down in the bullpen." Sutter was starting to warm up. Franks didn't like to use his All-Star closer unless the Cubs had the lead. He hadn't used Sutter in a tie game all season, much less a game they were losing, but this was no ordinary game.

Pinch-hitter Scot Thompson, a twenty-three-year-old rookie, had come to Chicago with gaudy minor-league numbers. He'd batted .316 over two seasons at Triple-A Wichita before hitting .417 in a brief trial with the Cubs at the end of the 1978 season. Batting .325 in limited duty so far in '79, Thompson was Franks's secret weapon off the bench. For one thing, nobody knew how to pitch him yet.

He took a strike at the knees from Reed.

Dave Kingman stood in the third-base dugout, looking past Bill Buckner in the on-deck circle. "*If Kingman came up in this inning with a man or two on, I'd put him on intentionally,*" Richie Ashburn said. "*Just walk him!*"

Thompson tried to bunt but missed. With a count of two strikes, Reed went into his motion, expecting to put the rookie away, but the ump waved his hands. One of Sutter's warm-up pitches had gotten away in the Cubs bullpen and was rolling toward third base. The world stopped while a batboy chased it.

Would the at-bat, the inning, the game have gone differently if that bullpen ball hadn't gotten away? Reed had to collect himself when time was back in. He went into his stretch and tried to repeat the same arm action and release. It seemed to work when his 0-2 fastball crossed the outside corner. Boone held it there for a full second, but umpire Cavenaugh did not react. Danny Ozark barked at him from the Phillies' dugout, to no avail. The count was 1-2.

Twice more Reed went for the kill. Thompson spoiled both tries, fouling them off. Reed's third 1-2 pitch, a fastball, was too close to take. Thompson took it, Boone framed it, and again the ump kept his hands on his knees. The Phillies figured they had the rookie struck out twice by now, but he was still up there.

Reed missed outside—another close one—and Cavenaugh got this one right. A count that was once 0-2 was now full. Boone wanted a fastball. So did Thompson, and with Buckner on deck he had reason to expect one. When it came, he connected over the plate's front edge, driving the ball to right. It sailed over Bake McBride's head as Thompson rounded first, thinking double, but McBride—a better outfielder than Kingman, who had let a carom play him an inning before—backed away from the wall at the last instant, giving Thompson's shot enough room to let it bounce right to him. He threw to second base in time to hold Thompson to a single. DeJesus took third.

Both teams now had twenty-three hits. The Cubs had runners at the corners as Buckner stepped to the plate, representing the tying run. Buckner was having a banner day: a grand slam and five RBIs. After batting .323 the previous season he had just emerged from one of the worst slumps of his life, finishing April with an average of .183. Three hits today got him to .264 and counting.

Rawly Eastwick began to throw in the Philadelphia bullpen.

Eastwick, a former closer for the Reds, didn't expect Reed to finish the game for a four-inning save. "I knew I was going in," he recalled. "I just didn't know when." Reed had already faced as many batters as both starters combined and was wading once again into the middle of the Cubs' order. He might be out of the game by now if not for his status as a fourteen-year veteran, not to mention being a cantankerous cuss whose opinions carried weight in the clubhouse. Danny Ozark didn't need to be on the Phillies veterans' bad side, not with the front office looking over his shoulder, telling him to win or else.

Buckner the count worker took a smooth practice swing. The Phillies wanted to get ahead of him, especially with Kingman's long shadow on deck. Knowing that the first pitch would likely be over the middle, Buckner swung and looped a single over second base. DeJesus scored, Thompson stopped at second, Buckner had lifted his average to .270, and up came Kong, taking a longer practice swing than Buckner's, looking as excited as a sleeping alligator and just as dangerous. The Phillies' lead was down to two, 22–20.

Few crowds of fifteen thousand, minus the unlucky few who had left, ever made more noise. "*I have never in my life seen anything like this,*" Ashburn said. "*Danny Ozark is out of the dugout, headed towards the mound.*"

Eastwick was sure he was going in. Instead, the mound conference ended with a pat on the shoulder for Reed, who stayed in to face his fifteenth batter. Eight of the first fourteen had reached base. That made it a curious decision by Ozark, who risked his job with every potentially game-turning move.

Reed started Kingman with a fastball on the outer half. Cavenaugh called it ball one. After eight innings of this, Phillies catcher Boone was getting tired of framing pitches on the black for this umpire to miss. He and Reed tried jamming Kingman with the next one, a fastball. Boone would have sworn in court that this one was also a strike. Cavenaugh called it ball two. Outside or inside, he was an equal-opportunity Magoo.

Reed had no good options. Hiding the ball in his glove, he stuck it between his thumb and forefinger. He stretched, ignoring the runners, and offered Kingman a slip pitch, his curvy changeup. Kingman swung from his heels and hit nothing but air. He took another lumberjack swing at a 2-1 slip pitch and missed that one, too.

With the count 2-2, what should Reed throw? Two pitches on the corners hadn't worked. Two slip pitches made Kingman look bad. The unwritten book of baseball wisdom says that if a guy looks bad on a pitch, you keep throwing it until he shows he can adjust. Which Kingman knew as well as anybody else, having been fooled as much as anybody else since he broke into the big leagues in 1971. Which Boone knew Kingman knew.

With a glance at the runner at second, Boone went through decoy signs before Reed nodded.

His fastball was just high enough to miss the sweet spot on Kingman's bat. Kong's fly ball sailed to center field, where Greg Gross hauled it in for the first out.

The noise level dropped. Fans sat down. You could hear vendors hawking beer. Steve Ontiveros waited for a slip pitch and punched it to the right of second baseman Rudy Meoli as the runners started for second and third. Ontiveros's grounder is a *This Week in Baseball* highlight if

Meoli can backhand the ball and get it to Bowa for an inning-ending double play. Bowa was already at second, reaching for the throw. But Meoli fumbled the ball. It boinged off his glove, another misplay in a day that had more than its share of them. Meoli found the ball in time to force Buckner at second, but there were two outs instead of three.

With runners at the corners, Jerry Martin sent a grounder up the middle. Reed stabbed at the ball but couldn't field it. Martin's single scooted into center field as Thompson scored from third with the Cubs' twenty-first run.

Barry Foote, the catcher with the walrus mustache and .196 average, said hello again to his old mentor Bob Boone. Foote had a habit of telling his Cub teammates about Boone, Schmidt, Carlton, the division-champion Phillies and their winning ways. It was a habit that made his manager feel like pulling out what was left of his hair. Franks didn't want to hear about the Phillies, he wanted to beat them.

Foote crowded the plate and fouled Reed's first pitch straight back. Boone and Reed answered with a fastball close enough to back him up. With the count even, Foote lunged at the next pitch, connecting too high on the ball for an ordinary grounder. The ball bounded off his bat with topspin that took it clear over Schmidt's head into left field. Ontiveros, running on contact, rounded third, turning for home, racing through sun into shadow down the third-base line.

Jack Brickhouse urged him on. "*Come on Steve, c'mon Ontiveros . . .*" Brickhouse said on Channel 9. "*He's gonna score! It's a tie game! Oh, brother!*" A yellow 3 joined the white 6 0 0 3 7 3 0 on the center-field scoreboard. The score was 22–22.

Eastwick had been hoping for a few more minutes in the bullpen, not because he wasn't loose but because he didn't want to enter the game looking like he'd peed himself. He'd been minding his own business in the bullpen down the right-field line when a front-row fan dumped beer on him. "I was hoping to dry off before I went into the game with yellow stains on my uniform."

Ozark had the pitcher's spot coming up in the next inning. He could double-switch a hitter into the lineup. The Cubs' next batter, Bobby

Murcer, had singled off Reed the inning before. Still Ozark left Reed in the game.

Reed's first pitch to Murcer bisected the strike zone. Cavenaugh called it ball one. A fastball dipped low. Cavenaugh called this one a strike, prompting a vocal protest from Murcer, who walked past the catcher to put his nose against the umpire's mask. Boos cascaded from the bleachers and grandstand.

A few pitches later, with the count 3-1, Reed got another strike with a chin-high fastball, and the count was full. With the shadow of the upper deck creeping toward the mound, Reed's nothing-much fastball went from sun to shade on its half-second transit to Murcer's bat.

Murcer swiped at a fastball he might have driven in his better days, sending a bouncing ball to Meoli, who threw him out.

Pete Rose spiked the ball and hustled to the dugout. Ron Reed followed with his head high. He'd allowed six runs on nine hits but had given his manager three and a third innings. His ERA had risen from 0.42 to 2.55. Reed's day would have been better if he hadn't spent the last hour fighting a lousy umpire, if Meoli hadn't kicked a double-play ball, if Ozark hadn't left him out there to give up three runs in the eighth—on five singles—but he could still win the game. Reed was the Phillies' pitcher of record.

TOP OF THE 9TH

PHILADELPHIA	7	0	8	2	4	0	1	0		—22	23	2
CUBS	6	0	0	3	7	3	0	3		—22	26	2

Due up for the Phillies: Boone, Meoli, Reed

Chicago's sixth pitcher was the one the Phillies never wanted to see. Sleepy-eyed with bushy sideburns and a Fu Manchu mustache, Bruce Sutter threw a split-finger fastball *Sports Illustrated* described as "unique and overpowering." The magazine called him "the best reliever in baseball—and, just possibly, the best in baseball history."

Appearing in his ninth game of the season, the first he'd entered without a lead to protect, Sutter had six saves and an earned run average of 1.06 through the season's first six weeks. Throwing the splitter almost exclusively, he had allowed eleven hits and struck out twenty in seventeen innings. According to his catcher, Sutter's specialty was three pitches in one. "It looks like a fastball," Foote said, "gets to the plate like a change, and then drops like a spitter." As *Sports Illustrated* described it, "Envision, if you will, an auto speeding on a pier, braking at the last moment and then plunging over the side into the drink." The pitch plunged due to its reduced spin, a result of Sutter's choking the ball between his long fingers. "A man trying this with ordinary-sized fingers would never play the piano again." The term *split-finger fastball* was a misnomer, of course, a relic of Fred Martin's coaching sessions. The minor-league pitching coach wanted his pupils to release it exactly as they released a fastball, so that's what he called it. In fact it was a changeup.

Sutter didn't throw the splitter as he took his warm-ups before the ninth inning. No need to give the Phillies any extra looks. His warm-ups, eight tempting batting-practice fastballs, kept his arm loose while the buzzing crowd cheered his name on the public-address system.

Bob Boone had faced Sutter a total of six times and was oh-for-six with four strikeouts. Still, he was upbeat as he led off the ninth. The Phillies catcher had added twenty-five points to his batting average so far today with a homer, a double, and a single. Anything more would be gravy. The best sort of gravy would be scoring the winning run.

He took a split-finger pitch in the dirt. The Phillies' game plan against Sutter was to try to wait him out. "Make him lift it. Make him throw it for a strike, that was the conventional wisdom," Boone recalled. Such an approach meant taking pitches that looked knee- or even thigh-high on their way to the plate, expecting them to drop. If they didn't—if a particular pitch was the poky fastball Sutter mixed in now and then to keep you honest—you looked bad. That look was described by some hitters as standing there with your dick in your hand.

With the count 1-0, Cavenaugh gave Sutter a borderline strike. His 1-1 splitter dipped into the dirt again. The Cubs were about to put the same grimy ball back in play when Boone called time.

"*Boonie wants the plate umpire, Dick Cavenaugh, who's had quite a workout today, to look over that ball,*" Harry Kalas explained on Phillies radio.

It wasn't easy to hit, think, and teach an umpire how to do his job at the same time, but Boone was trying.

Cavenaugh put a new ball in play. Sutter spent a few seconds rolling it between his oversized hands, massaging the leather. Some pitchers cheated by scuffing or scratching the cover, nicking it with a shard of razor or a thumbtack, or adding spit or Vaseline to change how the ball spun. Sutter got the same result without breaking the rules, thanks to his claw-fingered grip.

Boone took a strike to level the count.

The 2-2 splitter came in a little higher than the others. Boone had waited Sutter out and made him throw it for a strike. He looped it over the pitcher's head into center field. He thought it might be the leadoff single the Phillies needed, but the wind that had turned half a dozen pop-ups into Texas League singles and added thirty feet of superfluous distance to Boone's first-inning homer was doing no favors for lazy liners like this one. The ball hung up for Thompson, who snagged it for the first out.

Along with Del Unser and the Cubs' Steve Ontiveros, Philadelphia second baseman Rudy Meoli was one of only three starters who had only one hit in the game. His third-inning single had briefly lifted his batting average to .200, but he was now down to .188. A six-year veteran with a career total of two home runs and a .217 average, Meoli was trying to show he belonged in the big leagues for the rest of the season if not another year or two. He let an shin-high splitter go by. Cavenaugh called it strike one.

Meoli took a fastball outside that Sutter threw for show, then took a splitter for ball two. Sutter's 2-1 pitch was a second fastball, too high to swing at. Now Meoli had the count his way. Determined to stick with the game plan, he took ball four. It was the kind of at-bat hardly anybody outside the dugouts would notice: Rudy Meoli got the better of Bruce Sutter without swinging the bat even once. He jogged to first as the potential go-ahead run.

After Meoli came the pitcher's spot in the order. Here's why Danny Ozark had left Reed in to finish the eighth: if he'd brought Rawly Eastwick into the game, he'd have to pinch-hit for him now. Of course the Phillies might still be ahead if he'd used Eastwick in the Cubs' three-run eighth, but this was no time for second-guessing. There would be plenty of that after Ozark's team won or lost. At the moment the manager had other worries. For one, he was running out of pinch-hitters.

Batting .190 in limited duty, Tim McCarver had hit just one home run since 1977. The only man on either team to have played a big-league game in the 1950s, McCarver had broken in with the Cardinals in 1959, and almost a decade later caught Bob Gibson the year Gibson had a 1.12 ERA. Now thirty-seven, he was winding down his career as Steve Carlton's personal catcher. Carlton and Bob Boone were friends in the clubhouse and weight room but were too headstrong to work together, so McCarver caught Carlton every fourth or fifth day. He spent the other days pinch-hitting, advising younger players, and working on quips that would serve him well in his broadcasting career.

One benefit of Sutter's split-finger pitch, from the Phillies' perspective, was that it could be easy to steal on. The ball was often in the dirt, and when it wasn't it dived past the batter's shins toward the catcher's feet. And while Barry Foote had a strong arm, he had poor technique behind the plate. Unlike Boone, who worked out all winter and all season to stay limber, Foote moved like a bear.

Fans chanted, "We want an out!" Meoli broke for second on Sutter's first pitch to McCarver, who swung under the ball. Foote's peg was high, and Meoli, sliding headfirst, had his first stolen base of the season. Philadelphia had the lead run at second base with one out.

McCarver tapped a foul ball to fall behind in the count, 0-2. Moments later he took Sutter's next pitch, a letter-high fastball. The Cubs had the strikeout they needed—but only if the umpire ruled it a strike. Cavenaugh literally twitched this time, his right arm moving as if to ring McCarver up, but he couldn't go through with it. His hand went back down. Fans booed. The count was 1-2.

McCarver topped a 2-2 splitter, bouncing it to the right side. Second baseman Mick Kelleher, subbing for Steve Dillard, who'd been subbing for Ted Sizemore, threw him out. Meoli ran the tiebreaking run over to third.

Bake McBride came up with two away. It was his eighth at-bat of the afternoon. "*Bake has singled, popped up, singled, flied out, singled, struck out, and struck out,*" said Kalas, recounting McBride's busy day at the dish. Eight at-bats in a nine-inning game tied a major-league record.

"*Hard to believe you'd get up eight times in a nine-inning game,*" Richie Ashburn said. "*We've seen a lot of things today we've never seen before.*"

McBride flailed at a splitter. He fouled off the next pitch to fall behind nothing and two, cursing himself, then swung over another splitter but got enough of it to send the ball on two hops to second. McBride's grounder looked like a replay of McCarver's until the baseball struck a pebble, a dirt clod, or some bump in space-time designed to keep the Cubs from winning, and sprang straight over the second baseman's head. "*High hop—a brutal bounce!*" Kalas called it.

Meoli was halfway home from third.

Kelleher jumped for the ball, got a hand on it, came down with it, and threw to Buckner before McBride's foot hit first base. "*A crazy hop—it wanted to go over his head!*" Brickhouse shouted. Kelleher ran to the dugout to one of the loudest ovations of the day.

PHILADELPHIA	7	0	8	2	4	0	1	0	0		—22	23	2
CUBS	6	0	0	3	7	3	0	3			—22	26	2

Due up for the Cubs: Kelleher, DeJesus, Thompson

Danny Ozark paced the visitors' dugout while his team took the field. At fifty-five, the jowly, graying Philadelphia manager was no matinee idol. One sportswriter described him as "beagle-faced." Ozark didn't disagree. He counted every day he was alive as a good one. He'd won five Bronze Stars and a Purple Heart fighting in Europe during World War II. Then he'd returned to the Brooklyn Dodgers organization and spent eighteen seasons in the minors, hitting 238 homers, without a day in the big leagues. He'd nearly quit the game in despair after his son Dwain, a first-grader, lost an eye in a freak accident. (The boy was using a water hose to fill a milk bottle when the bottle exploded.) Ozark returned to baseball and put in eight years as a coach for Walter Alston's Los Angeles Dodgers before landing the Philadelphia job in 1973. Since '75 his Phillies were more than a hundred games over .500 at 315-203. He'd won the 1976 Manager of the Year Award but wasn't sure how much rope he had left after three straight losses in the playoffs. Ozark figured his win-or-else mandate meant he had to reach the 1979 World Series, if not win it, to keep his job.

He needed a shutdown inning from Rawly Eastwick.

Ozark knew one thing for sure: the Philadelphia papers would roast him for blowing a twelve-run lead if the Phillies lost this game. The press liked to portray him as a genial fellow, maybe a little dim, lucky to have a bunch of star players making him look smarter than he was. According to the *Inquirer*'s Frank Fitzpatrick, Phillies fans expected a manager to be like Gene Mauch: "tough, edgy, and smart—three qualities no one would ever attribute to Ozark."

The game was changing too fast for this manager's liking. A generation earlier, teams could count on the same writers who kept quiet about players' bar fights and road-trip trysts to clean up the skipper's grammar and make him look good in the papers. By the late '70s managers were supposed to talk on TV like sportscasters, and Ozark had a habit of putting his spikes in his mouth. After the Phillies were mathematically eliminated from the National League East race in 1975, he announced, "We're not out of it yet." Asked about team morale, he said, "Morality isn't a factor." He once said, "I'm being fascist," meaning facetious. Not that there wasn't wisdom in some of Ozark's views. He claimed he didn't listen to jeering fans at Veterans Stadium, calling them "the boo-birds of unhappiness." Of one disgruntled part-time player, outfielder Mike Anderson, he said, "Anderson's limitations are limitless."

His managerial moves often backfired. Today was an example. If Ozark had it to do over he'd take Ron Reed out of the game while the Phillies were still ahead. But so what? If managers got do-overs he might have saved some good young men at the Battle of the Bulge or found a way to be home the day his little boy lost his eye. This was just a ballgame. He sent Eastwick into the game and hoped for the best.

"Hey, Rawly," a fan shouted. "It's you and Bruce Sutter, and you're gonna lose!" According to Bill Conlin of the *Philadelphia Daily News*, it was the only printable thing the Chicago crowd yelled at Eastwick.

"I still smelled like beer," the pitcher recalled, "but the stains had pretty much dried." A scrawny righty who made his living with a sinking fastball, Eastwick had been tinkering with a split-finger pitch that broke like blazes, but he didn't yet trust it enough to throw it in a game. He'd spent his first four seasons with the Reds, winning a World Series ring with the Big Red Machine of 1976, the year he led the majors with twenty-six saves.

Three years later, finishing his warm-ups at Wrigley Field, he was eager to face the Cubs. Despite the wind, despite being Ozark's third option in the bullpen behind McGraw and Reed, despite the fact that he'd allowed nine runs in his last five and a third innings, Eastwick had no doubt he'd get the Cubs out. He never lacked confidence. "I liked pitching at Wrigley, never mind the wind," he said. "We played in so many of those bowls in those days—Riverfront, Three Rivers, Shea Stadium, the Astrodome. I liked a park with real turf and dirt."

Mick Kelleher led off the last of the ninth, illustrating the old saying that a guy who makes a great play to end a half inning leads off the next. The number 20 on his uniform was about all Kelleher had in common with Mike Schmidt, whose first-inning joke that their numbers might match today's score turned out to be on the low side. After seven years in the majors, Kelleher was still looking for his first career home run.

He didn't play much. Six weeks into the season, Kelleher had two hits in twelve at-bats. This was either his first or second ovation of the year. It was still the first if you count the Cub fans cheering his run-saving play in the top of the ninth who were still cheering when he came up against Eastwick.

Kelleher's job as leadoff man in a tie game was to get on base in any way possible. That went double for a slap hitter with no home-run power, so the odds of Mick Kelleher swinging at the first pitch in this particular situation were close to zero. At the same time, he knew Eastwick expected him to take the first pitch. If you're the pitcher in that situation, throwing your first pitch of the game to a guy who's certain to take it, you might lay one in there and start off with a strike.

Or not. "I wasn't taking anything for granted," Eastwick recalled.

Kelleher swung at a first-pitch fastball and grounded it to Bowa, who threw to first with plenty of time but missed his target. It would be hard to find a worse time for a low throw. An error now might make Bowa a bigger goat than Ozark. But Rose stretched for the throw, picking it off a short hop for the first out.

DeJesus came up for the seventh time, having singled twice, walked, and doubled. He was susceptible to sinkers.

Eastwick looked into the shadows for a sign from Bob Boone. "With Boone, I threw what he called," he remembered. "Some catchers, you put yourself in their hands."

DeJesus took a sinker for a strike. He dug down in the strike zone for the next one, popping it over the seats behind the Phillies' dugout. Rose chased it just in case the wind blew it back. He got to the dugout in time to see the ball angling back toward him and snapped it out of the air for the second out.

Scot Thompson, who had stayed in the game in a double switch, was the last batter who could keep the game from going to extra innings. Instead he tapped a sinker past the mound. Bowa charged in to field it and threw to Rose at first to finish off the game's first one-two-three frame.

"*We move to the tenth,*" Kalas said, "*with the score, and I'm saying this right, Phils twenty-two, Cubs twenty-two.*"

TOP OF THE 10TH

PHILADELPHIA	7	0	8	2	4	0	1	0	0	—22	23	2
CUBS	6	0	0	3	7	3	0	3	0	—22	26	2

Due up for the Phillies: Bowa, Rose, Schmidt

The flags atop Wrigley Field's scoreboard and foul poles pointed straight out to left as the wind freshened. There wasn't much more than two hours' light left. Bill Buckner had to doubt such facts would matter with Sutter pitching. After watching the split-finger fastball do its stuff for two seasons, Buckner said that there were only two outcomes when Sutter pitched: "He gets a strikeout or a ground ball."

Buckner stood well behind first base, near the foul line: a no-doubles defense. At bat was Larry Bowa, five-for-seven on the day. Bowa faked a bunt and took a splitter low for ball one. Steve Ontiveros at third base moved a step closer to the plate. "*Bowa's around the .320 mark now. He came into the game batting .287*," Richie Ashburn told Phillies fans. Bowa was actually at .309, but with no continuously updated stats on the scoreboard or anywhere else, it would have taken a pencil and paper to say for sure.

Sutter didn't bother to check the wind. He focused on his grip and the mechanics of delivering the splitter with the same motion as his fastball and wasted little time thinking about the weather, the score, or who was batting. Like the cocky Eastwick, who exuded a more obvious sort of swagger, Sutter always said he began each inning expecting to retire the side in order. "I never worried, I just pitched."

Bowa took ball two.

Sutter didn't trouble himself much about counts, either. "I feel like a pioneer with the split-finger fastball," he said later, "the first one to throw it pretty much a hundred percent of the time." He'd had arm trouble before learning the pitch. In 1972, barely hanging on in the Class-A Midwest League, he blew out his elbow. Not wanting the Cubs to know he was hurt, he paid for his own surgery to correct a pinched nerve and healed fast enough to report the next spring to Midland of the Double-A Texas League, where he and Donnie Moore met Fred Martin, the split-finger guru, and Sutter began his steep ascent to the major leagues and stardom. After that he was healthy until '78, when he slumped so badly that Martin was summoned to Chicago to look him over. "There's nothing wrong with him a little rest wouldn't cure," said Martin, spurring calls for Herman Franks to be fired. The papers blamed Franks for overusing Sutter. A few writers, coaches, and players thought the splitter might be hurting his arm, but what else could he rely on, his Double-A fastball? Sutter kept throwing the pitch that had gotten him to the show.

Bowa took a strike, then spanked a 2-1 splitter to Mick Kelleher at second, who threw him out. That brought Pete Rose up for the eighth time. A few fans booed. Now batting a league-leading .355, Rose had only a single in six career tries against Sutter. "Since there was no by-the-book way to hit him, you go by situation," he recalled. With one out in the tenth, "I don't want to let him get ahead in the count and wipe me out. So I was going to be aggressive. I'm gonna go up there swinging from my ass."

It was the right idea. Sutter's first pitch to Rose was a plump fastball. He started his swing but held up as it crossed at chin level, a little too high.

Rose was sure he wouldn't get two fastballs in a row. "He wasn't going to screw around with me, not with Schmitty up next," he reasoned. He fouled off a split. He took the 1-1 pitch for a strike to fall behind, one and two. Now Sutter had a chance to wipe him out. But Rose was no easy mark. He had struck out only nine times in 127 at-bats.

Sutter's 1-2 splitter was higher than he wanted. Rose, protecting the plate, overcompensated for its break, his downward slash popping the ball toward the left-field foul line. Third baseman Ontiveros turned and chased the ball while the wind pushed it toward Kingman, who came loping in from deep left. Ontiveros couldn't get to the ball. At the last instant, Kong reached down and caught it.

In the Cubs' dugout, Herman Franks applauded. Two up and two down. He had Buckner and Kingman due up in the last of the tenth.

Even with the bases empty, some in the crowd expected Franks to wave four fingers at Barry Foote now. One fan yelled from the bleachers: "Mike Schmidt? Nobody on? Walk him!" The Cubs had walked Schmidt four times, but the unwritten rulebook says you never put the lead run on base in the late innings. If they walked him and the next guy doubled him home, it would be Franks getting roasted in tomorrow's papers. With the game's best reliever on the mound, the Cubs would take their chances with Schmidt.

Both teams had numbers on their side. Sutter had owned the Phillies since emerging as a closer in 1976, holding them to three runs in thirty-six innings, an earned run average of 0.75. Schmidt seemed especially clueless against him. He had a single in sixteen at-bats for a career average of .063 vs. Sutter. But Schmidt had always loved hitting at Wrigley Field, where his career average was .315 with twenty home runs. "That ballpark—it was like walking into heaven for him," Ozark said. The one thing that bothered the brooding slugger about Wrigley was how much he liked hitting there. "You don't want to press and try to hit everything out," he said.

The Cubs played him to pull, with Ontiveros near the line and DeJesus in the hole behind him, almost close enough to shake the third baseman's hand. Sutter's first pitch to Schmidt was off the plate. So was his second, a high fastball. He got the strike he needed with a split-finger pitch at the knees, then missed again.

His 3-1 splitter started at belt level. Schmidt took a home-run cut as the ball ducked under his bat. The count was full. Sutter peered in for a sign, shaking off Foote's signal. Practically everybody in the park knew what was coming, but the Cubs thought enough of Schmidt to try to decoy him.

The 3-2 pitch started higher than the one before. It ducked to belt level, where Schmidt's bat compressed the ball's leather hide for a millisecond before sending it the other way. Without Statcast cameras to record the event, no one can say whether it left Schmidt's bat at a thirty-five-, forty-, or forty-five-degree angle or how fast it was going.

The WGN video shows the baseball as a blur even in slow motion. It leaves the bat at a high angle and keeps climbing as center fielder Scot Thompson starts toward the warning track.

"*A high fly,*" Brickhouse said, his voice rising. "*Look out, now. Look out . . .*" Sutter never turned to watch it go. Head down, he stepped off the mound.

Fans in the left-field bleachers stood up as the ball came their way, then watched it sail over their heads.

"*This is going to leave the park!*" Ashburn shouted. "*Schmidt hit it over the fence and over the bleachers!*"

At the corner of Waveland and Kenmore, ballhawk Rich Buhrke jumped out of his folding chair and took off after the ball. "It landed on the street and took a humongous bounce into an alley," he later recalled.

The game's eleventh home run tied a major-league record. Schmidt rounded the infield and touched home with the Phillies' twenty-third run. He slapped hands with on-deck hitter Del Unser. He slapped hands with half a dozen teammates on his way down the dugout steps.

After that, Sutter had no patience for Unser. He struck him out on three pitches, the last a splitter that Unser missed by a foot, but the damage was done.

BOTTOM OF THE 10TH

	1	2	3	4	5	6	7	8	9	10	R	H	E
PHILADELPHIA	7	0	8	2	4	0	1	0	0	1	—23	24	2
CUBS	6	0	0	3	7	3	0	3	0		—22	26	2

Due up for the Cubs: Buckner, Kingman, Ontiveros

Philadelphia's twenty-three runs tied a franchise record. The Phillies had beaten the Pittsburgh Pirates 23–8 in 1900, a record unmatched until they lost to Chicago at Cubs Park (as it was then known), 26–23, in 1922. As *Sports Illustrated*'s Bruce Newman put it, "Every 57 years or so, the Phils and Cubbies get together for one of these bashes."

It was up to Rawly Eastwick to nail down the win.

"They had their big hitters coming up," Eastwick recalled. "Was I worried? No, I don't get worried. But I wanted to be extra careful to hit my spots. That's even more important when you're pitching into the wind."

Buckner, four-for-six with three singles, a grand slam, and seven RBIs, took a strike. He called time to let his eyes adjust to the shadows that had crept over the mound. The game was four hours old, late-day sun settling into the gloaming behind buildings on Clark. Buckner stepped back in. He hacked at Eastwick's 0-1 pitch and popped it over third into foul territory. Bowa and Schmidt gave chase but the ball fell in the shadows near the Cub bullpen, where Lynn McGlothen was warming up. McGlothen was a starting pitcher who had thrown a complete game against the Phillies two days before, but Franks would rather use him on one day's rest than ask Sutter to go another inning.

Buckner was still alive, still dangerous. "You knew you had to bear down with him," Eastwick remembered. His 0-2 sinker was right where he aimed it on the x-axis, a little too high on the y. It came in over the outside black but above the knees. Buckner drove it to left-center, fans cheering what looked like a leadoff double until Del Unser gloved it for the first out.

Fans who'd been sitting stood up now, yelling for Kingman. Their cheers and applause carried through the announcers' microphones to radios in the Philadelphia area and cable TVs all over the country. Here was Kong's chance to hit his fourth home run of the game and match Schmidt's Wrigley record.

Eastwick respected Kingman's power but didn't fear it. "I'd had good success with him," he recalled. Kingman was hitless in seven career at-bats against Eastwick. They both recalled one in particular, a ninth-inning matchup at Shea Stadium four years before, when Reds manager Sparky Anderson summoned Eastwick to protect a 2–1 lead. That night, with two outs, the Mets had Gene Clines at second base, Joe Torre at first, Kingman at the plate. "And I stair-stepped him—threw him a low fastball, a higher one, and then a real high fastball" for strike three.

Bob Boone remembered that at-bat, too. He and Eastwick weren't teammates then, but it came up later, when they compared notes on Cub hitters in pregame meetings, with extra talk about Buckner and Kingman. Pitchers and catchers of their generation could ask the front office for basic statistics like batting averages, but that was about it, which was fine with Eastwick. Looking back years later, he said he considered working with Boone to be the best sort of analytics. "A catcher that good, you trust him to call the game. I was going to throw what he called."

Mixing sliders and sinkers, Eastwick threw strike after strike. Kingman let one go by and fouled one straight back to fall behind 0-2. He kept fouling off other pitches. One was a foul tip Boone couldn't quite hold. The catcher spent a second mentally kicking himself—hang on to that one and it's two out, bases empty. Instead Kingman's still looking for a pitch to hit out of sight.

The crowd noise went up a notch. "*It's hard to see around the home plate area where the shadows crossed the plate. You can hardly see the ball,*" Ashburn said. But his eyesight wasn't entirely impaired. "*Two young ladies, scantily clad, are walking down below us, and the fans are really reacting.*"

Eastwick looked in for another 0-2 sign from his catcher. "And he surprised me," Eastwick recalled. Boone wanted a changeup. On this of all days. Then, flashing back on the seven times he'd faced Kingman since 1974, Eastwick's rookie year, he remembered something. "I'd never once thrown him a changeup. So when I saw Boone's sign I thought, 'That's perfect.'"

He threw it with the same motion as his sinker, but his grip and limp arm at release took fifteen miles an hour off the pitch.

Finishing his delivery, setting his feet to defend himself against a line drive, the pitcher had the best view in the house. He saw Kingman plant his front foot and start the swing that produced tape-measure shots.

"He came out of his shoes swinging," Eastwick remembered. "And he wasn't even close."

Kingman's last long swing seemed to take the air out of the ballpark. Annoyed with himself after the strikeout, Kong flipped his bat toward the batboy. Fans who'd been standing sat down. A few started for the exits. Others stayed on their feet and clung to the hope that Steve Ontiveros could start a rally.

Boone expected Ontiveros to take a pitch. Whether he was taking or not didn't matter to the Phillies; he would get sinkers and sliders. First came a sinker falling off the outside corner. Ontiveros, undecided, checked his swing. In umpiring terms he offered at the ball. To his surprise, it ticked off his bat toward third base. He stutter-stepped, not sure he'd hit it fair, before digging for first while Schmidt fielded home ball. The three-time Gold Glover had already made two errors to go with his homers, so naturally the baseball found him. He threw across the diamond to first baseman Rose, who caught the ball and then held it up in his bare hand as if he were giving the sky a fist bump.

"*And that's it*," Brickhouse said. "*A very sad finish to one of the greatest games anybody has seen anywhere.*"

The Phillies piled into a happy clubhouse where the beer was flowing. Soaked in beer for the right reason this time, Eastwick got hugs and high fives for his two perfect innings. "Everybody was laughing. We had some vocal players and some quiet ones, but everybody was yelling that day," he said.

Schmidt, surrounded by reporters, said, "Talk about wacko games! Was there fourteen hits in the first inning?" Asked if the Cubs should have walked him in the tenth, he said no. "Sutter ain't gonna walk anybody in this league, not with that pitch he's got."

The Cubs filed into their roomier, equally dingy home clubhouse. Nobody had much to say. One sportswriter got a comment from Kingman, who said, "Get the fuck out of here."

The fans retraced their steps to their homes and jobs. Helen Rosenberg and her friend Pamela went separate ways on the El. In the press box, old-timers like Jerome Holtzman and Bill Gleason of the *Sun-Times* pounded at manual typewriters while younger writers like the *Sun-Times'* Joe Goddard and the *Tribune's* David Israel used first-generation portable computer terminals. Goddard's game story, transmitted from his microwave-oven-sized Teleram P-1800, read, "It was historical. It was hysterical." *Tribune* columnist Israel, typing on a Radio Shack TRS-80 with four kilobytes of memory, was more of a quipster. He was working on a column that claimed, "If baseball is the moral equivalent of war, Wrigley Field is the moral equivalent of Belgium," and blamed the Cubs' latest loss on "their whacked-out heritage."

The *Trib's* Dave Nightingale added a footnote to the Cubs' quirky history: "They set a major league record for most runs by a team rallying to tie in a losing cause."

Bruce Newman phoned his *Sports Illustrated* editor in New York. "You're not going to believe this," he said. Newman's story would be the first to describe the Phillies' 23–22 victory as The Game.

Herman Franks, lighting a cigar, told reporters he didn't know if coming back from twelve runs behind to tie only to lose the ballgame would help or hurt his job prospects. "Who knows?" he said. "Maybe Danny Ozark will be fired before me."

His team got back into street clothes and headed out to their homes and condos or to the restaurants and bars on Rush Street. Donnie Moore and Ray Burris were two of the last to leave.

"We didn't talk about the game," Burris remembered. That might be a sore spot after Moore allowed seven runs on one of the worst days a pitcher could pitch. Burris, who had worked an inning and two-thirds without giving up a run, asked Moore where he thought they should meet their wives that evening. One drawback of day baseball was that the Cubs finished their workday at rush hour. Instead of fighting traffic all the way home, Moore and Burris would wait out the traffic and take their wives, Tonya and Regina, out to dinner.

"Tonya was a dynamic person," Burris said, "and so supportive of Donnie. What happened later, I never saw that coming." Nobody could foresee the changes the rest of the 1979 season and the '80s would bring. For starters, the Phillies would fly home to face the Expos while the Cubs hosted a weekend series against Pittsburgh. Burris and Moore both hoped to pitch again over the weekend.

"We were still so young," Burris said, "just trying to prove our worth."

PART THREE

LEGACIES

LEGACIES

MIRACLE ON BROAD STREET

For the winners, Thursday was getaway day. One benefit of day games was getting home the same night, and this was bound to be a good night for the Phillies.

"Bowa, Boone, Rose—even McGraw was laughing afterward," recalled *Sports Illustrated*'s Bruce Newman. The *Chicago Sun-Times* billed the 23–22 game as "an afternoon delight" for Cub fans who "screamed their tonsils off." On their flight home the Phils traded tales of how they'd blown a two-touchdown lead only to pull it out in overtime. A contest the *Sun-Times* called "baseball at its best and worst" had seen the Phils and Cubs rack up ninety-seven total bases, the most in major-league history, on eleven homers, two triples, ten doubles, and twenty-seven singles. Their forty-five runs scored were second only to the forty-nine plated by the same teams during the Cubs' 26–23 victory in this same ballpark in 1922.

Danny Ozark couldn't help smiling. What could make an in-flight beverage taste better than dodging a bullet? "Guess we don't need the designated hitter in the National League," the manager said. Coming off a 10-4 road trip, his Phillies now led the division by three and a half games over Montreal and five over St. Louis. They were seven up on the fourth-place Cubs.

"A day like that can make your week," Rose recalled. "A *slugfest*—it even sounds good, doesn't it? Except to the pitchers, who were pissed."

"Looking at the scoreboard, you'd think it was a choose-up sandlot game," Boone said. "I could almost see my son out there."

That night the first-place Phils fanned out from Philadelphia International to their suburban homes. Several lived a half hour away in Medford, New Jersey. Boone drove home to Medford to hug his wife, Sue, and their sons, ten-year-old Bret and six-year-old Aaron, who had stayed up late to give their dad a hero's welcome.

In the morning the players checked the box scores and stats in the newspapers. Rose was leading the league with a .351 average. Schmidt led the majors with fourteen homers—two more than Kingman. The Phillies' 24-10 record was the best in baseball.

In June, with the Phillies in Chicago again, Kingman cracked his twenty-sixth homer of the season, a blistering pace that put him five ahead of Schmidt. The Cubs had been making a run at first place while the Phils, with their three straight division titles and $4.9 million payroll, fell into a tailspin. Upon their return to Philadelphia after the May 17 game, the Phillies won twelve games and lost twenty-three. In Newman's latest report for *Sports Illustrated*, he wrote, "The Phillies beat the Cubs in a 23–22 donnybrook, whereupon they dropped dead."

The Phils didn't like losing to lesser clubs like the Mets and Cubs. On June 27, when the Cubs' Mike Vail tried to steal second against them with an 8–2 lead, the Phillies saw it as a breach of the unwritten rule against running up the score. So Philadelphia's Kevin Saucier beaned the next batter, Steve Ontiveros. When Cub pitcher Mike Krukow came to bat, Saucier plunked him, too. (Krukow's crime was hitting his first big-league homer earlier in the game.) Next thing you know, both benches emptied and punches flew. The umps waved their arms and shouted, trying to restore order. The fans cheered.

Rose thought that scuffle might wake up his teammates. Three months into his tenure with the Phillies he still wondered at their so-cool approach. "I'd run out to first base when we took the field," he said, "and have to stand there two minutes before I had anybody to throw to."

When reporters asked Ozark how his highly paid team could be in fifth place, he blamed bad luck. "If you had seen the bad hops, bloop hits and freak plays that have beaten us in the last month, you'd think we were snakebit."

The Phillies briefly rebounded, but a six-game skid in August left them in fourth place. "The team everyone thought would run away with the NL East was eight games behind," the *Sporting News* reported. Ozark was now booed whenever he came out of the dugout at Veterans Stadium. Once, when he went to the mound to take the ball from Steve Carlton, the Phils' ace fired the ball at Ozark's foot.

As the losses mounted, underprivileged children treated to free seats in the Bull Ring, a section of left-field seats named for Greg "the Bull" Luzinski, booed Luzinski. Ozark took to sitting in his office with the door locked.

Schmidt wasn't worried. "If we are the cream, we'll rise to the top," he said.

Philadelphia fans weren't buying it. They booed Schmidt so avidly that he disguised himself with sunglasses and a floppy hat on trips to McDonald's. He could never quite understand what the fans had against him. He gave his best at the plate and in the field. But he wasn't the type to show his emotions, and his nonchalance sometimes came across as apathy. Looking back years later, Schmidt wished he'd showboated a little. "If I knew then what I know now, I would have dove into more bases, dove after more balls."

Larry Bowa was less introspective. When the home fans booed him, Bowa called them "front-running motherfuckers."

One night Tug McGraw allowed four runs and expressed his irritation with the Expos' hitters by sticking out his tongue at them. After the game, Bowa shoved him. "We're out there busting our butts and you're kidding around!" he yelled. Pitching coach Herm Starrette smashed a folding chair against the wall.

Losing eight of nine in August was Ozark's Waterloo. Despite three division titles in four years, owner Ruly Carpenter fired him.

"If Danny Ozark had one fault, he was too damn nice," Carpenter said. Nobody would say that about the manager who replaced him.

At forty-five, Dallas Green was just seven years older than Pete Rose. He was taller than all his players but Ron Reed, the six-foot-six pitcher he later challenged to a fight. Green was as ornery and foulmouthed as Bowa, as stubborn as Boone, bigger if not stronger than Schmidt. In his first team meeting he told the players, "The front office didn't fire Danny Ozark, you guys got him fired. You should be ashamed."

"Everything changed when Green replaced Ozark," the *Inquirer*'s Frank Fitzpatrick recalled. "Ozark was kind of a genial dunderhead. Green comes in and says, 'We've tried low-key. We need a little fire in the belly around here.' He told the players, 'I'm gonna make your life miserable,' and that's what he did."

The team improved in Green's month as manager but still finished fourth. That left Phillies fans worrying about 1980. According to one of them, the novelist James Michener (author of *Hawaii*, *The Source*, and other bestsellers), "When you root for the Phillies, you acquire a sense of tragedy." Michener said a friend of his had made him promise to carve a message on his tombstone: HERE LIES A PHILLIES PHAN, STILL HOPING FOR THAT ONE GREAT YEAR.

NINETEEN EIGHTY FELT different. The Phillies stayed close to the division lead all summer even as the home fans booed, sometimes jeering both teams in the same inning.

Tug McGraw relished being part of the spectacle. "I'm a sponge soaking it all in," he said. The shaggy-haired reliever thought his unusual background gave him perspective on what he called the "craziness" of his baseball career. When McGraw was a boy in blue-collar Martinez, California, his mother spent time as an inmate at Napa State Mental

Hospital, receiving shock treatments. One night she slipped out of the asylum and disappeared. After that Frank "Big Mac" McGraw Sr., a butcher turned firefighter turned sewage plant operator, raised their three sons on his own. One brother, Hank, grew up to be a hippie who dropped out of society; another, Dennis, became a convicted killer; and one, Tug, played big-league baseball.

"Maybe I'm fucked," Tug told a teammate in a hotel bar. "My family's brains are messed up. I'm a screwball surviving on a screwball."

Through his decade in New York, where he coined the 1973 Mets' motto, "Ya Gotta Believe," McGraw made TV spots for Schick razors and 7UP, cowrote *Scroogie*, a nationally syndicated comic strip starring a hapless screwballer, and stayed true to his family's unconventional ways. When his father died, Tug paid a baker to help fulfill Big Mac's last wish: "He wanted his ashes baked into loaves of bread and fed to seagulls at the pier so they could shit all over the city and his remains would be spread all over San Francisco."

Another sort of family loyalty startled McGraw in 1977, his third year with the Phils. That's when he heard from Betty Smith, who claimed that the happily married reliever was the father of her ten-year-old son, Timmy. Thinking back, Tug remembered Betty's "teeny bikini" and their one-night stand when he was in the minors. In those days he'd referred to baseball groupies in grocery terms, calling them "road beef," a term many players used, or, if they struck him as particularly ripe, as tomatoes. "I usually did all right in the tomato department. When it came to that type of produce, I was always able to pick one out of the bunch," he noted in his memoir, *Ya Gotta Believe!*

Eleven years after Tug's night with Betty, Timmy Smith was poking around in his mom's closet when he found his birth certificate, naming him "Samuel Timothy Smith." His abusive stepfather's surname had been written over another name, "McGraw."

Tug agreed to meet the Smiths on a road trip to Houston. He took them to the Astrodome to meet his teammates—the boy's eyes bugging out as he shook hands with Mike Schmidt and Greg Luzinski—but never admitted to being Timmy's father. Naturally his teammates gave him grief about the paternity question. Upon meeting Timmy, Bob Boone announced, "Tug, that's your boy for sure. He's your spittin' image!"

McGraw said it wasn't so. "What happened between me and your mom had nothing to do with you," he told Timmy. "Why don't you just tell everybody we're friends?"

The Smiths went home from the Astrodome to Delhi, Louisiana, where the boy tacked Tug McGraw baseball cards and magazine photos to the wall of his room. Three years later, while Timmy was singing in the school choir, he started writing his name with Tug's last name. He watched the Phillies whenever they were on TV.

Tug McGraw smiled and joked his way through a dramatic 1980 season. He even claimed he liked pitching at the Phillies' supremely unlikable Veterans Stadium, a cement bowl at the south end of Broad Street in South Philadelphia. The Vet was one of the generic multisport stadiums cities erected in the 1970s, along with Riverfront Stadium in Cincinnati, Three Rivers Stadium in Pittsburgh, ad nauseam. It had an Astroturf field, Plexiglas windows on the bullpens, and a squad of female ushers, the Hot Pants Patrol, decked out in short-shorts and go-go boots. The home clubhouse hosted baseball's second-best soap opera after the "Bronx Zoo" New York Yankees.

Much of the turbulence spun around the gravel-voiced Dallas Green. In his first full year as manager, Green imposed a dress code on road trips and a two a.m. curfew. He banned alcohol on team flights without his permission. He swore he'd bench anyone who acted too cool to play hard.

"Give Dallas credit. He was the kickass manager that team needed," Rose recalled.

"We hated him," Bob Boone said.

Green told them the clubhouse was his, not theirs. "He didn't really know what he was stepping into," one Phillie recalled. Green opened the 1980 season by hanging a sign in the team's spring-training clubhouse, a banner reading WE NOT I. Bowa thought that was pretty high school. "When do the fucking pom-pom girls get here?" he asked.

The jut-jawed manager's approach was an odd fit for a club led by headstrong union men. The players had elected Bowa as their union representative after Boone became player rep for the entire National League. Even free spirits like McGraw owed their new prosperity—and loyalty—to the union, not management. To make matters trickier for Green, his clubhouse was full of nonconformists. Steve Carlton, the irreplaceable ace, didn't need any advice from a washed-up ex-hurler like Dallas Green. (As the *Inquirer* noted, "Only an organization that hasn't won a pennant in thirty years would hire a former pitcher with a 20-22 record to instill a winning attitude.") Carlton ignored him. So did Boone, for the most part, and most of the pitchers followed Boone's lead. Rather than jog laps and do jumping jacks with other players, Boone and Carlton stayed flexible with yoga and kung fu. Carlton had a room of his own in the clubhouse, a soundproof sanctuary with blue walls where he reclined in an easy chair, listening to the sound of crashing surf and a recorded voice saying, "*I am courageous, calm, confident. . . .*" He was meditating and visualizing years before teams hired sports psychologists.

To have any sway in the clubhouse, Green needed to win over the Phillies veterans. He squandered any chance of that by challenging the stars to earn their places in the lineup. "Let's see who really wants to play," he told them.

Garry Maddox, for one, had already proved himself. The center fielder with five Gold Gloves and a .293 career average boarded team flights in a fur topcoat over a leisure suit, the height of late-'70s fashion, with a leather handbag over his shoulder. As often as not there was a Bible in the bag along with the charts Maddox kept on other teams' players. Alone among the infielders and outfielders, he sat in on pitchers-and-catchers meetings to see how the Phils planned to pitch particular hitters. He had a cat-quick first step in the outfield and the eyesight of a raptor. "I asked Garry how he got such a good jump on the ball," Bowa recalled. "He said he watched Boone's signals. He'd cheat toward right field on fastballs, to left on a curve. He's reading the catcher's signals from center field!"

Maddox feuded with Green, who reminded him of the tough-talking sergeants he'd met in the army. Green claimed Maddox was sullen—a charged word, like *moody* and *militant*, applied almost exclusively to black players. After that, Maddox said, "I was a disgruntled employee."

Most major-league clubhouses in the '70s divided along racial lines. The Phillies' clubhouse was an exception, but it hadn't started out that way. The team's racial dynamic dated to Dick Allen's second stint in Philadelphia in 1975–76. "We have rap sessions," Maddox said at the time. "We call them the Dick Allen Show because he does most of the talking." Allen was a seven-time All-Star (with three different teams) with no patience for baseball's plantation mentality. Exuding confidence, he enthralled the young Mike Schmidt. When the Phillies clinched the 1976 Eastern Division title, Allen, Maddox, and four others skipped the festivities. "Five black players plus Mike Schmidt, a white player who pals around with the blacks, held their own celebration," the *Daily News* reported. The Allen Show irked some white players, including Tug McGraw, who said, "Schmidt and a group of black players segregated themselves from the rest of the team."

By 1980 Allen was out of baseball and the Phillies were a more cohesive club. Schmidt and McGraw carpooled from Delaware County. "When I drove, Schmitty napped," McGraw recalled. "When he drove, I had to read him the sports page." McGraw preferred stories about his own late-inning escapes, but Schmidt wasn't impressed. "You load the bases to draw attention to yourself," he said.

Boone and Greg Luzinski carpooled from New Jersey across the Walt Whitman Bridge in Boone's turbocharged Datsun 280Z, often with their grade-school sons in the backseat. At the Vet they parked near Rose's Rolls-Royce and followed their boys into the stadium, where Ryan Luzinski, Bret Boone, and Aaron Boone often joined ten-year-old Petey Rose, nine-year-old Mark McGraw, kindergartner Garry Maddox Jr., and other Phillies kids for tapeball games under the stands. They'd fashion balls out of duct tape and smack them around with Wiffle bats. Sometimes the Phillie Phanatic, the team's seven-foot mascot (a PR intern in a fuzzy green costume), joined in, galumphing around the kids' paper-plate bases.

That summer the *Trenton Times* ran a story that embarrassed some of their parents. A minor-league team doctor had been writing illegal amphetamine prescriptions for Rose, Carlton, Luzinski, Tim McCarver, and pitchers Randy Lerch and Larry Christenson, as well as Jean Luzinski and Sheena Bowa. ("How do you think the wives stay so thin?" beat writers snarked.) Other teams' fans jeered the "Philadelphia Pillies."

A subsequent trial embarrassed the team. Asked why Luzinski needed pep pills, the doctor testified, "Greg had a problem with excessive weight, and he wanted Dexamine to help keep it down."

"Bowa said he was running out of gas, he was tired, he needed something to pick him up."

"Pete was having trouble with his weight and needed some help with his thirty-eight-year-old body."

Meanwhile the "Pillies" caught up with the Pirates and Expos in the division race. They seemed to thrive on friction. "Distractions galore!" Rose recalled with a laugh. "But remember, this is a veteran team with talent all over the field. That's why I went to Philly in the first place."

ON OCTOBER 12, 1980, Maddox waved his bat over the plate at the Houston Astrodome. After clinching the National League East in dramatic fashion—an extra-inning homer off Schmidt's bat on the season's penultimate day—the Phillies stood on the brink of another playoff loss.

The fifth and last game of the 1980 National League Championship Series matched the Astros' Nolan Ryan against a Phillies club that had survived three extra-inning fights to get to this point. When the Astros took a three-run lead in the seventh inning of the deciding game, the Houston crowd raised such a racket that Schmidt covered his ears. Said Rose, "I thought the Astrodome would fall down." Maddox, who had ducked artillery in Vietnam, called it "the loudest sound I ever heard." After the visitors rallied for five runs in the eighth, Maddox came up in extra innings with the score 7–7. He lined Frank LaCorte's first-pitch fastball to center for a double that drove in the winning run. After the last out, the Phillies hoisted the Secretary of Defense onto their shoulders. "I'd never been carried off a field before," Maddox said. The Phillies were going to their first World Series since the Whiz Kids faced the mighty Yankees in 1950.

THE PAPERS HAILED Philadelphia's favorite drill sergeant, but Green's harangues and WE NOT I sign had less to do with the team's success than career years by players who couldn't stand him. While most of the Phils had mediocre seasons, Schmidt led the majors with forty-eight homers and slashed .286/.380/.624. Carlton went 24-9, pitching 304 innings with a 2.34 ERA. Modern metrics rank Carlton atop all major leaguers in 1980 with 10.2 Wins Above Replacement, followed by Kansas City Royals third baseman George Brett at 9.4 (Brett hit .390 that season) and Schmidt at 8.9.

Whiz Kids manager Eddie Sawyer, who had made it to age seventy, returned to Philadelphia to lob the ceremonial first pitch of the 1980 World Series between the Phillies and Royals, two teams that had often fallen short in recent years. Both clubs were known for losing in the playoffs. In 1976, 1977, and 1978, as the Phillies were dropping the National League Championship Series to the Reds and the Dodgers, the Royals lost three straight American League Championship Series to the Yankees, often in dramatic fashion. (Chris Chambliss's walk-off home run came in Game Five of the 1976 ALCS.) Neither club had ever won a World Series. The Royals' excuse was that their franchise was only in its twelfth season. The Phillies were ninety-seven years old and counting.

Before the 1980 Series began, McGraw told *Inquirer* writer Bill Lyon he had a hunch: "We can't lose."

McGraw saved Game One, striking out Willie Wilson to preserve a 7–6 Phillies victory. He lost Game Three on a tenth-inning single. Two days later, with the Series tied at two games apiece, he came in again with the Phils behind by a run.

By then he had thrown 103 innings in sixty-five appearances since April, winning five games and saving twenty with an ERA of 1.46. And his arm was killing him. The human elbow and wrist are not designed to twist backward while throwing a five-ounce pill as fast as possible. Even so, Tug was jazzed to be playing in his third World Series. Here he was, a slopballer who never forgot being the littlest kid on his high school team, now facing the great George Brett. Better yet, McGraw knew that his trajectory with the 1980 Phillies had been an entertaining mashup, "like riding through an art gallery on a motorcycle." By the time he faced Brett in Game Five, Larry Bowa had ended a boycott of the press to announce that Phillies fans who booed the home team could fuck themselves. Green had benched Luzinski and told the press, "I love Greg Luzinski, and I'd love to play him. But I'm not the one who hit .228." Kansas City's U. L. Washington had become the first player in Series history to hit and run the bases with a toothpick in his mouth. But the biggest story of all was George Brett's hemorrhoids. Brett's piles had him limping around the bases. Before Game Three the Royals' All-Star third baseman went to the hospital for a lancing and came back to leg out a triple in Game Four. "My troubles are all behind me," he said.

McGraw would have enjoyed the spectacle even more if he could feel all his fingers. He would have preferred not to be hungover from a late night and early morning on the town. But he held the Royals scoreless in the seventh. He held them in the eighth.

Philadelphia got two runs in the ninth to take a 4–3 lead. McGraw stayed in the game, despite feeling "my arm hyperextend" with every screwball "and pinch my crazy bone. My fingers were numb."

He walked Royals second baseman Frank White to start the bottom of the ninth, bringing George Brett to the plate as the potential winning run. McGraw got ahead of Brett with screwballs, then sneaked an 0-2 Peggy Lee fastball over the outside corner for strike three. "One of the biggest thrills of my career," he called it. But then he walked Willie Mays Aikens to put the winning run on base.

At this point every screwball felt like "banging my elbow on the corner of a table," McGraw recalled. He hung one to the next Royals batter, Hal McRae, a spinner that didn't spin enough. McRae belted it over the left-field fence for a walk-off three-run jack that had forty-two thousand Royals fans yelling—

Until the ball curled foul.

NBC's cameras showed McGraw fanning his hand over his chest, miming a heart attack.

McRae bounced to short for the second out.

McGraw's third walk of the ninth inning loaded the bases. Bob Boone took a step toward the mound, giving him the hands-down sign that meant *Take it easy*. As if Tug would take it any other way.

McGraw struck out Jose Cardenal to send the Phillies home with a chance to win the Series at the Vet.

TUG MCGRAW WASN'T usually religious except while hungover, but he prayed he wouldn't be called on to pitch in Game Six. Let the Phillies win without him for a change. But after Carlton threw seven shutout innings, Kansas City opened the eighth with a walk and a single. With a four-run lead and six outs to go, Green waved to the bullpen for his best reliever, hoping Tug could shut down the Royals one last time.

McGraw's funny bone ached. He'd popped a few Tylenol before the game and a few more in the fourth inning. He allowed a sacrifice fly and then loaded the bases, but escaped the eighth inning with a 4–1 lead. As his cartoon alter ego Scroogie would say, "Handstands!" But Tug had barely found a seat on the bench before the Phils were out, one-two-three, in the top of the ninth. He took a gulp of air and went back to the mound.

There were 65,839 at the Vet that night, the biggest crowd ever at a baseball game in Pennsylvania, all of them on their feet. Another thirty million watched on NBC, the most ever to tune in a World Series game. McGraw looked around the stadium, taking it all in. The moment was "nerve-wracking," he said later. "But that's why you play sports. If they don't wrack your nerves, find something else to do."

Amos Otis, leading off the ninth for Kansas City, struck out on a screwball. Then Tug, being Tug, loaded the bases on a walk and two singles.

With one out Frank White, the potential go-ahead run, hit a pop foul. Bob Boone tossed his mask aside, looking straight up as he chased the ball to the lip of the first-base dugout. Boone reached up—and the ball bounced off his mitt. McGraw called it "another devastating error in the cursed Phillies' history—until, all of a sudden, Pete was right there." Hustling over from first base, Rose grabbed the ball before it touched the ground.

A moment passed while the Phillies fans processed what had just happened. Then they roared as never before at the Vet. Rose flipped the baseball to Boone, who walked it to McGraw on the mound.

"Tuggles," Boone said, "isn't this exciting?"

"Boonie, you sure talk funny when you're nervous."

The bases were still loaded. Boone wanted screwballs to Willie Wilson, who represented the potential go-ahead run as well as the potential last out of the game and the Series. McGraw shook his head, looking pained at the thought of a scroogie. "I might have one left," he said.

Boone said, "We'll throw him one, just to put it in his head, and get him with fastballs."

The catcher jogged back to the plate. He crouched and signaled for a screwball.

The pitcher shook his head. Again Boone gave the screwball signal. "He did it four times," McGraw said later. "I just kept shaking my head. Willie Wilson's standing there thinking, 'He ain't *got* that many pitches!'" Finally McGraw uncorked a screwball that caught a corner of the plate. Strike one.

Wilson fouled a slider off his foot. With the count 0-2, McGraw wanted to buzz Wilson under the chin—"shave his Adam's apple"—to set up a 1-2 pitch outside. To Tug's dismay his next "Cutty Sark" sailed too close to the plate. "A real meatball," he called it.

Wilson, looking surprised, took it. McGraw couldn't believe his luck. His catcher gave him a breather by coming out for another mound conference. When Tuggles asked Boonie what he thought of that last pitch, Boone recalled, "We looked at each other and broke out laughing."

Crowd noise almost drowned out the NBC broadcast. Boone called again for a fastball. He figured the last thing Wilson expected was two fastballs in a row.

McGraw nodded.

He looked around the stadium, taking it all in. "I look over at the dugout," he recalled, "and there's a horse." A dozen mounted police-men stationed around the Vet stood ready to stop any rioting if the Phillies won. "And this particular horse isn't stadium-trained. His tail went up, he did his thing, and I thought to myself, 'If I don't get Willie Wilson out, that stuff that's layin' on the turf below the horse is exactly what I'm going to be.'"

It was 11:29 p.m. on Tuesday, October 21, 1980. The pitch was one of McGraw's John Jameson fastballs, straight with a twist. "The slowest pitch ever thrown in Philadelphia," he called it. "It took ninety-seven years to get there."

Wilson swung and missed.

McGraw jumped, raising his fists toward the fireworks going off over the Vet. Schmidt ran over from third base and jumped into his arms. The Phillies hugged and danced, World Series champs for the first time.

In Delhi, Louisiana, thirteen-year-old Timmy McGraw Smith turned off the TV. He didn't know if he should cheer or cry. Timmy had sent letter after letter to the man he was sure was his father, address-ing them to TUG MCGRAW, C/O PHILADELPHIA PHILLIES, 3501 S. BROAD STREET, PHILADELPHIA, PENNSYLVANIA, the only address he could find. They were all ignored. His long-distance phone calls to Veterans Sta-dium got no reply. After two years of telling his friends to call him McGraw, he said he was Timmy Smith again.

KONG VS. THE MEDIA

On the day after the Cubs' 23–22 loss to the Phillies in 1979, Dave Kingman smacked his fourth home run in twenty-four and a half hours, this time against the Pittsburgh Pirates, in a 9–5 loss at Wrigley. Kingman was now only one homer behind Schmidt for the major-league lead, with each of them on a pace that would challenge Roger Maris's record of sixty-one in a season. Schmidt swore he'd rather lead the league in batting average than homers. Kingman had no such compunctions. When he swung, he swung for the fences. The improv comics at Second City had a riff: *"The count's oh-and-two on Kingman. There's a pickoff throw to first—Kingman swings and misses!"*

While the Phillies faded in the summer of '79, the Cubs dueled the Expos for first place in the National League East. "Nineteen seventy-nine was the year Kingman came close to his potential," said John Schulian of the *Sun-Times*. "He actually shortened his swing with two strikes and tried for a single! Dave Kingman's secret was that he was dying to be a .260 hitter."

Working with Cubs hitting coach Lou Fonseca, Kingman had revamped his stance and his swing. Taking a wider stance and moving closer to the plate, he found he could cover the outside corner and was still quick enough to jack inside pitches for homers to left.

Through seventy-six games, Kingman's twenty-nine homers projected to sixty-two over a full season. Chicago went cuckoo for Kong, a man *Sports Illustrated*'s Newman would recall as "an odd duck. He didn't smoke or drink or go skirt-chasing with the other bachelors, or tolerate the routine of postgame interviews. He lacked the patience, or the insincerity, to say 'It's all about the team,' or 'We'll take 'em one at a time.'"

Asked by a reporter why he spurned reporters, Kingman told the truth: "I'll admit it, I hate you guys. You have no idea how hard my job is. You ask all the same questions. You don't know who I am and I'm not going to tell you." Some of the beat writers were pleased when he twisted his knee and missed several games. That cut his pace down to a more plausible fifty-five home runs. Then the Cubs went to New York, where he konged a pair of homers one night and three more the next. It wasn't August yet and the man had thirty-five jacks. Almost as surprising was his .306 batting average—thirty points better than Bill Buckner's.

When a writer asked Buckner what he thought of Kingman, the first baseman said, "He's a teammate."

KINGMAN'S HEROICS BROUGHT the Cubs within a half game of the first-place Expos at the end of July. Then they lost six in a row. The press focused on the usual Cub follies, like a bad throw from outfielder Mike Vail that beaned the batboy.

The Cubs opened September by losing seven of eight. Two weeks later, on Fan Appreciation Day, they were mathematically eliminated. "I've had it up to here. Some of these players are crazy," said Herman Franks, waving a twenty-four-thousand-dollar check made out to the Salt Lake City Country Club. "Do you think I'd shell out twenty-four thousand dollars and then come back here? Next year I'll be playing golf every day." With that, he skippered his club to a 6–0 loss. Several thousand of the fans being appreciated booed the home team. After the game, Franks quit, telling reporters he was fed up with Vail's "constant whining" and Barry Foote's going on about "how they did it in Philly." As for Buckner, Franks was withering: "I thought Buckner was the All-American boy, the kind of guy who'd dive in the dirt to save ballgames for you. What I found out is, he doesn't care about the team. He couldn't handle Kingman's success this season. When Kingman had a great year, Buckner couldn't take it."

In the season's final week, with the Cubs sixteen and a half games out, interim manager Joey Amalfitano gave Donnie Moore a start. There were 5,827 fans and thirty-two thousand empty seats at Wrigley that day. Moore saw the start as a chance to prove he deserved a big-league job in 1980. The Mets had him on the ropes in the fourth, when New York's Bruce Boisclair looped a fly ball to right. Larry Biittner (the only player ever with consecutive double letters in his name, as announcer Jack Brickhouse loved reminding Cub fans) chased the ball toward the ivy. As he neared the warning track, his hat flew off. He turned, looked for the ball, and did a double take. Where was the ball?

Bleacher fans pointed and yelled, "Hat! Hat!" Finally Biittner ran to his cap, which had fallen on top of the baseball. He grabbed the ball and threw the runner out at third. It was the closest the bleacher bums ever got to recording an assist, but Moore lost the game anyway.

In the end the Cubs' 9-22 finish in 1979 was even worse than the collapse of '69. Kingman at least finished strong, closing his career year with forty-eight home runs, three more than Schmidt, to lead the majors. A .288 batting average, 115 RBIs, and a league-leading slugging percentage of .613 offset his strikeouts. "He might have been the best player in the league that year," said Schulian. Still Kingman came in eleventh in the writers' vote for National League MVP. More important to him, perhaps, the Cubs' paid attendance of 1.65 million was enough to trigger the fifty-thousand-dollar bonus in his contract.

At first, the 23–22 game was recalled as just one of the Cubs' eighty-two losses that season. Then a producer at WGN did some editing.

That winter, with the Hawk whistling past the empty ballpark,

Channel 9 rebroadcast the game. Again Jack Brickhouse narrated Dennis Lamp's nightmare outing, Buckner's grand slam, Kingman's three blasts, Barry Foote's single sending Steve Ontiveros chugging around third ("*C'mon Steve, c'mon Ontiveros!*"), and Schmidt's tenth-inning homer ("*Look out now, look out . . .*"). Then, in the bottom of the tenth, WGN cut to a ten-year-old tape of a different game. "*It's Ernie Banks!*" Brickhouse said. Spliced into the game tape eight years after his retirement and two years after his induction into the Hall of Fame, Banks drove a long fly to left. "*Back back back,*" said Brickhouse, who had come into the studio to record the new ending. "*Hey hey, he did it! A two-run homer by Ernie Banks and the Cubs win, 24 to 23!*"

KINGMAN AGREED TO an off-season interview with Chicago's WMAQ-TV on his forty-foot boat in San Diego Bay, where he spent winters. "First he poured a cold beer down my back. Later he threw me into his hot tub," recalled WMAQ producer Sandra Weir. "I had my clothes on and didn't think it was funny. Finally, he literally threw me into the Pacific Ocean. Luckily, I'm a good swimmer."

A couple of months later, when the union boycotted spring-training games, demanding fewer free-agent restrictions and a boost in the minimum salary of thirty thousand dollars, Bill Buckner, the Cubs' player rep, called a players-only meeting. Everyone attended except the National League's home-run king. "Kingman didn't have the courtesy to show up," Buckner said. Next, Kingman dumped a bucket of ice on a writer from the *Arlington Heights Daily Herald*. The club made him apologize. A month after that, he signed on as a guest columnist for the *Tribune*. Kingman's column mocked sportswriters. "Frustrated players at heart," he called them, "and this exposes itself in their writing."

Mike Royko, the *Sun-Times'* Pulitzer Prize–winning columnist, struck back with his own guest columnist, Dave Dingdong, "the tall, handsome left fielder who hits those towering homers." In Royko's spoof, Dingdong wrote, "You might wonder why I've broken my legendary silence. Well, I'm a frank and honest person. And to be frank and honest, I'll do anything for a buck. . . . I'd be a standout anywhere, but especially Wrigley Field, because most of my teammates are nothings."

Kingman tripped over a bat that spring and banged up his shoulder. He came off the disabled list in time to strike out and reinjure his shoulder in the All-Star Game at Dodger Stadium. He gave up his *Tribune* column. The 1980 Cubs fell into last place on the same day Dallas Green's Phillies pulled within a half game of first. Star-crossed franchises going in different directions, they crossed paths in an August game that found Kong with just eleven home runs, booed by dwindling crowds. "It didn't help when the club held a T-shirt giveaway in his honor and he didn't show up," Cubs historian Ed Hartig said. "He was out on Lake Michigan, fishing."

While most sportswriters tiptoed around him, some of the Cubs saw a better side to Kong. He was a clubhouse cutup, the kind of guy who loads up guys' caps with shaving cream and jocks with itching powder. Pitcher Mike Krukow told a writer about team parties Kingman hosted. "He was running around making sure the glasses were filled and the ashtrays were empty," he said. During a party on Kingman's yacht, Krukow, Rick Reuschel, and Bruce Sutter marveled at his strength. As Krukow recalled, "Dave had a keg of beer in a thirty-three-gallon trash can full of ice. To make room for guys, he picked it up and moved it. Later we all walked over to the trash can full of beer. None of us could budge it."

AFTER KINGMAN'S HOME-RUN total fell from forty-eight in 1979 to eighteen in 1980, the Cubs called an end to what the *Sun-Times* called the Kingman Experiment. General manager Bob Kennedy dumped Kingman and his $240,000-a-year salary on the New York Mets for part-time outfielder Steve Henderson. Mets manager Joe Torre was eager to get his old teammate in the lineup. "Dave Kingman is a quality home-run hitter we have been missing since we traded him," Torre said.

The New York press wasn't so sure. The *Daily News* columnist Dick Young called Kong "the most selfish man I have met in a game glutted with selfish people." But Young's colleague Mike Lupica welcomed another chance to enter "the disco that is Kingman's mind." To Lupica the Mets' new left fielder was "more fun to watch than any hitter alive."

"I'm at the peak of my career, and I'm overly excited," Kingman told reporters. This time, "the distractions won't affect me as much."

In his second tour with the Mets he belted several of the longest home runs in team history and had the shortest commute. He slept in a boat moored in the marina next to Shea Stadium, fished in the mornings, and walked to work. He kept another boat at Lake Hopatcong in New Jersey (teammates joked that the lake's full name was Hopatkingman), where he and other Mets fished and Jet Skied. One friend, pitcher Craig Swan, called Kong a freak of nature. "We were wrestling in the clubhouse one day," Swan told the writer Greg Prato. "He got behind me and picked me up in the air, turned me upside down, and stuffed me into a big old thing of towels! And I weighed 225."

In 1982, Kingman led the National League with thirty-seven homers (to Dale Murphy's thirty-six and Mike Schmidt's thirty-five), but caught flak for his league-worst 156 strikeouts and .204 batting average, the lowest ever by a home-run king. Pundits pointed out that Cy Young Award winner Steve Carlton outhit him by batting .218 that year. Even so, front offices dug the long ball. The Mets re-signed Kong for two more years, with a hefty raise.

Then, in June 1983, the Mets acquired All-Star first baseman Keith Hernandez from the St. Louis Cardinals. Kingman had been playing first after too many mishaps in the outfield; he went to the bench. The Mets released him at the end of the season, despite owing him $675,000 in 1984 whether he was on the team or not.

A week before Opening Day 1984 he was fishing in San Diego Bay, waiting to hear if anybody wanted him. Oakland was interested. With Rickey Henderson leading off and forty-year-old Joe Morgan batting third, the A's were looking for a power bat. They signed Kingman to a one-year deal for the major-league minimum of forty thousand dollars. It was a bargain for Oakland. Since his guaranteed contract with the Mets had another year to run, New York was on the hook for all but the minimum salary Oakland took on. In effect, the Mets paid Kingman $635,000 to play for the A's.

As Oakland's designated hitter, Kingman got off to the best start of his career. He was so pleased with his new role in life that he had a new name painted on the boat he moored in San Francisco Bay: *Designated Hitter*. His ten April homers, including a one-handed broken-bat shot over the Green Monster at Fenway Park, spurred renewed talk that Kingman might be the man to break Roger Maris's record. "Nobody can hit a ball as high and deep as he can," said his teammate Dave Lopes. California Angels pitcher John Curtis said, "Some game he's going to hit one of those towering pops and the ball's never going to come down."

That actually happened in 1984. Facing the Twins' Frank Viola in Minneapolis, Kingman launched a pop-up toward the Metrodome's fiberglass roof. Several Twins camped under the ball. "I was waiting for it to come down through the atmosphere," second baseman Tim Teufel said. Seconds ticked by. There was still no ball. The baseball had disappeared through an eight-inch hole in the roof. The umpires called it a roof-rule double.

Kingman clubbed thirty-five homers to lead the 1984 A's. He hit .268 with a career-high 118 RBIs and won the Comeback Player of the Year Award. That December he celebrated his thirty-sixth birthday by signing a $1 million deal to return to Oakland in 1985.

"SINCE JOINING THE A's, Kingman's relations with the media have been cordial and productive," *USA Today* reported, including this quote from the man himself: "Oakland writers are not New York and Chicago writers—those guys have bigger egos than the ballplayers. In Oakland, they do not have to manufacture a story. I may have learned it a little late, but I know now you can't control what's written."

He hit his four-hundredth career home run for the A's in 1985, a milestone widely viewed as a ticket to the Hall of Fame. He rounded the bases stone-faced as usual, then reared back to high-five the on-deck hitter, Alfredo Griffin. And his hand missed Griffin's hand. Even in his greatest moment, Kingman whiffed.

After the game, the man of the hour smiled and chatted with reporters until he spotted Susan Fornoff, a young writer from the *Sacramento Bee*.

"If she's here, I'm not talking," he said.

Fornoff was a twenty-six-year-old University of Maryland graduate who had covered sports for the *Baltimore News American* and *USA Today* before joining the *Bee*. She got along with most of the athletes she covered, but said she never felt welcome in the A's clubhouse. "One thing fans may not know is how a baseball clubhouse isn't just a place where players shower and dress. It's their living room. And some of them want to keep you out."

After his four-hundredth homer Kingman told her, "Don't come near me."

Notebook and pen in hand, she said, "Can't we just be professionals?"

He said, "Don't ruin this for me."

Fornoff had been ready to write something positive. Instead, she backed off and gave him his space. "Readers seem to like stories of reformed bad guys in the sports pages," she recalled. "They never like to hear so-and-so is really a prick."

KONG BANGED THIRTY homers for the A's in 1985, but his batting average fell to .238. Throughout the season he froze Fornoff out of interviews. "This is a men's clubhouse," he said. After her editor complained to general manager Sandy Alderson, Kingman chucked a tissue box at her and said, "Kleenex, anyone? Anyone crying?" When Fornoff approached Alderson himself, "he blew up at me," she recalled. "He said, 'I don't give a shit about you and Dave Kingman!'"

A year later the A's were on the road, going nowhere, sitting in sixth place in the seven-team American League West. Fornoff was in the press box at Kansas City's Royals Stadium when a messenger handed her a

Mike Schmidt led the first-place Philadelphia Phillies into Wrigley Field for their first trip of the season in May 1979.

Chicago Cubs slugger Dave Kingman was chasing Schmidt for the National League lead in home runs.

"Lucky Charlie" Weeghman, a luncheonette tycoon, built his team a North Side ballpark in 1914.

With player-manager Joe Tinker at short, Weeghman's Chi-Feds brought Federal League baseball to Chicago.

Manager Danny Ozark
began the 1979 season with
a mandate from the Phillies'
front office: win or else.

Herman Franks, the Cubs' grumpy skipper, knew a fourth-
place club when he managed one.

First baseman Bill Buckner, Dave Kingman's teammate and rival, took every out personally.

Pitcher Ray Burris met Cub fan Ed Hartig—later the team's official historian—at a Chicago-area Kmart.

Bruce Sutter went from sore-armed suspect to superstar after mastering the split-finger fastball.

The Phillies opened the vault—
eight hundred thousand dollars
a year!—to lure Pete Rose from
Cincinnati to be their sparkplug.

Combat veteran Garry Maddox played
center field so expertly fans called him
the Secretary of Defense.

Hot-tempered
Larry Bowa was the
Phils' slick-fielding,
slap-hitting, tantrum-
throwing shortstop.

In the third inning on May 17, Philadelphia catcher Bob Boone barreled into third base as the visitors padded their lead.

Kingman's second homer of the game was still rising when it cleared the left-field bleachers.

Reliever Ron Reed "hated everybody," a sportswriter said. When Reed entered the game in the fifth, he turned his ire on the Cubs' hitters, their fans, and the plate umpire.

Maddox and Schmidt at a meeting with players' union chief
Marvin Miller, who changed the game forever.

Tug McGraw and his carpool buddy
Schmidt celebrated the Phils' 1980
World Series win.

Troubled Donnie Moore
became the Angels' relief ace
and signed a million-dollar deal
before his life fell apart.

Phils dads McGraw, Boone, and Rose goofed around with Petey Rose (left), Mark McGraw and Boone's boys Bret and Aaron. That's five-year-old Aaron, the future manager of the New York Yankees, in the middle.

The next day, a banner headline in Philadelphia celebrated the twelve-run lead that almost got away.

box. It was a small paper box like the one her high school prom corsage came in. Someone had written SUE FORNOFF, SAC BEE on it.

Inside she found a live rat. The rat had a tag tied to its foot: MY NAME IS SUE.

When the story got out, Kingman called it a joke. "I'm a prankster," he said.

Fornoff and her editor went back to the general manager. This time Alderson apologized on behalf of the team and promised to fine Kingman. The fine was announced the next day: thirty-five hundred dollars. That sum represented a day's pay for Kingman. Fornoff had been expecting more zeroes. The club's announcement that the prank was "an affront to Ms. Fornoff and to the dignity of baseball" didn't keep one of his A's teammates from phoning Fornoff's hotel room at 3 a.m. to tell her, "Baseball is for men. You will never understand that or be part of that." It didn't keep Kong from handing out RAT PATROL T-shirts in the clubhouse.

Fornoff's colleague Pete Dexter wrote a scathing column about the rat and the man behind it. Unlike Dave Kingman, Dexter claimed, "the rat is not overpaid." The rat "has to have a better glove" and "probably did not live with its mother until it hit middle age." It hadn't "called in sick" on Dave Kingman Day at Wrigley "and spent the afternoon peddling motorized water skis at a Chicago lakefront festival while his team played a baseball game."

Claire Smith of the *Hartford Courant* told Fornoff they were in the same boat—in steerage. "You could take a bum off the street, shave him, clean him up, put a pad and pencil in his hand, and he could walk into a clubhouse you and I have worked for five years and be *instantly accepted* in a way you or I will never be," said Smith. They traded war stories like the one about another locker-room pioneer who kept trying to do her job while a player exposed himself to her, saying, "What about this? What do you think of this?" Finally she said, "It looks like a penis, but smaller."

Fornoff remembered Kingman "in his corner of the clubhouse,

staring at me as if he were Norman Bates plotting his next move in the shower." She would outlast Kong in the A's clubhouse but got tired of the baseball beat. She worked as an official scorer for the A's and Giants, the first woman to hold that position, and later founded a website for golfers. "And one of the rats in the story had a happy ending," she recalled. "I gave the rat he sent me to a five-year-old science nut who promised to take good care of it. I just had one request: I asked him to name the rat Kong."

IN 1986, KINGMAN's last big-league season, he batted .210. Tony La Russa, the A's new manager, wasn't keen on his thirty-seven-year-old DH. La Russa had gotten his big break in Chicago in the summer of Kong, but on the South Side. White Sox owner Bill Veeck, the sixty-five-year-old hustler who had planted the ivy at Wrigley Field back in 1937, made La Russa the youngest manager in the majors as well as the only one with a law degree and the first to crunch baseball stats on a computer. La Russa ran the ball club while Veeck goosed attendance with events like Disco Demolition Night in July 1979. Fans chanted "Disco sucks!" and sailed vinyl records through the air while a rock DJ dynamited a pile of disco discs. Fans stormed the field, setting a fire in center field and literally stealing bases. A South Side kid named Michael Clarke Duncan slid into third. Twenty years before costarring with Tom Hanks in *The Green Mile*, Duncan stole a bat from the Sox dugout before the riot police arrived. The umpires called off the game—one of just five big-league forfeits in the past fifty years.

Seven years later, after leaving Chicago for Oakland, La Russa piloted the A's to a third-place finish in the American League West. Kingman ran his career strikeout total to 1,816, fourth-most in history at the time. Even so, he still led the club with thirty-five home runs, and his 94 RBIs were second only to Rookie of the Year Jose Canseco's 117. But the A's didn't want him back. They had a pair of young power hitters who would be earning a combined $135,000 in 1987, compared to Kong's $730,000: twenty-two-year-old Canseco and the team's top prospect, twenty-three-year-old Mark McGwire.

Another reason, Fornoff said, was that "the front office finally gave a shit about their public image. That's why they didn't offer him a contract."

Again Kong waited for the phone to ring. He stayed in shape by water-skiing, playing tennis, and jogging, but got no offers. Why? The answer came nine years later, when an arbitrator ruled that major-league owners had conspired to limit offers to free agents in 1986–87. The arbitrator awarded Kingman $829,849.54 in lost wages, the highest sum to come out of the players' collusion case against the owners. Involuntarily retired, Kingman went hunting. His 442 home runs were the third-most among active players at the time, behind future Hall of Famers Reggie Jackson and Mike Schmidt.

Spy, the satirical magazine of the '80s and '90s, remembered Kingman as a "strikeout-prone galoot." Bill James named an award after him: the uncoveted Dave Kingman Award went to the hitter who "best exemplifies the idea of hitting home runs without doing anything else."

When a *Sporting News* reporter tracked him down, Kingman said he didn't miss playing and especially didn't miss talking to people like *Sporting News* writers. He retired to Lake Tahoe. He married, raised a family, and said he was a happy man.

"I had critics all my career," he said. "When their stories came out, I had a good laugh."

DISGRACE UNDER PRESSURE

Dave Kingman and Bill Buckner had something in common: they weren't baseball fans. Kingman had grown up without baseball heroes. He wouldn't dream of watching a ballgame if he could hunt or go fishing. Buckner looked up to pure hitters like Stan Musial and Pete Rose but never really understood fandom. Asked about the Cubs' die-hard fans, he said, "It's hard for me to fathom, but it's not for me to decide what infatuates them or occupies their time. The whole idea of professional sports is kind of crazy, really."

Buckner had his best year yet in 1980. With Kingman hurt and the Cubs tumbling to last place in their division, he went 114 at-bats before striking out. He was in the hunt for the NL batting title all year, bellyaching about how many ground-ball hits the infield grass at Wrigley Field, grown high to help the pitchers, cost him. "The grass is so long I could feed my cattle with it," said Buckner, who spent off-seasons at his ranch in Idaho. The head groundskeeper at Wrigley offered to let him use a mower.

"Buckner was a pro in the best sense," John Schulian of the *Chicago Sun-Times* recalled, "and incredibly brave, in my view. He won the batting title that year on one good leg." He could have sat out the last game to preserve his lead over the Cardinals' Keith Hernandez, but he played and edged Hernandez, .324 to .321. Later he took a few college classes and felt a personal connection to Hemingway's *The Old Man and the Sea*. According to his professor, "He talked about that last scene of the old man lying face down in the sand, the skeleton of the fish beside him, and how it reminded him of the last day of the 1980 season. At the moment of triumph he looked up and the stands were empty. He felt terribly alone."

A year later, after asking Steve Carlton about his fitness routines, Buckner adopted some of Carlton's methods, plunging his arms into sacks of rice and then flexing to build strength in his hands and wrists. Before the 1982 season, with Kingman gone, he signed a five-year contract for $2.6 million that made him the highest-paid Cub. He said life was "hunky-dory" but found the club's losing ways less lovable. "Sometimes I laugh off the losing. It's the only way to keep your sanity," he said. After bleeding Dodger blue for L.A. teams that contended for pennants year after year and played for big crowds, he never got used to seeing fans stretched out in the bleachers, sleeping. After five years in Chicago he agreed with the pundits who claimed that day baseball hurt the Cubs' chances. "As a player, I'd like to have lights here. We go on the road for night games, come home for day games. The body and mind get tired of making adjustments." He was also enough of a purist to dislike the winds at Wrigley as well as the grass. When the wind blew in, "You crush a ball and it's a pop-up. The batters scream. The next inning the wind shifts and a pop-up's a home run. The pitchers scream."

Schulian liked to talk hitting with him. The *Sun-Times* columnist would often show up early enough to hear the *snap-crackle-pop* of Buckner's ankles as he walked into the Cubs' cramped, leaky clubhouse. "Buckner could be difficult with writers," he recalled. "He didn't like hearing the same questions day after day. 'Do you think the Cubs can win?' That gets old. But if you catch him at the right moment he's an interesting guy. One day we sat in front of his locker and talked about his insecurity as a hitter. Every time he made an out, he thought he'd never get another hit. He envied guys like Dick Allen who expected to get a hit every time."

In 1982 the San Diego Padres' Tim Lollar threw a fastball under Buckner's chin. This was not something a kid like Lollar had a right to do, so Buckner had a word with Cub pitcher Dan Larson, who plunked the next Padres batter. Just protocol, except that Lee Elia, Herman Franks's successor as Cub manager, thought he should be deciding who got beaned. "Who's managing this team?" he barked when the Cubs came off the field. Elia and Buckner traded words. One of them threw the first punch. WGN's cameras caught their dustup in the moments before the other Cubs pulled them apart. Buckner missed the next game with a neck injury he blamed on Elia, who said Buckner was faking the injury.

The team's new general manager could barely believe the chaos he inherited. A year after managing the Phillies to their 1980 World Series title, Dallas Green signed a lucrative deal to turn the Cubs around. He hired Elia (a former coach for him in Philadelphia) but soon soured on him, canning him halfway through the 1983 season. A year later he traded Buckner to Boston for twenty-nine-year-old starting pitcher Dennis Eckersley in a deal long-suffering Cub fans would flash back on for years. Among other things, trading Buckner opened first base for Leon Durham, who would let a ground ball roll between his legs for a pivotal error in the 1984 National League Championship Series.

Red Sox third baseman Wade Boggs called Buckner a welcome addition to a team on the rise. "He's got a lot of fire under his butt. That battling part of him rubs off on us," Boggs said.

In 1986, using fistfuls of aspirin, massages, tape, stretches, and ice to play 153 games, Buckner batted .267 with eighteen home runs and 102 RBIs. In one writer's description, "There's ice on his knee, ice on his shoulder, ice on both thighs, and he plunges his feet into tubs of ice." Buckner hit .320 down the stretch to help lead the Red Sox to a division title. He was sore going into the American League Championship Series against the California Angels, then aggravated a thigh injury beating out an infield hit as the Sox won Game Seven and the pennant. Team doctors said he might not be ready for the World Series against the New York Mets, but he batted third and played first base in Game One.

Before that game, Buckner spoke on TV about the pressures of playing in the World Series. "The nightmares are that you're gonna let the winning run score on a ground ball through your legs," he said.

In Game Six, up three games to two and holding a 5–4 lead over the Mets in the bottom of the tenth inning, the Sox were on the brink of their first championship since 1918. A wild pitch with Mookie Wilson at the plate allowed the tying run to score. Three pitches later, Wilson bounced what looked like an easy inning-ending grounder to Buckner. Sox fans had wondered why Boston manager John McNamara hadn't replaced Buckner with Dave Stapleton, a more mobile first baseman who usually subbed for him in the late innings. Was it an oversight by McNamara? Did the manager doubt Stapleton's guts, as he later claimed? As it happened, Buckner took four steps toward the ball and got into perfect fielding position. Then his worst nightmare came true: the baseball sneaked under his glove and through his legs, letting in the winning run.

BUCKNER'S HERO PETE Rose watched the 1986 World Series on TV. After leading the Phillies to their first World Series crown in 1980 and to another pennant in 1983, he'd gone home to be player-manager of the Cincinnati Reds for $1 million a year. In 1985 he piloted the Reds to a second-place finish in the NL West and was runner-up in voting for National League Manager of the Year, one vote behind the Cardinals' Whitey Herzog. A year later Rose retired as a player with a record that may never be broken: 4,256 career hits. That was 65 more hits than Ty Cobb's total and hundreds more than anyone else's. In the more than thirty years since Rose's retirement, the closest anyone has come to his total is Derek Jeter—and he fell nearly 800 hits short, the equivalent of four All-Star seasons' worth. The Hit King, people called Rose. After 1986 his Rolls-Royces bore HITKING vanity plates.

He would have been elected to baseball's Hall of Fame in 1992 if he hadn't stayed in the game as a manager. In 1988, while still managing the Reds, he was investigated by the Commissioner's Office.

Like Buckner, Kingman, and plenty of other players, Rose never really understood why people would care who won a ballgame they weren't involved in. He was among the ex-players who stayed interested by betting, sometimes legally and sometimes not. Like many Americans, the Reds' manager had a bookie. In that way he was like millions of others, only he had more money—and he was still employed in the game.

He knew he was breaking baseball's first commandment. A sign posted in every major-league clubhouse spelled out Rule 21, a warning dating back to the 1919 Black Sox scandal:

> Any player, umpire or club official or employee, who shall bet any sum whatsoever upon any baseball game in connection with which the bettor has no duty to perform shall be declared ineligible for one year. Any player, umpire or club official or employee, who shall bet any sum whatsoever upon any baseball game in connection with which the bettor has a duty to perform shall be declared permanently ineligible.

So Rose kept his bets secret. He kept them affordable, a thousand dollars here and there, and rationalized breaking the rule by telling himself that it didn't apply to him because he never bet against the Reds. His rationalization made a sort of sense. After all, the rule's purpose was to keep players and managers from throwing games, and you can't throw a game by winning it.

There was a problem with that idea he didn't acknowledge, even to himself. What if he had a big bet down—would he manage a game differently? Would he use his top reliever, John Franco, in a tie game? What if Franco had thrown three nights in a row? What if Rose got so far in debt that the guys behind his bookie threatened to hurt him or his family if he didn't throw a game?

When rumors of his betting reached the Commissioner's Office, he denied everything. He denied betting on baseball even after the attorney John Dowd produced seven volumes of evidence that convinced Commissioner A. Bartlett Giamatti to ban Pete Rose for life. (Dowd would reemerge in the public eye three decades later as President Donald Trump's lawyer.)

Rose stepped down as the Reds' manager, agreeing to a proviso that he considered crucial: he could apply for reinstatement after one year. According to Rose, he and Giamatti had an informal agreement to review his suspension the following year. Unfortunately for him, the commissioner died of a heart attack eight days after announcing Rose was out of the game.

The hit king's troubles weren't over. After failing to report $350,000 in income from memorabilia sales and public appearances, he served a five-month prison term for tax evasion. He moved to Las Vegas, where he could bet legally, and watched the steroid era unfold. He couldn't help wondering if Mark McGwire, Barry Bonds, and other pumped-up cheaters were worse for the game than he ever was. He still followed the pennant races and pulled for gamers like Buckner who reminded him of himself.

"You know one thing I remember about that game at Wrigley in seventy-nine?" he said. "Bowa was yelling at Buckner when we were ahead—'We're kicking your ass!' And Buckner's looking like, 'We'll see.'"

THE RED SOX released Bill Buckner in July 1987, nine months after his World Series error. They had a first-base phenom named Sam Horn coming up from the minors. Buckner signed a one-year deal with the California Angels for four hundred thousand dollars. When a reporter asked how his thirty-seven-year-old legs were holding up, he admitted, "I'm definitely going to have trouble in later years. To some people it's not worth it. To me it is."

In a 1989 *Penthouse* story exposing an extramarital romp between Wade Boggs and a woman named Margo Adams, Boggs ripped his Boston teammates Jim Rice ("He thinks he's white"), Roger Clemens ("Mr. Perfect"), and Buckner ("a gimp"). Buckner, stung, said he never liked the five-time batting champ anyway. "It's not like we were close." Boggs, he said, was obsessed with hitting. "He'd just hang around with a guy he thought was giving him luck. He'd go eat with a younger player, and if he got three hits the guy had to keep going out to lunch with him."

After being released by the Angels early in the 1988 season, Buckner spent two forgettable years in Kansas City, then reported to the Red Sox' spring camp in Winter Haven, Florida, and made the roster at age forty. On Opening Day 1990, the fans at Fenway Park gave him a standing ovation.

On April 22 Buckner took a blow to the head in a first-base collision with the Brewers' B. J. Surhoff. He was clearly concussed ("I didn't know what year it was") but returned to pinch-hit in the Sox' next game. The next day he started at first and legged out an inside-the-park homer. But by June he was hitting only .186, and the Red Sox released him again. Buckner and his wife, Jody, sold their house in Boston. "I'm definitely out of Boston," he told a reporter who asked, like they all did, about his World Series error. "My kids are getting older. I don't want them hearing about that all the time."

He raised cattle on his ranch near Boise, Idaho, and tracked the price of hay, which had fallen since his years of complaining about the long grass at Wrigley Field. He hunted elk with a bow and arrow and fished the same streams Hemingway had fished, but whenever he left the ranch people only wanted to talk about his error in the World Series—not about his batting title or his 2,715 hits or how he'd played through pain for so many years. At an auction in 1992, the actor Charlie Sheen paid $93,500 for the ball that had gone between Buckner's legs. (Broadcaster Keith Olbermann lost with a bid of $47,000.) Reporters asked Buckner, then working as hitting coach for the Triple-A Syracuse Chiefs, about the sale. "No comment," he said.

The Chiefs fired him because he couldn't get along with the manager. From then on, every public appearance seemed to be about his error against the Mets. "That's a dead horse," he said. He was signing autographs at a card show one day when a fan piped up: "Don't ask him to sign that ball, he'll just drop it!" Buckner signed the ball, stood up, took hold of the guy's lapels, and lifted him off the ground. Suddenly the loudmouth had nothing to say.

Buckner hadn't seen Mookie Wilson for almost a decade when they crossed paths before a game in New York. It was awkward at first. Then Buckner said, "Want to hit me some grounders?" Wilson laughed.

In July 1999, during Hall of Fame Weekend in Cooperstown, New York, Pete Rose sat at a card table in a Cooperstown memorabilia shop. George Brett, Nolan Ryan, and Robin Yount were to be inducted into the Hall that Sunday. Rose planned to leave town before the ceremony—"It's their day, not mine"—but for now he was still hustling, signing balls and bats for cash.

During lulls between handshakes and autographs, he denied ever betting on baseball. Yes, he'd agreed to a suspension, but when he and Giamatti negotiated the ban, "They said it'd be twenty-two years till I could apply for reinstatement. We got it down to eleven, then to one year, and that's when I signed." Then Giamatti died. The Hall's board of directors promptly passed a new rule: players who were suspended from the game were no longer eligible for induction. Fay Vincent, the new commissioner and a Hall of Fame board member, claimed with a straight face that the rule wasn't aimed at Pete Rose.

"I'll kiss your ass if that's true," Rose said, adding that Hall of Famers like Ty Cobb and Babe Ruth "weren't altar guys." Still, Vincent's successor, Bud Selig, wouldn't return his phone calls. Why? Rose swore he'd quit betting illegally and associating with crooks. "Bart Giamatti told me to reconfigure my life, and I have."

Had he? Five years later, in 2004, he finally admitted that he had bet on baseball when he was managing the Reds. He then stooped to signing balls a new way: *I'm sorry I bet on baseball.* (Available at Amazon and eBay for $89 to $242.49.) A decade later he would show off his still-keen baseball mind as a TV commentator for Fox Sports, but he lost that gig after a former girlfriend revealed that they'd had an affair during his playing days, before she turned sixteen.

Rose turned seventy-seven years old in 2018. Still a hero in Cincinnati and at memorabilia shows where fans paid a hundred dollars for an autographed ball and a handshake, he was asked which he thought was worse, steroids or gambling on baseball. He took a few seconds to think about it.

"I'll say steroids were worse than *my* gambling," he said. In his view, "one sacred thing baseball has is its history," and steroids changed the game's history in a way his betting never did. "There's nothing worse than gambling on your team to lose, but I bet on my team to win."

BUCKNER WAS LATE to the memorabilia market but liked what he discovered there. At one card show he told a *Boston Globe* reporter, "I made more money this weekend than I did in my rookie year—ten thousand five hundred." In New York he raked in more than $70,000 in two days of signing his name. The market heated up further in 2011, the silver anniversary of his error. He and Mookie Wilson appeared together on CBS's *The Early Show*. They signed everything in sight. They joked that they should have tracked down the ball that went through Buckner's legs and claimed it when they had the chance. Instead, Charlie Sheen wound up selling it to a buyer who resold it for $418,250.

Both men were puzzled to see their careers boil down to one play. Billy Buck had a better career—twenty-two years with a career average of .289 and a batting title to Mookie's twelve years and .274—but Wilson stole 327 bases and played a key role in the World Series that had the highest TV ratings ever recorded. Even so, he said, "It's like all I ever did was hit a ground ball."

Revisiting the '86 Series was less pleasant for Buckner. When a *Boston Globe* writer asked if he had "learned any karmic lessons" over the years, he said, "Catch the ball, I guess."

He went on to appear in a 2011 episode of HBO's comedy *Curb Your Enthusiasm*. In the show, Larry David lets a grounder go through his legs in a softball game. Buckner consoles him. Buckner graciously reaches for a ball to sign for Larry and drops the ball. But this time he redeems himself. At the end, Buckner saves the day by catching a baby thrown from a burning building.

MOORE AND THE SPLIT

Donnie Moore didn't have to wait long to find out if the Cubs wanted him back after his lackluster 1979. Two weeks after the season ended, they traded him to St. Louis.

Moore proved himself to the Cardinals in spring training. They made him part of their 1980 bullpen, but once the season began he couldn't get anybody out, and they sent him to the minors.

Still only twenty-six, he felt like a failure. After pitching for crowds of thirty or forty thousand in the big leagues, and millions more on cable, he labored in dollar-beer ballparks in Evansville, Indianapolis, Omaha, Des Moines, Denver, Wichita, and Oklahoma City. The Triple-A Springfield Redbirds played home games at Robin Roberts Stadium, a gussied-up high school field where the Phillies' ace of the 1950s and '60s had once pitched for Lanphier High. The park held forty-five hundred but was often half empty. Sometimes seventy-four-year-old Satchel Paige, a Redbirds vice president and goodwill ambassador, sat in the stands with his old Homestead Grays teammate Josh Johnson.

As a starter for the Redbirds, Moore went 6-5 with a 3.07 ERA. His fastball and slider were too much for minor-league hitters. The big club showed how little that meant by selling his contract to the Milwaukee

Brewers in the middle of the next season. After a brief audition there (four innings, three runs), the Brewers sent him back to the Cardinals, who flipped him to the Atlanta Braves in 1982 for another minor-league pitcher. That was the trade that changed his life.

The Braves didn't want him, either. They assigned Moore to their Triple-A club in Richmond, Virginia, where he continued to pitch like a minor-league ace against younger hitters like the Syracuse Chiefs' George Bell and Tony Fernandez, the Columbus Clippers' first baseman Steve Balboni, and Balboni's twenty-one-year-old backup, Don Mattingly. Moore wasn't well regarded enough for Richmond's starting rotation, so he pitched out of the bullpen. He began to drink more after losses. And after wins. His wife, Tonya, reminded him to stay positive. She told him he was still blessed. How many men had an arm like his? One in a million. She told him to keep believing in himself—that's how he'd get back to the big leagues.

Moore had been a jealous husband in Lubbock, Chicago, Springfield, and everywhere else. It got worse when he drank. If he and Tonya went to a team party, he kept a sharp eye on her. He told teammates to address her as "Mrs. Moore." Tonya tried to laugh it off, but he was serious. She'd be in trouble if he caught her flirting, he said.

Moore knew he needed more than confidence and the best-looking wife in the International League. He needed a third pitch. His fastball and slider were enough in Triple-A, but not enough against major-league hitters. He had tried every changeup grip in the book, but nothing worked. Finally he returned to the split-finger pitch he'd tried five years before. He stuffed the ball between his index and middle fingers and threw it like a fastball.

Johnny Sain, the Braves' pitching coach, saw him throwing the splitter in the bullpen and asked if he used it during games. Moore shook his head.

"Well, you should," Sain said. "It's a hell of a pitch." And this wasn't any old pitching coach saying so. This was the Boston Braves right-hander who'd teamed with Warren Spahn on the mound and in the immortal line about the perfect pitching rotation: "Spahn and Sain and two days of rain." Sain had been the first major-league hurler to face Jackie Robinson. He'd been a twenty-game winner four times. Now sixty-four, he was jowly, slow-moving, and a little stooped, but still opinionated as hell. When Moore said he didn't trust the pitch enough to use it in games, Sain told him to wake up. "That's why you're in Triple-A," he said. "You should be working on it. Throw it."

Moore tried. He threw it and threw it until something clicked. Now, when he released the ball with a hard downward flap of the wrist, as if he were swatting a fly, it nose-dived like Bruce Sutter's splitter. Sharply. Consistently. The Richmond Braves made him their closer. Atlanta called him up for the second half of the 1983 season; he finished sixteen games and saved half a dozen, pitching well enough to make the big-league roster in 1984.

That was the year Atlanta manager Joe Torre called Donnie Moore aside. "I want you to be our closer," Torre said.

Donnie and Tonya rejoiced. Conaway Moore installed a satellite dish at his little house in Lubbock so he could watch his son pitch on superstation WTBS.

Moore saved sixteen games for the '84 Braves and had a 2.94 ERA. Former closers Steve Bedrosian, Gene Garber, and Terry Forster served as his setup men. Still, the Braves lost him after the season. Under the game's fast-evolving free agency rules, teams that lost a premier "Type A" free agent got a consolation prize: a pick in a postseason "supplemental draft." Each club was allowed to protect twenty-four to twenty-six players; anyone else was pluckable. The Braves left Moore unprotected because he was a thirty-year-old journeyman with one good season to his name.

The California Angels had lost outfielder Fred Lynn when Baltimore signed him as a free agent for $6.8 million. That gave them first choice in the supplemental draft, and here is where luck or answered prayers gave Donnie Moore's career a boost. The Braves had fired Torre, who signed on with the Angels as a TV commentator. Torre told Angels owner Gene Autry and general manager Mike Port how much he liked Donnie Moore. The Angels made him their supplemental draft choice. It was a move they would celebrate until they regretted it.

CALIFORNIA ANGELS OWNER Autry, the seventy-seven-year-old singing cowboy of old-time radio and TV, was tickled to shake hands with the new arrival. "A fellow Texan!" said Autry, whose residuals from hits like "Back in the Saddle Again" and the original 1949 recording of "Rudolph the Red-Nosed Reindeer" helped pay for the team.

Autry had lost his manager when John McNamara left to join the Red Sox. His new hire was an old one: Gene Mauch, the snakebit skipper of the famously folding 1964 Phillies. The fifty-nine-year-old Mauch, often called the best manager never to have won a pennant, was as lean and hungry as ever. One of his first moves was a phone call to Donnie Moore.

"We can win our division," Mauch said, "and I want you to be our stopper." Moore signed a one-year, $407,500 contract that turned out to be a bargain for the Angels.

As California's closer in 1985, he blew away American League hitters. He wasn't sure why, but after years of topping out at ninety-three or ninety-four miles an hour, his fastball occasionally reached ninety-seven. His splitter—the pitch that made his wife give up catching—was one of the deadliest in the American League. That July, he was the Angels' only All-Star.

He and Tonya could barely believe their good fortune. They hobnobbed with baseball royalty over the All-Star break in Minneapolis, Donnie getting handshakes and pats on the back. Look, there's Nolan Ryan! Dwight Gooden! Pete Rose! Moore's heart was pounding when American League All-Star manager Sparky Anderson sent him into the game in the seventh inning, but he was ready. His split was working. His two All-Star innings went like this:

Jack Clark grounded out. Willie McGee grounded out. Dave Parker grounded out.

Tim Wallach struck out. Pete Rose grounded out. Ozzie Smith flied out.

After thirteen up-and-down years in pro ball, Moore was a celebrity. When a *Sports Illustrated* writer asked Mauch to pick the MVP of his first-place Angels, he said, "Donnie is the one most responsible for our success." The magazine described the Angels' closer as "one of the best slam-the-door relievers in baseball . . . a burly, pleasant man who much prefers to talk about his team rather than himself." The magazine even gave Moore the last word on his success: "Maybe I'm just a survivor."

Moore finished the 1985 season with thirty-one saves, a 1.92 ERA, and an owner who sure looked smart for signing him. Autry rewarded him with a three-year, $3 million contract.

It was more than Donnie and Tonya from South Lubbock ever imagined. They splurged on an $850,000 house on an acre and a half in the hills east of the Big A, Anaheim Stadium. The Moores' dream house had a swimming pool, a trampoline for the kids, and a private lake he stocked with catfish. Tonya looked after their fourteen-year-old daughter, Demetria, and her brothers, Donnie Jr. and Ronnie. Donnie drove a black Mercedes he kept to a mirror shine. Sometimes he'd bring his friend and teammate Reggie Jackson home for dinner.

The man of the house often strode around in purple shoes and purple satin warm-up pants, compliments of an endorsement deal with Puma. He was by all appearances a good husband and father. "Every morning when the team was home, I'd kiss him on the cheek as I went off to school," recalled Demetria. "Sometimes he'd come with me for Show and Tell, and talk about being a baseball player. He was sponsored by Bubble Yum, and he'd bring a bunch of whatever new flavor they had. Everybody wanted to be my friend."

"Donnie was low-key," said Randall Johnson, Moore's attorney. "But there was a side of him most people didn't see. At home, he was volatile."

Moore was a mean drunk. After the fifteen-minute drive home from Anaheim Stadium, win or lose, he'd pour himself a whiskey, down it, and pour another. On off days he'd drain a bottle of Jack Daniel's.

Tonya learned to stay out of his way when the bottle was running low. She still thought her husband was a good man. It was the combination of Donnie and Jack that scared her.

Teammates knew he was a wife beater. They saw the bruises on Tonya, though he never hit her in the face—he didn't want to ruin her looks. During one clubhouse confrontation George Hendrick, the Angels' six-foot-three outfielder, challenged Moore to fight him instead. "You want to *hit* somebody?" Hendrick said, getting within inches of the pitcher's face. But Moore kept his cool, the threat passed, and he went home to Tonya.

If she spoke at the wrong time, he hit her. If a teammate, waiter, or gas station attendant smiled in what seemed to him a flirty way, he waited until he had some fire in his belly and hit her.

At first her flirtations were all in his mind. "I never looked at another man," she remembered. He always apologized afterward for giving her a beating. Sometimes he cried like the kid he'd been when he got a beating.

She stayed because she loved him. She also worried that if she left, "he would find me and kill me." One day he told her that if she ever cheated on him, he'd tie rocks around her and throw her in the pool. "That's why I took swimming lessons," she said.

His arm hurt. The team trainer told him not to worry about it. A cortisone shot in the elbow helped, but he felt twinges under the numbness.

By then the splitter Bruce Sutter made famous had become the Pitch of the Eighties. Tony Gwynn, Wade Boggs, Keith Hernandez, Steve Garvey, and *Sports Illustrated* all said so. Dozens of pitchers around the majors tried it. For a few, most of them blessed with long fingers, it was a magic bullet. The Tigers' Jack Morris threw split after split while winning twenty games in 1983 and nineteen the next year. "Morris was already a good pitcher. With the split-finger, he's a great one," said Tigers pitching coach Roger Craig, who became the game's split-finger guru after Fred Martin died in 1979. (Soon the Tigers' whole pitching staff was throwing the pitch.) In 1984, after pitching a pair of complete games to lead Detroit to its first World Series title in sixteen years, Morris wondered aloud if Babe Ruth could have hit his split. "I've seen Ty Cobb swing on film, and I know he couldn't have," Morris said.

In 1986, *Sports Illustrated* estimated that half the pitchers in the majors had at least experimented with the splitter. The Mets' Ron Darling developed a good one. Boston's Bruce Hurst went from mediocrity to All-Star after learning the pitch. So did Houston's Mike Scott. At age thirty, Scott had a career record of 29-44 and an equally tepid 4.49 ERA. After mastering the split he enjoyed five seasons as one of the game's dominant starters, with three All-Star appearances, a Cy Young Award, and a no-hitter (the only no-hitter ever to clinch a division title). According to minor-league pitcher-turned-sportswriter Pat Jordan, Scott made the pitch "an art form. His oversize hands allow him to get a comfortable grip on the ball for better control, and he can throw it with consistently high speed, usually in the mid-80s. More important, perhaps, was the realization that he had to surrender his career to the pitch."

Old-timers said the trendy new weapon was a forkball by another name. In fact it was thrown harder, with the ball between the fingers rather than farther back toward the palm. *Sports Illustrated* reported that it was also easier on the arm, "since throwing it involved none of the twists of elbow and wrist that curveballs and sliders require." A few pitching coaches disagreed. They heard barking coming out of their pitchers' elbows.

Like Scott, Donnie Moore surrendered his career to the pitch. In 1986, the year after his All-Star season, he needed more frequent cortisone shots. He was also getting migraines. "Donnie was quiet. He didn't say much, but there was something going on inside of him," a teammate recalled. "He took things hard, especially bad things." He complained that his back was killing him, but team doctors couldn't find any reason for his back pain. (It would take more than a year for them to discover a bone spur the size of a quarter near his spinal cord.) Even so, he pitched almost as well as he had the year before, treating the pain with acupuncture and liquor. But the ache in his back made him change his pitching motion, and then his elbow hurt worse.

He spent five weeks on the disabled list in 1986. Still he saved twenty-one games for the Angels, who won the American League West. Whenever the manager asked how he was feeling, Moore said he was good to go.

HIS CATCHER DOUBTED it. "Donnie was hurting," Bob Boone said.

Boone had put his 1980 World Series ring, with its eight diamonds in the Phillies' capital-P logo and a ruby in the middle, in a safe-deposit box for his kids. Boone expected to be a Phillie for life, but after he hit .211 in '81, the Pope sold the fading thirty-four-year-old catcher to the California Angels for three hundred thousand dollars. Boone was annoyed and a little impressed. "That was pretty good money," he recalled. And he made the Angels pay to keep him. After he took charge of the pitching staff, they rose from fifth place in 1981 to first place in 1982. Coincidence? The Angels didn't want to take the risk of finding out. They paid $2.75 million over three years to keep him.

With Boone calling signals, the Angels won another division title in 1986. To him, Donnie Moore was an elite closer with issues. Not mental issues, like some pitchers. As far as Boone could tell, Moore's troubles were physical. "At his best, Donnie was throwing his fastball in the mid-nineties, using the split like a changeup," he recalled. "Then his back started hurting and affected the split."

Moore used to have mental issues on the mound. He could be indecisive. He'd get a hitter on the ropes with the splitter and want to show off his fastball. With Boone, those issues went away. In California, Moore was happy to let his catcher outthink the other guys. "Pitching to Bob Boone is like a love affair," he said. He never shook off Boone's signals.

Late in 1986, the catcher thought Moore looked like Tug McGraw in 1980—spent. Still he saved Game Three of the American League Championship Series against the Red Sox. He looked shaky in the

eighth inning, balking in a run and allowing another on a Rich Gedman single as the Sox pulled within a run at 4–3. With two out in the
ninth, he faced his old Cubs teammate Bill Buckner, now Boston's first
baseman. Moore got him on a fly ball to end the game.

The Angels won the next night to take a three-games-to-one lead.
After that, Mauch said he had no plans to use his sore-armed closer in
Game Five.

Between games, Moore got another cortisone shot.

Sixty-four thousand fans packed the Big A for Game Five. Boston
took an early 2–0 advantage that Boone cut in half with a solo homer.
The Angels took the lead in the sixth on one of those accidents that can
turn a season or a career upside down. With two out and a runner on
second, Bobby Grich sent a fly ball to the warning track. Red Sox center fielder Dave Henderson drifted back. Henderson was playing only
because Boston's regular center fielder, Tony Armas, had sprained his
ankle earlier in the game. He jumped and caught the ball for the third
out. A split second later his glove bumped against the top of the fence.
The ball popped out and dropped on the far side for a two-run homer.

An inning later, California got two more. They led 5–2 in the ninth.
With Mike Witt on the hill, the Angels were three outs from the first
World Series in their twenty-five-year history. And Gene Mauch was
on the brink of his first pennant. Helmeted security guards stood ready
to keep the fans from storming the field. Champagne was chilling in
the Angels' clubhouse. Mauch stood in the dugout next to DH Reggie
Jackson, who put an arm around the manager as if to say, *We got this.*

But the Red Sox weren't finished yet. Buckner hobbled to the plate
and led off the ninth with a single. Boston manager John McNamara,
who'd given Mauch his chance by leaving the Angels for the Red Sox
job, sent Dave Stapleton in to run for Buckner.

Jim Rice struck out. Don Baylor, the Red Sox' massive DH, known
for crowding the plate and getting hit by pitches, leaned out and golfed
an outside curveball over the left-field fence.

Mauch looked stunned. He left Witt in to face Dwight Evans, who
popped out to third. Two out. Now Mauch sent his pitching coach,

Marcel Lachemann, to the mound. It was Lachemann who waved his left hand toward the bullpen. In came left-hander Gary Lucas to secure the last out.

It was the right move. The next hitter, Rich Gedman, had batted .282 against right-handed pitching that year, but only .186 against lefties. Lucas had struck him out in Game Four. In three career at-bats against Lucas, Gedman had struck out all three times. But even the best stats are no guarantee of future performance. Lucas plunked him with his first pitch. Gedman was the first batter Lucas had hit in his seven-year career.

With right-hand-hitting Dave Henderson coming up, Mauch once again played the percentages, calling for Donnie Moore to nail down the victory.

None of the Angels had expected to see Moore come into the game. According to third baseman Doug DeCinces, "He wasn't supposed to pitch." DeCinces challenged Lachemann on the mound, asking, "What's going on?"

"It's not my move," Lachemann said. "Gene's making the move."

Moore took the ball. He always took the ball. Sixty-four thousand voices cheered him on. A TV camera caught Tonya in the wives' section, praying. In the dugout, Reggie Jackson folded his cap and put his glasses in his pocket, expecting a riot any minute.

Moore threw a fastball low, then blew two more past Henderson, the substitute outfielder who had barely played in a month. One more strike and the fireworks could start. After a taste pitch outside, he looked past Henderson for his catcher's sign. Four fingers. Boone wanted a split to finish him off.

Henderson swung over the ball but got a piece of it to stay alive.

Boone called for another split, but Moore had a flicker of doubt. Why not blow another fastball past him? But he threw what his catcher called. The pitch ducked across the outside corner, knee high, a little higher than he and Boone wanted. Henderson slung the barrel of his bat at it. "*To left field and deep,*" Al Michaels called it for thirty million viewers watching the game on ABC. The ball was carrying. *"And it's gone! Unbelievable! You're looking at one for the ages."*

A 5–2 ninth-inning lead was now a 6–5 deficit. That said, the Angels weren't beaten yet. They still had last ups. But they felt beat. The way the stadium went quiet after Henderson's home run "was almost scary," Grich said. In interviews, Tonya remembered watching the Boston wives hugging and jumping around while she sat there wondering whoever had had the bright idea of seating both teams' wives in the same section.

The Angels tied the score in the last of the ninth and had the bases full with one out, but didn't score again. Moore lost the game on a sacrifice fly in the eleventh. The home fans booed him.

He spent that night thinking and drinking while the kids stayed out of sight. His parents were there for the playoffs along with Tonya's mother, keeping their voices down as if it were a funeral. It was late when Tonya sent her mother to a guest bedroom. "Mama," she said, "whatever you hear, do not come out of this room." If Donnie was going to beat her up, she didn't want her mother to see it.

Instead he stayed quiet that night and in the months ahead. "He brooded over it all winter," Tonya said.

He'd done what a ballplayer was supposed to do. He had pitched hurt, played through pain. But he was the goat—especially after Boston went on to beat the Angels in Games Six and Seven to advance to the 1986 World Series. Like many players, he didn't enjoy watching baseball on TV. It was slow, and the announcers said so many ignorant things. It would have been a special torture to watch the Red Sox against the Mets in that Series, so he never saw Bill Buckner let Mookie Wilson's grounder go through his legs.

The next spring, Moore admitted he wasn't over Game Five yet. Maybe he should have shaken off Boone's sign and thrown a fastball. "More than likely," he told the *Orange County Register*, "I'll think about that until the day I die."

There were scattered boos at the Big A when he pitched, but he saved three Angels victories in April 1987. His earned run average was 2.08. He celebrated saves with three or four cocktails on team flights.

It didn't last. Despite cortisone shots, his elbow hurt almost as much as his back, and now he had a new ache under his ribs. He spent weeks on the disabled list, throwing only twenty-seven innings all season. The Angels, who had been one pitch from the World Series the year before, finished sixth. General manager Mike Port laid some of the blame on Moore. "Instead of whining about his rib cage," Port told reporters, "he should have been out there earning his money. What do we pay him a million dollars for?"

"When I read that, I felt like decking Mike Port," said Moore's teammate and friend Rod Carew.

The next year—the last on his three-year contract—was no better. After that he was a sore-armed thirty-four-year-old free agent. Nobody wanted him. He signed a minor-league deal with the Kansas City Royals, who assigned him to their Triple-A club in Omaha.

Moore hated returning to minor-league life. He paid extra for a single room on road trips—Donnie Moore wasn't rooming with some twenty-year-old kid. But it wasn't all bad. His Omaha teammates nicknamed him "Million Dollars" and treated him like a star. He still had big-league friends like Bill Buckner, who stayed in touch. They went hunting together, a couple of postseason goats stalking ducks.

Moore knew his arm was shot. In twelve minor-league innings in the spring of 1989, he gave up seventeen hits, including three long home runs. "He was throwing his fastball eighty-three to eighty-five miles an hour," Omaha manager Sal Rende said. "He tried to throw the split-finger pitch, but it wasn't effective enough to make up for the lack of velocity."

Rende called his oldest player to his office in June.

"We're releasing you," he said.

Moore nodded.

"He was almost relieved," the manager recalled. "He said he had some things to take care of."

The *Lubbock Journal* reported that Tonya Moore moved out of their California home as soon as she learned that Donnie had been released.

She didn't want to bear the brunt of his disappointment and anger. They had agreed to separate, but Donnie still called Tonya his wife.

"Donnie had problems on top of problems," said Randall Johnson, Moore's attorney. "He'd injured his arm. He had marital problems. Money problems. I'd tried to get him interested in managing his money. I tried to get him into a Popeye's Chicken franchise, but he said no."

Just months after throwing his last big-league pitch, Moore was broke. He had no choice but to sell the house in Anaheim Hills. Tonya was all for it—she had three kids to think about. And so on July 18, she volunteered to show a prospective buyer around the place.

Demetria, a new driver at sixteen, dropped her mother off that morning. Tonya was dressed in a white blouse and skirt. Her husband was there with their sons, ten-year-old Donnie Jr. and eight-year-old Ronnie. Donnie was wearing his purple Puma pants. She could tell he'd been drinking. The buyer never showed up, which aggravated Donnie. Soon he and Tonya were arguing.

Tonya hoped he wouldn't hit her in front of the kids. She phoned Demetria. "Come get me. I need to get the fuck out of here," she said.

She was relieved when Demetria pulled into the driveway again. Donnie loved seeing their daughter. But Donnie didn't see Demetria drive up. He'd gone to another room. He didn't know their daughter was on her way into the house when he came at Tonya with a handgun she'd given him for Christmas.

He shot his wife through the neck and chest. She ran to the laundry room, wounded, with a hole in one lung. He kept shooting.

Tonya staggered to the driveway.

Demetria drove her injured and bleeding mother to the hospital. She would remember "freaking out, trying to stay on the road, and my mom is calming me down. She's saying, 'It's OK, everything will be OK,' trying not to choke on her blood. We get to the hospital and they hand me a clipboard. I said, 'My mother got shot. She's dying!'"

Tonya didn't wait for help. As Demetria pleaded and pointed at her, she got out of the car and walked into the ER.

Donnie sat in the kitchen of his dream house. He had another bullet left. According to Don Ware, a neighbor who hurried over when he heard shots, "Little Donnie comes in the kitchen, screaming and yelling. Ronnie's there, saying, 'What happened? Where's Mom?' Donnie says, 'Don't worry. I'm gonna be with Mommy.' And in front of his kids he shoots himself in the head."

BALL IN THE FAMILY

Donnie Moore's last big-league catcher remembered him at his best. "That first year in California, Donnie was unhittable," Bob Boone said. "I think he was happiest when he was on the mound." Boone didn't know much about Moore's life off the field. He was shocked by the headlines and TV news stories about Moore's suicide, actually an attempted murder-suicide. "I'd rather think of him in the year he had thirty-one saves."

While Moore had been a brooder, Boone was a pragmatist. In baseball, he said, "You can't afford to get down. You don't stop and reflect because there's always somebody coming up to take your job."

Boone batted .295 and won his sixth Gold Glove in 1988, his last season with the Angels. Still they let him go. Who wants a forty-one-year-old catcher?

The Kansas City Royals did. They wanted to make him their everyday catcher. Boone was thrilled, but he hadn't gone through the labor wars with Marvin Miller to take whatever a team offered. He told the Royals he'd be damned if he'd sign for less than the $883,000 the Angels had been paying him. After a quick negotiation, he signed for $883,001.

In his first year with the Royals, Boone hit .274 and won a seventh Gold Glove. He led the American League by throwing out 43 percent of the runners who tried to steal on him. Peter Gammons of *Sports Illustrated* called him "baseball's best catcher," praising him as a fitness pioneer and pitch framer, a term new enough that the magazine had to explain it: "a technique in which a catcher moves his glove gently to catch the ball in the webbing while most of the mitt stays directly behind the strike zone." Gammons wrote that Boone was nearing the end of "a career that makes him a cinch for the Hall of Fame."

Bob Boone played the last of his 2,264 major-league games at the Big A on September 27, 1990, as a member of the visiting Royals. He went two-for-three with a pair of singles off Jim Abbott, retiring with 1,838 hits, a .254 career batting average, and 105 home runs in nineteen big-league seasons. He had caught more games than anyone else in major-league history. (Carlton Fisk and Ivan Rodriguez would later eclipse his record.) He'd caught a perfect game by Mike Witt, who gave Boone much of the credit. Bill James described Boone as a man who "worked as hard to stay in shape as anyone who ever played baseball . . . not much of a hitter, but one of the five greatest defensive catchers of all time."

Sue Boone kept her husband's Gold Glove awards, framed magazine covers, and other mementos in the den where Bret and Aaron had grown up playing keep-away with autographed baseballs. During his playing career, Bob never had time to school them in the game he worked at for a living. Now he could turn more attention to the boys, who had become promising players in their own right, twenty-one and seventeen years old.

"But we weren't looking for tips from Dad," Bret Boone recalled. "I mean, he had a great career as a catcher, but I could *hit*."

Two years after Bob retired, Bret came up from the minors to join the Seattle Mariners, making the Boones the first family to send three generations of players to the big leagues. By then Aaron was a big-league prospect playing for USC, Dave Kingman's alma mater, and third son Matt was a travel-team phenom. "We never pushed the boys to play baseball," Sue Boone said. "We didn't have to." Sue had known she was joining a baseball family when she married Bob. They'd been high school sweethearts, the star athlete and the beauty queen. At Sue's bridal shower her future mother-in-law, Patsy Boone, gave her "a seat cushion, a blanket and thermos for cold nights, a scorebook, and a box of pencils," Sue recalled. "Welcome to the world of baseball wives!"

Bob and Sue's first child was precocious. "Bret started walking at six months," Sue remembered. "When he was two he'd go to the local pool with us, climb up the ladder to the high dive, and jump off." Bret spent hours in the yard, knocking Wiffle balls over the house with his grandpa Ray, then a scout for the Red Sox. Ray said Bret "came out of womb hitting." At age ten the boy had his own Phillies uniform and a highlight at the 1979 All-Star Game: shagging fly balls in the outfield before the game, he caught several behind his back—a trick he'd learned from Tug McGraw—and got an ovation.

Bret would recall his boyhood as "mainly baseball. Gramps and I watched Dad's ballgames on TV while Aaron was crawling around, absorbing whatever it is that makes you live and breathe baseball. The 'It Factor,' I call it. Whatever it is, we had it in our bones."

In 1991, with Bret in the minors and Aaron finishing high school, Sue was glad to have Bob home more often. After twenty years of juggling his career along with the endless duties of rearing three boys, she was thrilled to have her husband around to work on the car or drive Matt to a schoolboy all-star game.

But Bob got antsy being away from the game. A year later he was back on the road, managing the Triple-A Tacoma Tigers. After that he spent a season as the Cincinnati Reds' bench coach, then returned to the majors as manager of the Kansas City Royals in 1995.

The Royals' lineup that year had an average age of thirty-four. They had Wally Joyner at first, Gary Gaetti at third, and Vince Coleman in the outfield—all past their prime. They finished second in the American League Central, but it was a distant second, thirty games behind the Cleveland Indians. After that they got worse. On the day the Royals fired him in 1997, Boone's record as a manager was 181-206.

Asked if he could have done better, he said, "Yeah, if I had a better team."

He followed his father's example and became a scout.

AFTER HIS OWN thirteen-year career ended in 1960, Ray Boone spent decades driving around the Southwest, making thousand-mile circuits of high school, junior college, and college diamonds, panning for the It Factor. Scouts spend years hunting for the one in ten thousand high school stars good enough to climb six rungs of minor-league baseball to the majors. The pay is lousy and the job gets frustrating even for bird dogs with eyes as keen as Ray's. Sometimes you see a raw, gawky teenager oozing It, but you can't convince your bosses to draft him. Sometimes you stick your neck out (some scouts mention another body part) for a kid, putting your good name and maybe your job on the line, and win the argument, only to lose the kid because another team takes him higher in the draft.

For all the dust scouts eat, they have their moments. Ray signed future major leaguers Marty Barrett, Sam Horn, and Phil Plantier, as well as a skinny kid he found pitching for Yavapai College in Arizona. "He liked telling me about Curt Schilling," Bob remembered. "Dad called the front office from Phoenix: 'This kid's only 140 pounds, but when he puts on weight he'll really be something.'" In 1986, on Ray Boone's recommendation, the Red Sox made Schilling their second-round pick in the amateur draft. That left Ray the task of getting the kid to sign. He drove to the Ramada Inn where Cliff Schilling, Curt's father, worked as a desk clerk, and offered fifteen thousand dollars for Curt's signature on a Boston Red Sox contract. It was more than Cliff earned in a year, but Curt wanted more. Finally Ray told the nineteen-year-old pitcher, "Son, if you're as good as we both think you are, fifteen thousand is going to be meal money in a few years. But if you're going to jerk me around, I'm going home."

Curt said, "Where do I sign?"

He went on to a twenty-year career with the Orioles, Astros, Phillies,

Diamondbacks, and Red Sox, winning 216 games and rising to crucial occasions with an 11-2 record and 2.33 ERA in nineteen postseason starts.

In 1998, a dozen years after his father signed Schilling, Bob Boone sat in a room full of Cincinnati Reds scouts. The Reds had the seventh choice in that year's draft of high school and college players. Everyone knew who the top few players off the board would be: Philadelphia was going to take Pat Burrell, with Mark Mulder going to the A's and Corey Patterson to the Cubs. After that the draft got interesting. "Everybody was loving Austin Kearns," Boone recalled. Kearns was a Kentucky phenom who'd batted .577 at Lexington's Lafayette High School. But Boone had his own "pick to click," as he called his hunches. The Reds' general manager, Jim Bowden, asked each scout for his top choice. "Everybody says Austin Kearns. Until it's my turn," Boone recalled. He had a hunch about a pitcher at Vallejo High in the Bay Area. "So it's Kearns, Kearns, Kearns. Finally it comes around to me. I said, 'C.C. Sabathia.'" The Reds chose Kearns, who went on to have a fine rookie season and a respectable if unspectacular major-league career. Meanwhile, Sabathia was still going strong in 2018, a 246-game winner. Boone went on to rib Bowden for years: "Hey, did you see C.C. last night?"

Bowden admitted no regrets. "It was just business," he recalled of the 1998 draft. "Bob got outvoted."

Boone got another chance to manage in 2001, when Bowden and Reds CEO Carl Lindner Jr. handed him the keys to an improving Reds team that had Ken Griffey Jr. in center field, Barry Larkin at short, Sean Casey at first, and a part-time third baseman named Aaron Boone.

"Playing for Dad was weird at first," Aaron recalled. Still, he hit .294 with fourteen home runs and sixty-two RBIs for his dad's team. What bothered him was hearing his father get booed as the Reds finished fifth in 2001 and third in 2002.

The *Cincinnati Enquirer* thought the manager deserved a few boos. Boone was "stubborn," the paper reported. He tried "unorthodox managerial moves, using power hitter Adam Dunn and slow-footed Sean Casey as leadoff hitters, and going to a four-man pitching rotation." In fact he was ahead of his time. Dunn had an on-base percentage of .400 that season. Casey reached base almost as often, but on-base percentage was a little-known stat. The Reds' fifth starters had a combined ERA of 5.55. But no stack of printouts outweighed a losing record.

Boone expected to turn the Reds around in 2003. Then Griffey dislocated his shoulder in April and Larkin strained muscles in both legs. Still the stubborn Reds stayed close to the lead in the National League Central. On July 2, with Griffey and Larkin back in a lineup featuring Dunn, Jose Guillen, Aaron Boone, and Austin Kearns, Cincinnati pulled within two and a half games of first place.

Two weeks later, Aaron Boone represented the Reds at the All-Star Game in Chicago. Big brother Bret was there for the Mariners. They posed for pictures with former All-Stars Bob and Ray. The first family to send three generations to the big leagues was now the first with four All-Stars.

Ray's health was failing. He soon suffered what he called "a little heart attack. But it'll take more than that to bring a Boone down."

BOB BOONE'S REDS were in the thick of the division race as the season's second half began. Then the bottom fell out. Griffey ruptured his Achilles tendon on a play at the plate. Kearns, woozy from a home-plate collision, was reduced to pinch-hitting. The Reds lost eight straight. They saved Boone's job with a three-game sweep in Milwaukee, then lost eight of nine.

Nobody tells a manager he's in trouble, but he knows. The weather changes in the clubhouse. It gets quieter while everybody waits to hear his last words. For Boone, one of the worst things about getting fired was getting asked about it beforehand. He knew the front office was looking for his replacement, but he was still the club's main spokesman. When reporters asked if he expected to get fired, he had to play PR man. As he recalled his duties in his last days in Cincinnati, they included saying, "We'll take 'em one at a time. We're looking for a winning streak, blah blah."

Boone never minded talking to the press. He was a newspaper reader and crossword puzzler, a Stanford psychology grad who had almost quit baseball for medical school. He stayed with baseball after Marvin Miller and the players' union made ballplayers richer than doctors. But the PR side of management was making him feel more like his old friend Dave Kingman.

When the axe fell, he shook hands with reporters on his way out of Cincinnati's Great American Ball Park. This time he wasn't talking. "I might say something I shouldn't," he said.

"Bob Boone was the consummate professional," said Reds COO John Allen, speaking for the team. "I have tremendous respect for Bob as a person."

The Reds' third baseman was relieved the drama was over. "I don't think he's been treated the best. Everything was always his fault," Aaron said of his father. "Now he gets to go home and see his grandkids and do normal, less stressful things."

Instead, Bob stepped up his workouts. According to Bret, who hit thirty-five homers for the Mariners that year, "Dad's hair was starting to go gray but he'd still bench-press his weight with ease. He'd knock out five hundred sit-ups, take a coffee break, and do five hundred more." Bob Boone had played two decades in the majors without spending a day on the disabled list. He'd played with torn cartilage in both knees. He'd broken a finger on his throwing hand, taped it to the next finger, and still led the league in throwing out baserunners. His sons remembered the day Bob built them a backyard swing set. "He was almost done when his back seized up," said Bret. "Dad fell down like he'd been shot. Greg Luzinski had to carry him to the car. But he played that night and got two hits."

FOUR DAYS AFTER firing his dad, the Reds traded Aaron to the New York Yankees. Three months later, with the Yankees facing the Red Sox in the 2003 American League Championship Series, Aaron was batting .125 in the series, two-for-sixteen.

Before Game Seven, Aaron's wife, Laura, let Bret into the New York hotel room they were calling home. Laura, *Playboy*'s Miss October 1998, was now a full-time mom and part-time counselor for her slumping husband. "He's having a tough time," she told her brother-in-law.

Aaron told Bret he was scuffling. "I've lost my swing."

"I wanted to shake him," Bret remembered. "I told him, 'Wake up! Are you gonna sit there like a little bitch?'"

Bret headed to Yankee Stadium. His Mariners hadn't made the playoffs, so he was serving as a color commentator for Fox Sports. Once he got to the booth he saw that Aaron wasn't in the lineup. Yankees manager Joe Torre had replaced him at third base with Enrique Wilson, a .230 hitter.

The Yanks trailed 5–2 in the eighth, and the Red Sox looked to be on the way to their first World Series since 1986. Derek Jeter, sitting next to Aaron in the dugout, told him not to worry. Weren't they wearing the same pinstripes as Ruth, Gehrig, DiMaggio, and Mantle? "The ghosts'll show up eventually," Jeter said. Sure enough, the Yankees came back to tie the game.

Aaron went into the game in the ninth. He led off the eleventh against Red Sox knuckleballer Tim Wakefield.

Bob and Matt Boone were sitting in a hunting lodge in Montana, watching the game on TV. They jumped as Aaron pulled a knuckler high and deep to left, raising his hands as the ball carried into the seats. Bob and Matt hugged and danced. Bret, sitting in the Fox booth with Joe Buck and his dad's old teammate Tim McCarver, stood up. Overcome with emotion, listening to the cheers for his brother, he heard the director's voice in his earpiece: "Say something!" For once the chattiest Boone couldn't speak.

Aaron, the quiet one, told reporters in the winners' clubhouse, "I can't even talk."

That night, standing on a table in a Manhattan bar, Bret raised his drink. He looked around at Jeter, Torre, Roger Clemens, Mariano Rivera, Jason Giambi, Andy Pettitte, and the rest of the team. "Gentlemen," he said, "for one night, and one night only, I am proud to be known as 'Aaron Boone's brother.'"

The Boone men compete with one another as much as with anyone else. After Aaron's epic homer, the Boones' greatest hit in the fifty-five years since Ray broke in with the Cleveland Indians, Bob said he wasn't all that impressed. "That knuckleball from Wakefield didn't knuckle. I mean, *I* could have hit that ball out."

Bret disagreed. "Dad never had Aaron's power. I'm saying warning track for Dad, *maybe.*"

AFTER THE SEASON, Aaron signed a $5.75 million deal to return to the Yankees in 2004. A month after that, he blew out his knee playing basketball, a game specifically banned in his new contract. He could lie—tell the Yankees he tripped—in hopes of saving the contract. "That never occurred to me," he said. He phoned Bob and then called Yankees general manager Brian Cashman to confess what had happened.

Cashman voided his contract. Aaron was out $5.75 million. To replace him, the Yankees traded for the Texas Rangers' Alex Rodriguez. Meanwhile, Aaron missed the season but hooked on with the Cleveland Indians for 2005. He would go on to play for the Indians, Florida Marlins, and Washington Nationals before signing with the Houston Astros. He was going through a routine physical before the 2009 season when tests showed a faulty valve in his heart. "It hits home," he told reporters. Before undergoing open-heart surgery, he wrote a letter to his four-year-old son, Brandon, to say how much he loved him.

Aaron came back to go 0-for-13 for the Astros that season and retired with a slash line of .263/.326/.425 in twelve seasons, with 126 homers and 555 RBIs, the least of the big-league Boones.

As for Bret, he had troubles of his own after his brother's pennant-winning home run. In 2005 Jose Canseco named Bret as one of his fellow steroid abusers. In his book *Juiced*, Canseco told of a 2001 spring-training game when he slid into second and got a look at Bret's new, improved muscles. He recounted an exchange that went like this:

Canseco: "Oh my God. What have you been doing?"

Boone: "Shhh. Don't tell anybody."

Reporters pointed out that Canseco had never reached second base in any game between their teams that spring. Asked about that discrepancy on the *Today* show, Canseco said, "Um . . . they may have made a mistake in the actual book, but this incident did happen."

Bret admitted to having taken greenies "and a ton of supplements." He acknowledged that he was also a heavy drinker, a "for-real alcoholic" who put booze in Pepsi cans to sip in the dugout. But he swore he never juiced. "If I knew I could use steroids, hit better, and get away with it, I might have done it," he said. "I mean, substances have been part of baseball since the invention of the spitball. But I was scared of getting caught. Getting exposed would mess up everything I cared about. My career. My family."

BOB BOONE SAW his family through four decades in the majors and the death of his father, Ray, in 2004 at the age of eighty-one. One key to lasting so long, he said, was keeping his feelings in check. "You train yourself to keep an even keel." Especially as a catcher. The catcher has to hit, field, throw 127-foot strikes to second base, and be field general, cheerleader, and psychologist for a rotating cast of pitchers, some hurt, some moody, some crazy.

He stayed close to Tug McGraw, who retired in 1984 and was diagnosed with brain cancer twenty years later. When Boone visited him in the hospital, he ribbed McGraw about the day Tug brought an eleven-year-old kid into the clubhouse. "Spittin' image!" Boone recalled, laughing. Tug had finally accepted Timmy Smith as his son in 1984, when the kid was seventeen. To Tug's surprise, Tim McGraw—the name Tim reclaimed after Tug admitted he was Tim's father—went on to become one of the biggest stars in country music. They appeared on magazine covers as father and son. "Timmy is a nice, courteous, respectful young man," Tug said. Obviously he didn't take after his father. "His mother, Betty, has the credit for that." Tim had gone to Northeastern Louisiana University on a baseball scholarship, and it was on the campus in Monroe where he tried strumming a friend's guitar. He'd sung in choirs growing up, but this was more to his liking. Tim McGraw dropped out of college and drove to Nashville, where his first demo led to a record deal that would lead to twenty-five number-one singles on *Billboard*'s country charts. Tug called the latest chapter of his family story "crazy."

Tug McGraw was fifty-eight when headaches led to the worst possible news: he had a brain tumor. In his last public appearance, he walked to the mound at Veterans Stadium on September 28, 2003, to throw out the last ball. The Vet was set to be demolished as the Phillies moved to the new Citizens Bank Park.

Tug died three months later. Tim spread some of his ashes on the field before a Phillies game.

Tim McGraw stayed in touch with some of his father's old teammates. He made sure Bob Boone and his family had good seats the night they went to one of his concerts.

Boone was enjoying himself that night until Tim began singing his number-one single "Live Like You Were Dying," a song he wrote for his father. As Tim sang in front of a video showing highlights of Tug on the mound, "I lost my even keel a little," Bob admitted. "Okay, I cried like a baby."

Pragmatic as ever at seventy, Boone learned a lesson that night.

"I'm not going to any more concerts."

BOONE ROSE TO his current post, vice president of player development for the Washington Nationals, in 2011. At the team's spring-training meetings, where executives introduce themselves to the players, he says, "I'm the vice president of making guys better."

Boone flies and drives to the Nationals' minor-league locations, watching hitters in the batting cage, reminding them, "Snap your hips."

As for pitchers, "We're going to give them all Tommy John surgery, just to get it over with," he says. He's joking.

Asked if any aspect of the game was better in his playing days, he said, "How about everything?" The players he sees coming up from the minors may be bigger and stronger, but they've had help, too. "Bats are harder and the balls are juiced," he said. Talk of baseball's so-called three true outcomes—home run, strikeout, walk—spurs a simple answer: "Doubles are good, too." And don't get him started on shifts. "I'd like to see you try shifting on the 1980 Phillies. We'd beat you with singles all day. Today they can't hit a ground ball the other way. Or won't."

Boone's latest pick to click was Ian Sagdal, a sixteenth-rounder out of Washington State University. In 2018 Sagdal batted .319 to lead the Class-A Carolina League. And Bob had his eye on an even younger player, Princeton infielder Jake Boone, Bret's son. "It's too early to tell" if Jake might become the game's first fourth-generation major leaguer, Bob said. "But he's got talent."

Meanwhile, Aaron Boone finished his first season managing the New York Yankees in 2018, leading them to a 100-win season and a wildcard berth. For Bob, that meant questions about which team he'd pull for if his Nationals ever faced the Yankees in the World Series. His answer: "Washington, obviously. But my wife will be for the Yankees."

THE LAST TIME Bob Boone visited the Baseball Hall of Fame, he met up with Bret and Bret's eleven-year-old twins, Judah and Isaiah. The twins swung a couple of Babe Ruth's huge bats. They pointed at the baggy "pajamas" players wore in their great-grandfather's day. They saw their uncle Aaron's home-run bat from 2003. After that they rounded a corner and came across a box score on the wall: the 23–22 slugfest at Wrigley Field the *New York Times* dubbed "the wildest game in modern history."

Bret ran his finger down to the seventh slot in the Phillies' lineup: BOONE 4 2 3 5. "There's your grandpa," he told the twins. "Three-for-four with five RBIs. The wind was blowing out like crazy."

EPILOGUE:
MONEY, METRICS, AND MUSIC

Today's Wrigley Field is the hub of a neighborhood called Wrigleyville. When real estate agents coined the term in the 1970s, they thought it beat the previous name, Lakeview. They were right. Today, real estate near the ballpark is some of the priciest on the North Side. Motorists still park in nearby driveways and side streets, but now it costs forty dollars instead of five.

The first sign of Wrigley Field from any approach is the banks of lights over the grandstand. After forty years as the only major-league park without them, Wrigley got lights in 1988. They turn the sky purplish white on game nights. Music blares from open-air pubs—there are forty-four bars in a four-block radius. Vendors hawk RIZZO and BRYANT jerseys. The lights, music, and crowds give the old neighborhood a Las Vegas vibe. A city block on the west side of Clark Street has been razed to make room for the high-end Hotel Zachary, named for Wrigley Field architect Zachary Taylor Davis. A block from there stands the sprawling Budweiser Brickhouse Tavern (Homerun Nachos $14, Margarita Pitchers $36), named for WGN announcer Jack Brickhouse, who died in 1998. Around the corner, a sign on a stadium wall reads CHICAGO CUBS, WORLD SERIES CHAMPIONS 1907 1908 2016.

On Waveland and Sheffield Avenues, tar-paper roofs where fans once held cookouts have been replaced by rooftop bleachers co-owned by the Cubs. The owners of a dozen apartment buildings warred with the team until 2004, when they agreed to share revenue. Fifteen years later the Wrigley Rooftops aren't apartment buildings anymore. They are four- and five-story sports bars full of HD monitors and memorabilia, with bleacher seats on top—another part of Wrigleyville's conversion from a lived-in neighborhood to a theme park devoted to the Cubs. The Ricketts family, which made its fortune in finance, bought the team in 2009 for $875 million, spent another $850 million modernizing the park, and now owns eleven of the buildings beyond the outfield walls.

Before one night game in 2018, ballhawk Rich Buhrke sat in a folding chair at the corner of Waveland and Kenmore. He remembered seeing Dave Kingman's sixth-inning blast come over the bleachers forty years ago. "I got outrun for that one," said Buhrke, now seventy-one years old and dressed in a Cubs cap and a sweatshirt with WRIGLEYVILLE over his heart. He still chased home-run balls to sell to fans. "I've lost a step, but I make up for it in anticipation," he said.

Inside the old ballpark, the ivy Bill Veeck planted in 1937 still eats an occasional ground-rule double, but the nets that kept crumbling mortar from conking Cub fans are long gone. In today's Wrigley, even the old-fashioned steel-trough urinals in the men's rooms gleam. A 4,600-square-foot Jumbotron outshines the old manual scoreboard. A playing field manicured down to the quarter inch makes bad hops a rarity, though you may wonder about the clouds of dust kicked up by base stealers. For years, Cub fans have sneaked loved ones' ashes into the park and strewn them on the field while groundskeepers looked the other way.

Attendance now averages almost three times the 14,952 who turned out on Thursday, May 17, 1979. Today's fans, who pay from $49 to $119 for bleacher seats, hardly ever get into fights. The bleacher bums of the '70s used to get bored during blowouts and chant back and forth: "Left field sucks!" "Right field sucks!" "Rain sucks!" They might have chanted worse at the fat cats in luxury boxes if there had been luxury boxes then. Today's Cub Suites on the mezzanine level rent for $9,000 to $13,000 per game. On the other hand, the old bleacher bums might say it's better to win.

In 2011 the Ricketts family hired general manager Theo Epstein away from the Red Sox. Epstein was the very model of the modern general manager, a Yale grad conversant in economics, sabermetrics, two-seam and four-seam grips, and clubhouse politics. His Red Sox had broken their own curse in 2004, when the thirty-year-old Epstein was the game's youngest general manager. He jumped to Chicago for a record $18.5 million over five years. Five years later the Cubs finally broke the Curse of the Billy Goat: they beat Ray Boone's old Cleveland Indians to win their first World Series since 1908. All three of their home games in the 2016 Series were night games.

The Cubs are now overdogs—a normal big-market franchise that behaves like one. They pay top dollar for free agents. Manager Joe Maddon deploys pitchers in unusual ways dictated by deep stats, and uses shifts as often as any major-league manager. The Cubs contend year after year. Some of their success is likely due to the fact that thirty-five to forty-three of their eighty-one home games each year are played at night. At least Maddon thinks so. He wants more night baseball at Wrigley Field. "Night games benefit us. I just want my players to be rested," says Maddon, who sometimes greets reporters before day games by saying, "Good yawning."

AFTER EXORCISING THEIR demons in 1980, thanks to heroics from Mike Schmidt, Steve Carlton, Pete Rose, and Tug McGraw, the Phillies lost to the Montreal Expos in a divisional playoff the following year. They lost the 1983 World Series to the Baltimore Orioles, and soon returned to last place. From 1987 through 2000 they had a winning record in only one season, 1993, when a Phillies team led by Curt Schilling, John Kruk, Lenny Dykstra, and Mitch Williams captured the National League pennant. (They lost the '93 World Series when Williams, with

'79 Phillie Tim McCarver calling the game for CBS, gave up a walk-off three-run homer to the Toronto Blue Jays' Joe Carter.) But after Chase Utley, Jimmy Rollins, Ryan Howard, and Cole Hamels led the franchise to its second championship in 2008, the Phillies also became a normal modern ball club—not as rich as the Cubs but equally driven by metrics and money management. By then Schmidt, now a celebrated figure in Philadelphia, was an occasional presence in the Phillies' TV and radio booths. Generally considered the best all-around third baseman of all time, he often groused about modern players' shortcomings.

Bruce Sutter, the other Hall of Famer to appear in the 23–22 slugfest of '79, has kept a lower profile. By 2018 the split-finger fastball pioneer had been retired for thirty years. Sutter was sixty-five, sporting a full white beard that made him resemble an Old Testament prophet, but unlike Schmidt and others of their generation, he was still getting paid to play ball. Back in 1984, when he signed a six-year, $9.1 million free-agent contract with the Atlanta Braves, he had all the money deferred, with interest and inflation factored in. The arrangement helped the Braves at the time by lowering their payroll, but left them on the hook for $1.12 million a year over thirty years. The deal will continue to pay Sutter through 2021.

WHEN THE PHILLIES returned to Chicago for a three-game series in June 2018, they were in contention again thanks to their $25-million-a-year ace, the former Cub Jake Arrieta, and young stars like Aaron Nola and Rhys Hoskins. Due to the modern game's salary structure, Nola—who would outperform Arrieta in 2018—and Hoskins earned a combined $1.1 million, their salaries a fraction of what they would be in a free market because they weren't yet eligible for salary arbitration. (Players need three years in the majors to qualify for arbitration. That's why teams keep their best prospects in the minors for a week or two every April, to give the club an additional year of control over them.) In effect, younger players earn less than market value so veteran free agents like Arrieta can earn tens of millions more. The Players Association favors this system.

By any accounting the Phillies were no match for the 2018 Cubs, whose $189 million payroll ranked fourth behind the Red Sox, Giants, and Dodgers. (Philadelphia's payroll stood at $104 million.) Not even Arrieta could brag much in light of what the Cubs were paying outfielder Jason Heyward, whose $28-million-a-year salary was ten times what the 1979 Cubs paid their entire roster and coaching staff.

There were 40,275 fans at Wrigley the night Nola faced off against Cubs lefty Jose Quintana. The fans would see no split-finger fastballs from either starter. Three decades after its heyday, the Pitch of the Eighties was considered an arm killer. Angels phenom Shohei Ohtani threw a wicked split, and the Yankees' Masahiro Tanaka had one that was almost as good, but both had elbow troubles. Too many who threw the pitch ended up needing surgery. But if the split was endangered, the screwball was extinct. By 2018 there were no screwballers left in the major leagues. Yu Darvish, the Cubs' $126 million pitcher, had relied on a screwball before switching to a split to preserve his arm. (He was soon out with a sore elbow.) Brent Honeywell, one of the Tampa Bay Rays' top prospects, had been ready to bring his screwball to the big leagues when he blew out his elbow. And the scroogie wasn't just feared as a health risk; some players doubted such an unnatural delivery existed. "I don't think it's physically possible," said Giants catcher Buster Posey. His teammate Madison Bumgarner agreed: "If anyone actually could do it, they'd last about three pitches." Christy Mathewson, Carl Hubbell, Fernando Valenzuela, and Tug McGraw might disagree.

On this night Nola would need all four of his pitches—fastball, sinker, curve, changeup—against a bigger, stronger Chicago lineup than the one Randy Lerch faced in 1979. Cubs first baseman Anthony Rizzo and third baseman Kris Bryant were almost as tall as Dave Kingman but denser with muscle. Forty years after the Phillies pumped iron on Nautilus machines in the majors' first weight room, the Cubs' posh clubhouse featured "so many rooms you could get lost," Bryant said.

With its hot tubs and hyperbaric chambers, the Cubs' 30,000-square-foot underground clubhouse was "part Las Vegas nightclub, part Star Trek spaceship, part luxury spa," according to the *Washington Post.* Rizzo, who wore cleats with blinking red lights in the soles, stood six foot three and weighed 240—thirty pounds more than the six-foot-six Kingman in his playing days. Bryant stood six foot five and outweighed Kong by twenty pounds. Injuries were up—too many tight muscles?—but so were home runs. And strikeouts.

Decades of data crunching dating back to Tony La Russa's White Sox days had turned baseball into a smarter game. Above all, modern metrics showed the full importance of the home run. For many if not most hitters, the most effective tactic is to damn the strikeouts, uppercut the ball, and swing for the fences.

"It's Kingman all over again," said Cubs historian Ed Hartig. "Homers and strikeouts—that's the modern way."

According to *Deadspin* founder and *New York* magazine columnist Will Leitch, "Dave Kingman is one of those baseball players spoken of in whispers, a certain sort of awe; he is a slugger from another time, another planet." Leitch noted that Kong's "embarrassing" strikeout totals "wouldn't even have gotten him in the top 40 in strikeouts" today. "When he played, he was a bit of a joke. But if you took Kingman's numbers and gave them to a hitter playing today . . . well, we might just award him the MVP."

In 2017 the Yankees' six-foot-seven, 282-pound outfielder Aaron Judge struck out 208 times and won the Rookie of the Year award. Judge deserved it, too. He slashed .284/.422/.627 and led the American League with fifty-two homers. Kingman's league-leading 131 strikeouts in 1979 would have placed him fifty-sixth among major-league hitters in 2017. A year later, sixty-one hitters would strike out at least 131 times. In 2018, for the first time ever, there were more strikeouts than hits in the majors. The Nationals' Mark Reynolds, who held the all-time mark with 223 in a season, joked that he was the "original gangsta" of swinging all-out all the time. According to Leitch, however, Reynolds was only "a down-brand version of Kingman."

In 1992 the Baseball Writers of America elected Tom Seaver and Rollie Fingers to baseball's Hall of Fame with 425 and 349 votes, respectively. Kingman got three votes, falling far short of the minimum required to stay on the ballot in future years. His fans always point out that he was the first player with four hundred or more home runs not to make the Hall. (Later sluggers excluded by the voters, including Barry Bonds, Mark McGwire, and Sammy Sosa, were rumored or admitted steroids users.) Kingman's defenders sometimes neglect to mention the owners' collusion against him: coming off a thirty-five-homer, ninety-four-RBI season for the 1986 A's, Kong got no offers in 1987. Given another year or two in the majors, how many more homers might he have hit?

BOTH TEAMS SWUNG like Kong at Wrigley Field in June 2018. By the end of the game the Phillies and Cubs had struck out twenty-five times—fourteen more whiffs than in the slugfest of '79.

Both starting pitchers were long gone by the time the Phils took a 5–3 lead in the ninth inning. In the last of the ninth, the Cubs loaded the bases with two out. Their last chance was Jason Heyward—the biggest bust of GM Epstein's revamp of the franchise. A Gold Glove outfielder with a Garry Maddox beard and mustache, Heyward was almost as fast as Maddox, but bigger: six foot four and 240 pounds to Maddox's six foot three and 175. After signing the richest contract in Cubs history—eight years, $184 million—he'd spent two and a half seasons flailing at National League pitching. His herky-jerky swing produced so many grounders and pop-ups that a few of the generally polite fans of 2018 booed as soon as they heard his walk-up music.

Heyward was 0-for-4 on the night. (Groundout, groundout, groundout, strikeout.) After Phillies left-hander Adam Morgan ran the count to 2-2, the Cubs were down to their last strike. At that moment, according to the latest metrics, their chance of winning the game was 18 percent.

The fans stood up. They hooted and applauded. Some put their hands together in prayer.

"*Heyward's hitting just .139 against lefties,*" announcer Len Kasper said on NBC Sports Chicago.

Morgan threw a ninety-seven-mile-an-hour fastball. Heyward took a big cut. "*And there's a drive!*" Kasper said as the ball flew into the night—the Cubs' first walk-off grand slam in a decade.

RAY BURRIS WAS rooting for the Phillies that night. After his fifteen-year career ended in 1987, the former Cubs, Yankees, Mets, Expos, A's, Cardinals, and Brewers pitcher—the only Chicago pitcher to survive the '79 slugfest without allowing a run—joined Philadelphia as a minor-league pitching coach in 2013. In 2018 the sixty-seven-year-old Burris served as the organization's rehab pitching coordinator, helping injured pitchers get back to the mound. He had a professional interest in Adam Morgan, who had rehabbed his shoulder on Burris's watch four years before. But Burris, who came to the majors as a Cub in 1973, couldn't help being happy for Heyward and the thousands of fans singing "Go Cubs Go" after Heyward's grand slam.

Burris sometimes thought back to the times he'd spent with Donnie Moore. So did Bill Buckner. "I had an inkling," Buckner said after Moore shot his wife and himself. Thinking back to their last hunting trip in the 1988–89 off-season, Buckner said, "It was a lot of things. His wife left him. He lost all his money, plus his arm was hurt." After Moore's attempted murder-suicide a sportswriter phoned Buckner's ranch in Idaho and asked his wife, Jody, if Bill ever thought about killing himself.

Tonya Moore never remarried. Now living in Corona, California, she plays doting grandma to six grandchildren. Sometimes she drives an hour from Corona to Newport Beach, where her daughter, Demetria, works as a real estate agent. Mother and daughter, both survivors, talk mostly about family, hardly ever about baseball. "We talk about happy things," Demetria says. Thirty years after the shooting, she keeps her dad's baseball card on the nightstand by her bed. It's the 1985 Donnie Moore card, his All-Star season.

Moore's old friend Burris was looking forward to 2019, his forty-seventh season in professional baseball. Looking back to 1979, he said, "Chicago was a special place to play." One of Burris's favorite memories is of driving home after a win with Moore, his best friend on the club. Traffic was awful but they didn't care. "We talked about how cool it was to be in the big leagues. Donnie had a white Ford van with plush seats and a tape deck. This is when music was *music*. We'd turn up the Temptations, James Brown, the Four Tops, Aretha, and just sing and sing. And that was a good day."

	ab	r	h	bi		ab	r	h	bi
PHILADELPHIA					**CHICAGO**				
McBride rf	8	2	3	1	DeJesus ss	6	4	3	1
Bowa ss	8	4	5	1	Vail rf	5	2	3	1
Rose 1b	7	4	3	4	Burris p	0	0	0	0
Schmidt 3b	4	3	2	4	Thompson ph-cf	2	1	1	0
Unser lf	7	1	1	2	Buckner 1b	7	2	4	7
Maddox cf	4	3	4	4	Kingman lf	6	4	3	6
Gross pr-cf	2	1	1	1	Ontiveros 3b	7	2	1	1
Boone c	4	2	3	5	Martin cf	6	2	3	3
Meoli 2b	5	0	1	0	Sutter p	0	0	0	0
Lerch p	1	1	1	1	Foote c	6	1	3	1
Bird p	1	1	0	0	Sizemore 2b	4	2	2	1
Luzinski ph	0	0	0	0	Caudill p	0	0	0	0
Espinosa pr	1	1	0	0	Murcer rf	2	0	1	0
McGraw p	0	0	0	0	Lamp p	0	0	0	0
Reed p	0	0	0	0	Moore p	1	0	1	1
McCarver ph	1	0	0	0	Hernandez p	1	0	0	0
Eastwick p	0	0	0	0	Dillard ph-2b	1	2	1	0
					Biittner ph	1	0	0	0
					Kelleher 2b	1	0	0	0
Total	**53**	**23**	**24**	**23**	**Total**	**56**	**22**	**26**	**22**

```
Philadelphia   7 0 8   2 4 0   1 0 0   1— 23
Chicago        6 0 0   3 7 3   0 3 0   0— 22
```

E—Schmidt 2, DeJesus, Kingman. DP—Philadelphia 2. LOB—Philadelphia 15, Chicago 7. 2B—Bowa 2, Rose 2, Maddox 2, Boone, DeJesus, Martin, Foote. 3B—Gross, Moore. HR—Schmidt 2 (14), Maddox (6), Boone (2), Lerch (1), Buckner (4), Kingman 3 (12), Ontiveros (1), Martin (3). SB—Bowa, Meoli. SF—Unser, Gross.

PHILADELPHIA	IP	H	R	ER	BB	SO
Lerch	⅓	5	5	5	0	0
Bird	3⅔	8	4	4	0	2
McGraw	⅔	4	7	4	3	1
Reed	3⅓	9	6	6	0	0
Eastwick W, 1-0	2	0	0	0	0	1
CHICAGO						
Lamp	⅓	6	6	6	0	0
Moore	2	6	7	7	2	1
Hernandez	2⅔	7	8	6	7	1
Caudill	1⅓	3	1	1	2	3
Burris	1⅔	1	0	0	0	1
Sutter L, 1-1	2	1	1	1	1	1

HBP—by Hernandez (Boone). T—4:03. A—14,952.

A NOTE ON SOURCES

In addition to interviews with players, sportswriters, Cubs historian Ed Hartig, and fans who were at the game on May 17, 1979, I turned to the Giamatti Research Center at the National Baseball Hall of Fame and Museum in Cooperstown, New York, for help while researching and writing *Ten Innings at Wrigley*. My play-by-play sources were the Cubs' WGN telecast, with Jack Brickhouse and Lou Boudreau, and the Phillies Radio Network broadcast with Harry Kalas, Richie Ashburn, and Andy Musser. I also relied on a shelf full of books that aided my work on various chapters. In rough order of importance they include *The New Bill James Historical Baseball Abstract* (New York: Free Press, 2001), Rob Neyer and Bill James's *The Neyer/James Guide to Pitchers* (New York: Fireside, 2004), Frank Fitzpatrick's *You Can't Lose 'Em All* (Lanham, MD: Taylor Trade Publishing, 2001), *The Baseball Encyclopedia* (New York: Macmillan, 1996), Stuart Shea's *Wrigley Field: The Unauthorized Biography* (Dulles, VA: Potomac Books, 2006), George F. Will's *A Nice Little Place on the North Side* (New York: Three Rivers Press, 2014), Mike Sowell's *One Pitch Away* (New York: Macmillan, 1995), Robert Gordon's *"Then Bowa Said to Schmidt . . ."* (Chicago: Triumph Books, 2013), Peter Golenbock's *Wrigleyville* (New York: St. Martin's Press, 1999), *Ya Gotta Believe!* by Tug McGraw with Don Yaeger (New York: Signet, 2005), and *Screwball* by Tug McGraw and Joseph Durso (Boston: Houghton Mifflin, 1974). I often consulted the Society for American Baseball Research's player biographies, courtesy of the invaluable SABR BioProject, and the stats and other information at Baseballreference.com.

I found important details in other sources, including those listed below.

PROLOGUE: MAY 1979

I consulted temperature readings at O'Hare and weather reports in the *Chicago Tribune* and *Chicago Sun-Times*, as well as attendees' memories. I reminded myself of the hit songs of the day by consulting Billboard.com. Longtime *Philadelphia Inquirer* sportswriter Frank Fitzpatrick shared details concerning the '79 Phillies. Some details about the growth of sports TV in the '70s owe a debt to my sources for my earlier book *The Last Headbangers*, including Al Michaels and Don Ohlmeyer. The acceptance of amphetamines in baseball in that era has been confirmed to me many times over the years; I reconfirmed it for this book with several players, none currently active. The founding of the original Rotisserie League is sometimes dated to 1980, and the first Rotisserie draft was that spring, but the idea sprang from the founders (not "founding fathers," because Valerie Salembier was among them) the previous off-season. The founders' memories are cloudy on whether their famous lunch at La Rotisserie Française was in late 1979 or January 1980; I framed the text accordingly. Regarding Pete Rose's being the best-paid player in the game, the Pirates' Dave Parker wound up earning $1 million in 1979, becoming the first player to do so, but much of it was in deferred payments and bonuses. Rose had the highest salary.

PART ONE: NATIONAL LEAGUE LEAST

For "The Cubs: Foiled Again," I often turned to Shea's *Wrigley Field* and Golenbock's *Wrigleyville*. A few details of the "cafeteria craze" appeared in the *Tribune*. The story of Charlie Weeghman's horse Queen Bess has been told by the *Tribune* many times over the years. I have opted to call Grover Cleveland Alexander by his given name, which appears on his Hall of Fame plaque. His nickname was "Ol' Pete," and lately he has been called "Pete Alexander" in many if not most references. In my book he's G.C.A. until further notice. The exploits of crime boss Arnold Rothstein and his minions occupied me during work on another book, *Titanic Thompson*, for which David Pietrusza was a great help. His *Rothstein: The Life, Times and Murder of the Criminal Genius Who Fixed the 1919 World Series* (New York: Basic Books, 2011) is a cracking read. My account of Joe Tinker's career owes details to his file at the Hall of Fame and his SABR biography by Lenny Jacobsen. My account of Opening Day 1914 at Weeghman Park is drawn from Shea's *Wrigley Field* and contemporary news accounts. Mordecai Brown's story is well told in his SABR biography by Cindy Thomson. That of Weeghman's Ku Klux Klan rally was told, complete with a scary photo, by the *Tribune's* Ron Grossman on January 23, 2015.

I gleaned several details about Gabby Hartnett and Al Capone in William McNeil's *Gabby Hartnett: The Life and Times of the Cubs' Greatest Catcher* (Jefferson, NC: McFarland Publishing, 2004). The *Sporting News* covered the debut of the first ballpark organ on April 26, 1941; a recap appears in Sam Pathy's *Wrigley Field Year by Year* (New York: Sports Publishing, 2016). Cubs historian Ed Hartig shared stories of Bronko Nagurski bonking his head on the wall at Wrigley and the remarkable ski-jumping event there in 1944. Interested readers should Google "ski jump Wrigley" for some striking pictures. The tale of the Curse of the Billy Goat is told by Shea, Golenbock, and many others. There's a nice encapsulation and several priceless photos at Billygoattavern.com. Some details of Bill Veeck's remarkable life appear in his autobiography *Veeck as in Wreck* (Chicago: University of Chicago Press, 2001).

Ernie Banks's story is well synopsized in Joseph Wancho's SABR bio. I found details of Banks's life and career in his own *Mr. Cub* (Westchester, IL: Follett, 1971) and a well-timed 2016 Ernie Banks Tribute Issue by *Sports Illustrated.*

I relied on my own research for *Electric October* (New York: Henry Holt, 2017) for background on the inimitable Leo Durocher. Anyone discussing his sign stealing with help from Herman Franks owes a debt to Joshua Prager's work in the *Wall Street Journal* and Prager's *The Echoing Green* (New York: Vintage, 2008). Durocher's calling Ken Holtzman an anti-Semitic name appears in many sources, including Paul Dickson's *Leo Durocher: Baseball's Prodigal Son* (New York: Bloomsbury USA, 2017). That and other details also appear in a 2015 *Tribune* recap of the 1969 Cubs' collapse. Ed Hartig shared tales of the brief reign of Salty Saltwell as the Cubs' GM. Bob Boone provided memories of the early days of Marvin Miller and the Players Association. So did Miller in his *A Whole Different Ball Game: The Inside Story of the Baseball Revolution* (Chicago: Ivan R. Dee, 2004). I'm grateful to Miller's daughter, Susan, for a phone conversation I'll never forget. It's a crime that her father isn't in the Hall of Fame.

Ed Hartig gave me interesting perspectives on Dave Kingman. John Kuczaj, who created and runs Kingman's exhaustive, fascinating website, shared his insights with me on his homer-hitting hero. Susan Fornoff shared her less flattering memories of Kingman. Jane Leavy's 1980 story in the *Washington Post* and Greg Prato's *The Seventh Year Stretch: New York Mets, 1977–1983* (New York: Greg Prato Writer, Corp., 2015) provided other views of Kingman. Helen Rosenberg recalled El conductors' calling the Addison stop "Kong Stadium" in 1979.

Frank Fitzpatrick was helpful to "The Phillies: Unloved Losers" in three ways—by phone, in his vivid book *You Can't Lose 'Em All*, and his *Inquirer* work of the late '70s and early '80s.

Ed Delahanty's untimely end has been recounted many times. It's vividly told in Tobias Seamon's *Morning News* story of August 13, 2003. As for Bill Veeck, who reappears trying to buy the Phillies during the war years, it's important to note that some baseball historians doubt that Veeck came close to breaking baseball's color line with the Phillies before Jackie Robinson went to Brooklyn. Veeck's doubters cite a lack of evidence beyond Veeck's own version. Others see such a stunt as perfectly in keeping with the rest of Veeck's career. There's no doubt he tried to buy the team, that he was rebuffed when the National League took it over and sold it, and that baseball would have to wait for Commissioner Landis to die before the color line could be broken. I have tried to be fair to both sides by saying, "According to Veeck . . ."

C. Paul Rogers III and Bill Nowlin's *The Whiz Kids Take the Pennant* (Phoenix: The Society for American Baseball Research, 2018) is the source of many details on the 1950 Phillies. Grover Cleveland Alexander's brief speech at the schoolboy sports banquet attended by Robin Roberts appears in C. Paul Rogers III's SABR bio of Roberts. My account of Dick Allen's difficult trip from Wampum, Pennsylvania, to the majors is drawn from multiple sources, including Rich D'Ambrosio's SABR bio and an entry in the online *Encyclopedia of Arkansas History and Culture* by Bob Razer of the Bill Clinton State Government Project of the Central Arkansas Library System. Gene Mauch's profane comment about Chico Ruiz is cited in John Florio and Ouisie Shapiro's *One Nation Under Baseball* (Lincoln: University of Nebraska Press, 2017). Mauch's parting words to Howard Cosell come from Robert Gordon, author of *"Then Bowa Said to Schmidt . . ."* Frank Fitzpatrick and Pete Rose provided several details of the Phillies' 1979 season as well as the championship season a year later.

PART TWO: TEN INNINGS

Much of Part Two comes from the Cubs' and Phillies' broadcasts of the game. Readers can see a twenty-five-minute highlight reel as well as the full WGN broadcast, and hear the Phils' radiocast, on YouTube. I never appreciated Harry Kalas enough until I spent hours listening to every minute of his work that day with Richie Ashburn and Andy Musser. I also relied on the work of the *Sun-Times'* John Schulian, Bill Gleason, Joe Goddard, and Jerome Holtzman and the *Tribune's* David Israel, Dave Nightingale, and, yes, Dave Kingman. The incomparable Mike Royko wrote entertainingly about the Cubs even before he took on "Dave Dingdong" in print.

My account of Donnie Moore's life owes much to his daughter, Demetria, his attorney Randall Johnson, and his teammates Ray Burris and Bob Boone, with details from two magazine stories, Loren Feldman's "What Broke Donnie Moore?," *GQ*, February 1990, and Michael McKnight's "The Split," *Sports Illustrated*, October 9, 2014, as well as Tonya Moore's 2015 talk with *Cosmopolitan*. Umpire Dick Cavenaugh's self-published *Just About— But Not Quite* (Bloomington, IN: AuthorHouse, 2011) is the source for his hangover. Bruce Sutter described learning the split-finger fastball from Fred Martin in his 2006 Hall of Fame induction speech. Information on the Cubs' clubhouse from the 1970s to today comes from Hartig and a Wrigley Field employee who asked not to be identified. My view of the Phillies then and now got clearer after I talked with Doug Glanville. The author of *The Game from Where I Stand* (New York: Times Books, 2010) was generous with his time on the phone, sharing takes that made me see baseball in smarter ways.

Sources including the *Tribune* (May 3, 1988) and *New York Times* (August 21, 1985) detailed Jerry Martin's experiences with cocaine and the Royals' subsequent scandal. Martin told Jim Kaplan how he visualized pitches while in prison, as Kaplan reported in *Sports Illustrated*, May 28, 1984. The quote I use about greenies ("I took them . . .") is from a retired player who spoke about them on condition of anonymity. Winners' win expectancy (wWE) numbers are from Baseballreference.com. To get an idea of how Statcast might treat 1979 launch angles and exit velocities, I spoke with Cory Schwartz, vice president of stats at Major League Baseball Advanced Media.

Tug McGraw's quotes and exploits pepper McGraw's autobiographies, the other Phillies books cited above, Frank Fitzpatrick's memories, my conversations with former Phillies including Boone, Rose, Ray Burris, and Rawly Eastwick, and a collection of McGraw's *Scroogie* comic strips (New York: Signet, 1976). Bill Caudill's relationship with the agent Scott Boras is part of Rory Costello's SABR bio of Caudill, and matched my recollections of my own conversations with Boras. Steve Dillard's praise for Fenway Park and Wrigley Field appears in Bill Nowlin's SABR bio of Dillard. Details of Bobby Murcer's life and career are drawn from *Yankee for Life: My 40-Year Journey in Pinstripes*, by Murcer with Glenn Waggoner (New York: HarperCollins, 2008), and Clifford Blau's SABR bio. Ray Burris and Rawly Eastwick provided pitch-by-pitch memories of their appearances on May 17, 1979. Scot Thompson assured me that he played center field in the late innings that day. His recollection matches the play-by-play accounts on WGN TV and Phillies radio; the box score and Baseball Reference, which both show Murcer in center and Thompson in right, got that detail wrong. I have corrected the box score you'll find at the end of the book.

PART THREE: LEGACIES

In addition to the sources noted above, "Miracle on Broad Street" features material found in Betty Trimble's *A Mother's Story* (Nashville: D'Agostino/ Dahlhauser/Ditmore Publishing, 1996). The Phillies' amphetamine scandal was reported first by the *Trenton Times* on July 8, 1980. The *New York Times* followed up on February 5, 1981. McGraw's recounting of the 1980 World Series can be seen in a wonderful YouTube clip, "The Last Pitch 1980 World Series." Mike Schmidt shared memories of being booed and wearing disguises around Philadelphia with Frank Fitzpatrick. Schmidt expressed his regrets about looking nonchalant on the field ("I would have dove into more bases . . .") to Bill Madden of the *New York Daily News*, January 10, 1995. James Michener's essay on the futility of being a Phillies fan appears in *The Phillies Reader* (Philadelphia: Temple University Press, 2005).

In addition to sources noted above, I consulted Susan Fornoff's *Lady in the Locker Room* (Champaign, IL: Sagamore Publishing, 1993) while working on "Kong vs. the Media." Fornoff was also generous with her time on the phone, as was John Kuczaj, who was nicely profiled by the *Chicago Reader* on March 13, 2003. Herman Franks's parting rant was reported by the *Tribune* on September 25, 1979. *Tribune* media columnist Gary Deeb reported Sandra Weir's encounter with Kingman ("He literally threw me into the Pacific . . ."). Randy Harvey reported Second City's Kingman joke in the *Sporting News*, June 7, 1980. George Castle told of Kingman's lifting a trash can full of ice in *When the Game Changed: An Oral History of Baseball's True Golden Age: 1969–1979* (Guilford, CT: Lyons Press, 2011). Ron Davis, formerly of the Yankees, Twins, Cubs, Dodgers, and Giants, described pitching to Kingman to me. The *Sporting News* reported on the end of his career ("I had a good laugh") on June 16, 1986. *Spy* called Kingman a "strikeout-prone galoot" in its August 1990 issue.

"Disgrace Under Pressure" owes a debt to Ed Hartig, John Schulian, and Bruce Newman. *Penthouse*'s Wade Boggs–Margo Adams story appeared in May 1989. Along with my conversations with Pete Rose, I referred to two books of his, *The Pete Rose Story* (Cleveland: World Publishing, 1970) and *My Prison Without Bars* (New York: Rodale Books, 2004). I reported on Rose's 1999 appearance at Cooperstown in *Sports Illustrated* that year. Bill Buckner's professor Richard Astro recalled the ballplayer's connection with Hemingway in the *New York Times*, July 16, 1993. Buckner's fateful quote before the 1986 World Series appears in Jeff Pearlman's *The Bad Guys Won* (New York: Harper Perennial, 2011). Rose expressed his view of steroids and gambling ("Steroids were worse than *my* gambling . . .") in a conversation with me. The Associated Press reported on Charlie Sheen's purchase of the Buckner ball for $93,500 on August 6, 1992. (Also sold at Lelands Auction House that day: a toothpick used by Tom Seaver for $440 and "a black leather crotch protector worn by Mike Tyson" for $1,650.) The Associated Press reported Buckner's icebreaker to Mookie Wilson on July 27, 2002. Buckner's *Curb*

Your Enthusiasm cameo appeared on HBO on September 4, 2011. The *Boston Globe*'s Stan Grossfeld asked Buckner about karmic lessons and reported his reply ("Catch the ball . . .") on October 28, 2011.

"Moore and the Split" owes details to sources mentioned above as well as my conversations with Demetria Moore and Randall Johnson and their descriptions of Tonya Moore's experiences. Donnie Moore's teammates Ray Burris and Bob Boone were also helpful; both spoke highly of Moore as a teammate. I listened again to Al Michaels's call of the 1986 American League Championship Series and appreciate baseball conversations I've had with Michaels over the years. Neighbor Don Ware described Moore's suicide in an ESPN report, "The Donnie Moore Story."

In addition to my talks with Bob Boone, "Ball in the Family" includes details from Peter Gammons's profile of Boone in *Sports Illustrated*, July 4, 1988. I have also enjoyed and employed many conversations with Sue Boone and their sons Bret and Aaron. Aaron's comments on Bob's firing by the Reds were to the Associated Press's Joe Kay, July 29, 2003. Bob recalled his father's scouting Curt Schilling; I also drew on a day I spent with Schilling for *Playboy* in 2002. Jim Bowden and I corresponded by email. Jose Canseco spoke with Matt Lauer on the *Today* show on February 22, 2005. Tug McGraw's quote about Betty's deserving the credit for raising Tim appeared in *Country Weekly*, June 1994. Tim McGraw's "Live Like You Were Dying" reached number one on Billboard's country music chart on July 17, 2004.

EPILOGUE: MONEY, METRICS, AND MUSIC

The costs of the Ricketts family's renovations of Wrigley Field were well reported by the *Tribune* and *Sun-Times*. Rich Buhrke shared his ballhawking stories with me at the corner of Waveland and Kenmore. Bruce Schoenfeld spoke to Madison Bumgarner and Buster Posey for a story on the vanishing screwball in the *New York Times*, July 10, 2014. Will Leitch's views on Dave Kingman ("a slugger from another time . . .") ran at Sportsonearth.com on February 23, 2015. Mark Reynolds referred to himself as the original gangsta of strikeouts in Tyler Kepner's column in the *New York Times*, May 19, 2018. Reynolds said "O.G.," which Kepner translated. I used "original gangsta" to avoid slowing down for the translation. (It was Kepner's May 16, 2009, story on the 23–22 game of 1979 that dubbed it "the wildest game in modern history.") Dan Lewis of the *Athletic* reported Bruce Sutter's deferred payments from the Braves. Ray Burris remembered a good day with his friend Donnie Moore when we spoke in 2018.

ACKNOWLEDGMENTS

In Chicago, Helen Rosenberg and Joel Frankel gave me a place to sleep and a rescue dog to curl up with. Many thanks to Helen for being such a smart fan and good quote. The great John Schulian, who went from the *Sun-Times* to TV and movies (while winning the PEN/ESPN Lifetime Achievement Award for Literary Sports Writing), shared his memories of the 1979 Cubs. Team historian Ed Hartig is someone any Cub fan would love to know; here's an "Ed *woo!*" for him. Bud Newton met me at the Ernie Banks statue and gave me an insider's tour of the new Wrigley Field. I'm grateful to John Rezek and his staff at the *Rotarian*, including Geoff Johnson, who tracked down the origins of "Wrigleyville," as well as Cubs media chiefs Kevin Saghy and Peter Chase, ballhawk Rich Buhrke, concessionaire Russel Nelson, and the helpful staff at the Chicago Public Library.

Bob Boone, one of the best catchers and conversationalists in baseball history, was indispensable to my understanding of the Phillies and the way the game was played in the 1970s and '80s. I could also count on his sons Bret and Aaron for smart takes on the game's evolution since their dad's era. Frank Fitzpatrick was a prized resource. Thanks to Phillies media director Bonnie Clark and her staff, and Alex Trihias at the Major League Baseball Players Alumni Association.

My boyhood hero Pete Rose was generous with his time and

thoughtful about his answers to my questions. Many thanks to him and his business manager, Joie Casey.

At Henry Holt and Company, Paul Golob is the DiMaggio of editors, making a hard job look easy. I'm lucky to have his intellect, heart, and baseball know-how to rely on. I'm also indebted to Holt's publisher, Stephen Rubin, along with Phil Passcuzzo for his fine jacket, Maggie Richards, Pat Eisemann, Gillian Blake, Kelly Too, and Fiora Elbers-Tibbitts.

My agent, David Halpern, has been an advocate and friend. I'm also a devoted fan of Kathy Robbins, Lisa Kessler, and their colleagues at the Robbins Office.

Thank you to Demetria Moore for sharing memories of her father, to Ray Burris for memories of his career and friendship with Donnie Moore, and to Susan Fornoff, Randall Johnson, Rawly Eastwick, Doug Glanville, Pat Manaher, and John Kuczaj.

Bruce Newman, who covered the game for *Sports Illustrated*, was such a good interview I went back to reread his stuff in the SI Vault. It's terrific. Our *SI* coworkers Rob Fleder, Dick Friedman, Jim Herre, Leigh Montville, and Jim Kaplan broadened my perspective.

At the national level, the Society for American Baseball Research provides writers a trove of historical material that gets better every year. At the local level, baseball historian Duke Goldman, who breaks new ground with his own research, helped by playing pepper with me on some of the book's ideas. Cassidy Lent was my guide to the archives at the National Baseball Hall of Fame and Museum. John Horne was a great help in providing photos from the Hall's archives. I'm also grateful to Tricia Gesner at AP.

I owe nods to Gregory Heisler and Jennifer Masters, Jim Kreutzer, Tribe fan Allison Burnett, Cub fans Tom and Kelly Cook, Randy Phillips, Phil Sullivan and Alexis Johnson, Peter Kreutzer, Steve Randall, Ajay and Sylvia Khanna, Ellen Stirnweiss Pittman, Judge Stanley Harris, and the Kubik Circle: Ken Kubik, Doug Vogel, and Chris Carson.

Thank you, Cal Cook and Lily Cook, for being who you are. Take me out to a ballgame and I won't care if I ever get back.

As always, I'm grateful to Pamela Marin, my partner in work and life. Any errors are mine, but every page of my work is better thanks to her.

INDEX

ABOUT THE AUTHOR

KEVIN COOK is the author of *Electric October* and five other books on sports and the people who play them, including *Tommy's Honor* and *The Dad Report*. A former senior editor at *Sports Illustrated* who has written for the *New York Times*, *Men's Journal*, *GQ*, *Smithsonian*, and many other publications, he has appeared on CNN, ESPN, and Fox TV. An Indiana native, he now lives in Northampton, Massachusetts.